D1202582

REVEALING WHITENESS

AMERICAN
PHILOSOPHY
John J. Stuhr, editor

EDITORIAL BOARD

Susan Bordo

Vincent Colapietro

John Lachs

Noëlle McAfee

Cheyney Ryan

Richard Shusterman

HT
1575
.S85
2006

6147 9582

REVEALING WHITENESS

THE UNCONSCIOUS HABITS OF RACIAL PRIVILEGE

Shannon Sullivan

Indiana University Press

BLOOMINGTON AND INDIANAPOLIS

This book is a publication of
Indiana University Press
601 North Morton Street
Bloomington, IN 47404-3797 USA

http://iupress.indiana.edu

Telephone orders   800-842-6796
Fax orders   812-855-7931
Orders by e-mail   iuporder@indiana.edu

© 2006 by Shannon Sullivan

All rights reserved

*No part of this book may be reproduced or utilized in any form or
by any means, electronic or mechanical, including photocopying and
recording, or by any information storage and retrieval system, without
permission in writing from the publisher. The Association of American
University Presses' Resolution on Permissions constitutes the
only exception to this prohibition.*

*The paper used in this publication meets the minimum
requirements of American National Standard for Information
Sciences—Permanence of Paper for Printed Library Materials,
ANSI Z39.48-1984.*

MANUFACTURED IN THE UNITED STATES OF AMERICA

Library of Congress Cataloging-in-Publication Data

Sullivan, Shannon, date
Revealing whiteness : the unconscious habits of racial privilege /
Shannon Sullivan.
p. cm. — (American philosophy)
Includes bibliographical references and index.
ISBN 0-253-34738-6 (cloth : alk. paper) — ISBN 0-253-21848-9
(pbk. : alk. paper)
1. Whites—Race identity. 2. Racism. 3. Race discrimination.
4. United States—Race relations. 5. United States—Ethnic relations.
6. Habit—Social aspects. I. Title. II. Series.
HT1575.S85 2006
305.809—dc22
2005026132

1 2 3 4 5   11 10 09 08 07 06

For Sophia and Phillip

CONTENTS

ACKNOWLEDGMENTS

I greatly appreciate the suggestions made by Dee Mortensen, John Stuhr, Noëlle McAfee, and several reviewers for Indiana University Press, many of which are incorporated in the pages that follow. I especially benefited from John's help on an earlier draft of the manuscript. I am grateful for Carol Kennedy's skillful copyediting and thoughtful suggestions. I thank the following people for discussing issues and providing comments on essays related to this book: Jim Albrecht, Kaarina Beam, Sherry Brennan, John Christman, Vincent Colapietro, Brent Crouch, Michael Eldridge, Marilyn Fisher, Kim Garcher, Bill Gavin, Lisa Heldke, David Kim, Pauline Kaurin, Terrance MacMullan, Steve Martinot, Erin McKenna, Phillip McReynolds, Charles Mills, Gregory Pappas, Scott Pratt, John Shuford, David Vessey, and Emily Zakin. Special thanks go to Andrew Cutrofello for bringing to my attention Nicolas Abraham and Maria Torok's work on the phantom. I have learned much from conversations with other friends and colleagues in ways that are difficult to pinpoint. I regret not being able to thank them individually.

I would not have had the courage to write this book without the love and support of my family: my sister, Jennifer; my mother, Bettye; and my father, Alex George. And above all, my husband, Phillip, has made this book possible. Thank you, Phillip, for believing in this project but also insisting that it could be better. Sole authorship can never credibly be claimed, but my work truly is woven out of our combined voices and conversations. I share credit for this book with Phillip but take responsibility for its flaws. It is lovingly dedicated to him and our wonderful daughter, Sophia. I hope that most of the transgenerational habits that we are nurturing in her are ones that she will enjoy, and that the others are ones for which she can some day forgive us.

Parts of this book previously have been published elsewhere. The section of chapter 1 that discusses John Dewey's definition of racial prejudice as aversion to the strange is adapted from "From the Foreign to the Familiar: Confronting Dewey Confronting Racial Prejudice," *The Journal of Speculative Philosophy* 18(3) (2004): 193–202. Chapter 3 is an expanded and modified version of "Enigma Variations: Laplanchean Psychoanalysis and the Formation of the Raced Unconscious," published in *Radical Philosophy* 122 (November/December 2003): 20–33. Chapter 7 is an expanded and modified version of "Reciprocal Relations between Races: Jane Addams's Ambiguous Legacy," published in *Transactions of the C.S. Peirce Society* 39(1) (Winter 2003): 43–60. All three essays are reprinted here with permission.

REVEALING WHITENESS

Introduction

This book examines how white privilege operates as unseen, invisible, even seemingly nonexistent, and suggests that because of this hidden mode of operation, something more indirect than and much different from conscious argumentation against white privilege is needed to combat it. This latter claim is somewhat ironic, of course. Arguing against argumentation to a certain degree, I recognize that the conscious, deliberate reasoning of much philosophical prose, including my own, is not sufficient for combating white domination. In that sense, this book partially points beyond itself—or, at least, beyond its direct, rational argumentation—to the need for other genres that often significantly impact unconscious habits. Literature, art, and film, for example, can be particularly useful to critical race theory because their images, tones, and textures often perform subtle emotional work that richly engages the nonreflective aspects of white privilege. But philosophy also has an important role to play, sometimes by performing similar emotional work, but also by clarifying the structures of human experience that contribute to white privilege. One the most significant of those structures is unconscious habit. As unconscious habit, white privilege operates as nonexistent and actively works to disrupt attempts to reveal its existence. Given this modus operandi, habits of white privilege are more likely to be changed by indirect, rather than direct, assaults upon them.

Due also to the constitutive role that the world plays in the formation of habit, the particular type of indirect assault needed is one that transforms the social, political, institutional, economic, aesthetic, physical, psychological, and other conditions for the composition of white privileged habits. Habit can never be separated from its environment, in other words. But even this characterization of habit can be misleading because the word "environment" suggests something outside of habit that encloses or envelops it. As an envelope, environment would influence or shape habit, but only secondarily, from without. By contrast, the concept of environment that I use in my account of habit is no mere container. Habits are not "in" the world like water is in a plastic cup. Because humans are habituated beings, the world inhabits us as much as we inhabit it.

By characterizing white privilege as an environmentally constituted habit, I do not mean that white privilege is merely a "bad habit" in need of elimination—something like overeating or interrupting others—although it is that. I am claiming something much stronger about white privilege as constitutive of the self, whatever race a particular self may be. Habits, whether those of race or of other characteristics of contemporary human existence, such as gender, sexuality, and class, are not some sort of veneer lacquered onto a neutral human core. They are dispositions for transacting with the world, and they make up the very beings that humans are. If the self can be understood as a complex tapestry of woven fibers, habits are the various threads that make up the tapestry itself. Or, to stretch the metaphor, habits are the various threads that help constitute each other as they also make up the tapestry as a whole. Habits of race and gender, to take just two examples, are not separately formed only to come into later contact with one another. My particular habits of whiteness concern my particular habits as a woman, and vice versa, and both have a great deal to do with my being middle-class and Texan (and the list could go on). White privilege will help constitute a different person—say, a black man—in different ways from me, but in both cases our habits (our selves) are composed in transaction with a world that privileges white people. Not all white people have identical habits of white privilege since other characteristics of their selves, their particular experiences, and the particular time and place in which they live often vary. But since the late eighteenth to early nineteenth century, when modern forms of race came into existence,[1] general patterns of white people being privileged and non-white people being disadvantaged have existed.[2]

Because of this, some scholars have argued that the concept of race should be abolished and the concept of ethnicity used instead.[3] But I think it is important to retain the concept of race even though it originated in practices of racism and white supremacy. The concept is needed to accurately capture historical and contemporary relationships between certain groups of people in the United States. Many ethnicities that today are thought of as white have not always been so. Ethnic groups such as the Irish, the Italians, the Greeks, the Poles, and the Jews were often considered black, or "off-white," in the United States until well into the twentieth century. Whiteness for Italian-Americans, and perhaps also for others such as the Jews, continues to be "site specific" to this day, varying in different cities and neighborhoods.[4] Substituting the concept of ethnicity for that of race risks neglecting the reality of white privilege and ignoring the fact that some ethnicities in the United States have been "allowed" to become white, while others have not.[5]

The advantages of understanding white privilege as unconscious habit are at least fivefold. First, since habits are both psychical and somatic, thinking of white privilege as habit avoids mind-body dualisms and explains the operations of racism as simultaneously and complexly bodily and mental. One of the aspects of white privilege that I explore in this book is how it comes to constitute ways of "bodying" as well as ways of thinking and how racist bodying and thinking mutually implicate each other. As an activity grounded in physicality, bodying tends to take on racist meanings in a world filled with white privilege, and those meanings likely will transform the activity of bodying, which will create new meanings that impact the world of white privilege, and so on.[6]

Second, habit construes ontology as historical, allotting an appropriate weight to race and white privilege without making them static, acontextual necessities. Ontology—or, simply, what things are—too often has been thought of as the eternal, unchanging, and "essential" characteristics of a being, in contrast with those that are historically produced, culturally situated, and therefore "accidental." This false dilemma does not adequately capture race or white privilege. Because the self, whatever its race, is not an atomistic bubble sealed off from the world around it, in a raced and racist world human beings will be raced and racist, albeit in often very different ways depending upon the particular environments they inhabit. Habits of white privilege currently are a historical necessity; they cannot be totally avoided given the white-privileged world that exists. Yet for something to have a weighty history does not mean that it is set in stone. Among other things, being historical means being capable of having a different future. To take seriously the historical and contemporary significance of race and racism is not to claim that their emergence was inevitable, nor to suggest that they can never be eliminated. Habits of white privilege are both capable of transformation and incredibly difficult to change because they are dynamic, temporal compositions of the self.

A third, related advantage is that thinking of white privilege as habit helps demonstrate how white domination is located, so to speak, in both the individual person and the world in which she lives. Since habits are formed through transaction with the world and since habits compose the self, habit at once is intensely personal and involves much more than the mere individual. In a world filled with white privilege, habits that privilege whiteness will result, and these habits in turn will tend to reinforce the social, political, economic, and other privileges that white people have.

Understanding white privilege as habit explains how oppressive structures such as white domination take root in people's selves. Racism is not located solely in the individual person; it has a long history of perpetuating itself through political, economic, national, global, educational, and other institutions that are much larger than any individual. Yet part of the way that these institutions are able to so effectively privilege white people and exploit non-white people is through the development of individual attachments and commitments to them. Here is a fourth advantage to an account of white privilege as habit: it can explain both how people become personally invested in racist institutions and structures and how they might try to combat this "internal" investment by changing their relationship to the "external" world. Much more than individual, psychical change is needed to eliminate white domination, but changes to larger, impersonal institutions ultimately will be effective only if the roots they have planted in people's psychosomatic habits have been dug up.

Finally, the concept of habit helps explain how white privilege often functions as if invisible. Habits are the things we do and say "without thinking." They are the mental and physical patterns of engagement with the world that operate without conscious attention or reflection. They fly under one's conscious radar, so to speak, and are all the more effective precisely because they tend to function unnoticed. This is not necessarily a bad thing. Human beings could never survive if, for example, they had to consciously guide every muscular movement that it takes to get out of bed in the morning. While the nonconscious aspect of habit enables organic flourishing, it also can limit it by allowing all sorts of destructive habits to operate undetected. White privilege is one such habit.

In the early twenty-first century, white domination increasingly gains power precisely by operating as if nonexistent. This has not always been the case. One hundred years ago, for example, when Jim Crow reigned in the United States, white domination tended to be fairly easily visible to all. Lynchings were well-attended social affairs for white people, who openly celebrated the vicious hangings of black people with picnics and photographs to proudly send to friends and family.[7] After the civil rights movements of the 1960s, the move from de jure to de facto racism meant not the end of white domination, but a significant shift in its predominant mode of operation. It was no longer socially acceptable in most white circles and institutions to openly proclaim racist beliefs. The "good" (= nonracist) white person was supposed to treat everyone equally, which was taken to mean not noticing a person's race at all. In this atmosphere of alleged colorblindness, racism continued and continues to function without the use of race-related terms. Race supposedly is not at issue in a society that obsesses over urban ghettoes, crime, the resale value of one's house, welfare queens, the drug war, the death penalty, and a massively growing prison industry.[8]

The shift from de jure to de facto racism corresponds with a related shift from habits of white supremacy to ones of white privilege. As I use the term "white supremacy," it refers to conscious, deliberate forms of white domination, such as those found in the law but also in informal social mores. Although racist groups such as the Ku Klux Klan and Aryan Nation offer some of the most obvious examples of white supremacy, one need not be a member of them to be a white supremacist. All one needs, so to speak, is a style of transacting with the world in which white domination is consciously embraced and affirmed. White supremacy has not disappeared with the shift from de jure to de facto racism. As long as white domination endures, there probably always will exist a mix of white supremacy and white privilege, on both the micro level of the person and the macro level of societies, cultures, and nations. But that mix is one with increasingly high proportions of unconscious white domination.[9] While big-booted forms of conscious oppression still exist, in the early twenty-first century white domination tends to prefer silent tiptoeing to loud stomping.[10]

It is no accident that it is difficult to hear the soft patter of white privilege. White privilege goes to great lengths not to be heard. Habits of white privilege are not merely nonconscious or preconscious. It is not the case that they just happen not to be the object of conscious reflection but could relatively easily become so if only they were drawn to one's attention. This overly optimistic picture implicitly denies the possible existence of formidable obstacles to the conscious acknowledgement of certain habits. It omits the strong resistance to the conscious recognition of racism that characterizes habits of white privilege. As unconscious, habits of white privilege do not merely go unnoticed. They actively thwart the process of conscious reflection on them, which allows them to seem non-existent even as they continue to function.

An experience a few years ago drove home for me the stubborn and willful resistance that raced habits can mount to their acknowledgement and possible transformation.[11] I was presenting a paper on racism and the Roma at an international conference in Slovakia, and upon completion of the paper, a Czech member of the audience proceeded to ask critical but sympathetic questions about my analysis. When doing so, he repeatedly referred to the Roma ("Gypsies," as most people at the conference called them) as "Jews" without hearing his slip of the tongue. After a second reference to the "Jews" in a comment that clearly concerned the Roma, a few members of the audience interrupted him to correct him, and he, embarrassed, said that yes, of course, he meant the "Gypsies." We all laughed away our discomfort and he proceeded with his comment. As he did so, he referred to the Roma as "Jews" for a third time without hearing what he said. The rest of us were so surprised by this that we said nothing, and I answered his question assuming (correctly) that the group he referred to was the Roma. He was followed by another Czech member of the audience who asked critical but supportive questions about my paper. In the course of doing so, he too referred to the Roma as the "Jews" twice without hearing his slip of the tongue. The audience and I did not correct him since, by that time, such correction felt pointless. After five occurrences, the substitution of "Jew" for "Gypsy" seemed to have roots too deep and stubborn for conscious correction to eliminate.

Understood as the product of merely nonconscious or preconscious habit, these slips of the tongue can be seen as the result of a style of transaction with the world that unreflectively associates Roma and Jews. This association is not innate to the human psyche, nor do the Roma or Jews have any sort of ahistorical racial or ethnic essence that would necessitate their conflation. The association instead is the product of a co-constitutive relationship between psyche, soma, and world in which historical events have shaped the way the Roma and Jews are negatively perceived; reciprocally, deprecatory stereotypes of the Roma and Jews have been used to facilitate and justify their oppression. More specifically, the slips are evidence of a habit of thought in the European mind that involves the scapegoat role that Jews and Roma have been assigned in Europe for hundreds of years. The most extreme example of this role can be found in Nazi Germany's attempted extermination of the Roma and Jews during World War II. A more complicated and equally sinister instance of it has emerged the last fifteen years, in which guilt about Europe's treatment of the Jews coexists with acceptance of rising violence and discrimination directed toward the Roma in Central and Eastern Europe in particular.

I find this account both very compelling because it is situated in European politico-economic history and somewhat dissatisfying because it is incomplete. While I find it helpful to understand the slips of the tongue as the verbal sign of complex habits that were not under the speaker's conscious control, I also think that more in-depth analyses of the repetition, mechanics, and inaudibility (on the speakers' parts) of the slip is needed. What is the significance of the slip's reoccurrence and "contagion"? Why couldn't the speakers hear their mistakes? Can the substitution of "Jew" for "Gypsy" plausibly be explained by verbal mechanisms that omit reference to unconscious habit? These questions are all the more pressing given the case of a third audience member who made comments that were openly hostile to my antiracist reading of the Roma's situation. If she had called the Roma "Jews"—which, interestingly, she did not—her doing so could be seen as motivated by conscious reasons that involved deprecating the Roma by means of antisemitism. In contrast, the first two speakers' lack of hostility toward my paper makes it unlikely that conscious antagonism toward the Roma resulted in their substitution of "Jew" for "Gypsy." An adequate explanation of the multiple slips must include an account of their unconscious operations and motivations.

My experience in Slovakia displays the forcefully compulsive and deviously obstructionist character that some habits—especially socially unacceptable ones, like those related to racial privilege—can have. It is to capture this particular character that I use "unconscious" to describe habits of white privilege. But unlike some psychoanalytic uses of the term, my use of "unconscious" does not mean that what is unconscious is necessarily and completely inaccessible to consciousness. I prefer to remain something of an agnostic practitioner about the level of accessibility of the unconscious. Whether and to what degree unconscious habits can be examined and possibly reworked can be found out only in practice. To declare that unconscious habits are in principle inaccessible creates a dangerously self-fulfilling situation in which no attempts at transformation are made because they are thought pointless, which then ensures that unconscious habits remain beyond the reach of conscious influence.

On the other hand, to declare that all unconscious habits are in principle entirely accessible to intelligent inquiry is dangerously naive. Such a declaration underestimates the devious resistances that both psychical and bodily habits often put up in the face of their possible transformation, resistances that go beyond mere inertia and tend to be strongest when the habit in question involves personally and politically charged issues, such as those surrounding white privilege. It is these resistances that the terms "nonconscious," "subconscious," and "preconscious" (which I will use interchangeably) tend to omit. Let me be clear in my criticism of these concepts that I recognize their limited usefulness and do not misunderstand their implications. I know that characterizing habit as nonconscious does not imply the possibility of a Cartesian razing of the slate; one cannot focus on all one's habits at the same time. It also does not imply the transparency of the body. I usually am not consciously aware of my internal organs' transactions with their environments or of my phenomenologically lived body as I unreflectively move throughout my day. But my concern is that characterizing habit as exclusively nonconscious implies that all habits are in principle available for conscious examination, even though practically that process must proceed in piecemeal fashion and, in some cases, will require the assistance of biofeedback, endoscopes, and other techniques and tools of technoscience.

The Alexander Technique, to which I appeal in my earlier work on transactional bodies, provides an excellent illustration of this point.[12] The technique operates on the principle that a person's body is the nontransparent, nonreflective basis for her lived experience. Its call for greater reflective awareness of one's body in order to improve its comportment posits the body as wholly subconscious. While I still think that this kind of work is important to do, its limitation is that it implicitly denies that some of the body's habits might be unconscious. I realize that it is unusual to speak of the body as unconscious, but I think it is important to do so. In part, this is because the dismantling of mind-body dualisms effected by the concept of habit means that the notion of the unconscious cannot be reserved for the psyche alone. It also is because restricting the body to the domain of nonconscious habit makes it difficult to consider the reasons why and examine the ways by which a body might fight attempts to make it more transparent. To do so, one would need to explore whether a particular aspect of a person's bodily comportment is the result of either disturbing experiences or socially unacceptable values (or both) that are retained in it, which the person would find painful to consciously remember and which the reconfiguration of her bodily comportment would help recall. In a case where that is so, bodily habits are not merely the nonreflective backdrop to lived experience, nor do they continue unchanged solely because of inertia. They instead are a site of repression that actively subverts attempts at transformation because such transformation would risk bringing the traumatic event or shameful values to conscious attention. In cases such as these, the body is an expression not just of "I can," but also of "I won't."[13]

Herein lies the problem that results when habit is treated as exclusively nonconscious. When that happens, what is lost is the notion that the ugliness of a habit can trigger forceful but evasive psychosomatic resistance to conscious examination of it. This resistance makes it much less likely that a person who wants to change her habits will be successful, for only if she realizes that irrational obstacles and blockages will try to thwart her can she possibly attempt to bypass or subvert them. Unless she recognizes the stubborn, manipulative resistances that arise from the desire to ignore the repugnant aspects of her habits, those resistances are likely to derail her efforts to change them.

This is not to say that merely having good intentions ensures that change will occur. Nor is it to claim that one can fully expose the hidden operations of unconscious habit. It is to suggest that the hidden, subversive operations of unconscious habits require indirect, roundabout strategies for transformation. One of the main claims of this book is that changing unconscious habits of white privilege requires altering the political, social, physical, economic, psychological, aesthetic, and other environments that "feed" them. Correspondingly, a white person who wishes to try to change her raced and racist habits would do better to change the environments she inhabits than (to attempt) to use "will power" to change the way she thinks about and reacts to non-white people. Whatever will power human beings have with regard to white privilege or any other habit is found in those habits themselves. A person cannot merely intellectualize a change of habit by telling herself that she will no longer think or behave in particular ways. The key to transformation is to find a way of disrupting a habit through environmental change and then hope that the changed environment will help produced an improved habit in its place.

I say "hope" because there is no way to totally control the process of habit transformation. This type of control is what direct methods of rational argumentation implicitly promise, which can make indirect methods of environmental change seem inadequate by comparison. Tempting though direct methods may be, they tend to fail because one cannot completely micromanage the complex transaction of psyche, soma, and world that produces unconscious habits. This is not to say that the formation of habits must be completely arbitrary and chaotic—although it often can be when little attention is given to the role that environment plays in their composition. Whatever significant control over unconscious habits exists is found in the indirect access one has to them via environment. And while many aspects of one's environment cannot be deliberately controlled, the development of at least some of them can be deliberately influenced and guided. The books that a person reads, the films that she sees, the histories that she studies, the people with whom she socializes, the neighborhoods in which she lives, the social and political work to which she contributes—all of these things are environments that help shape a person's habits and on which a person can have some impact.

In particular, relocating out of geographical, literary, political, and other environments that encourage the white solipsism of living as if only white people existed or mattered can be a powerful way of disrupting and transforming unconscious habits of white privilege.[14] It can also be, paradoxically, one of the most powerful ways to reinforce them. This is because one of the predominant unconscious habits of white privilege is that of ontological expansiveness. As ontologically expansive, white people tend to act and think as if all spaces—whether geographical, psychical, linguistic, economic, spiritual, bodily, or otherwise—are or should be available for them to move in and out of as they wish. Ontological expansiveness is a particular co-constitutive relationship between self and environment in which the self assumes that it can and should have totally mastery over its environment. Here can be seen the devious maneuvers of unconscious habits of white privilege to obstruct their transformation. The very act of giving up (direct) total control over one's habits can be an attempt to take (indirect) total control over them by dominating the environment. The very act of changing one's environment so as to disrupt white privilege paradoxically can be a disruption that only reinforces that which it disrupts. When a white person makes a well-intentioned decision not to live in an all-white neighborhood, for example, doing so can simultaneously disrupt her habit of always interacting with white neighbors and augment her racial privilege by increasing her ontological expansiveness. The sheer fact that she is able to make a choice about which neighborhood in which she lives is, after all, an effect of the privilege she has because of her race and economic class. That privilege is only strengthened by attempts to change her environment.

This paradox cannot be completely eliminated. There is no way to ensure that a challenge to white privilege does not simultaneously support it, and in part, this is because there is no way in any particular situation to totally master the complex organism-world transaction that is habit. I do not think that this realization should lead to despair, although it does snuff out any Pollyannaish dreams of the easy elimination of racism. I also do not think that it should lead to the conclusion that one should never try to alter one's environments in an attempt to alter one's habits. While the need for control is a significant aspect of habits of white privilege, giving up all attempts to control or impact one's environment only ensures that those habits will continue relatively unchanged. Since habits constitute agency and will, the attempt to eliminate white privilege must involve habits of white privilege themselves. Rather than despairing or giving up, a person needs to engage in an ongoing struggle to find ways to use white privilege against itself.

A significant part of that struggle involves trying to understand one's own complex relationship—and complicity—with white privilege, and this is true whatever one's race. One of the key motivations for my initial work in critical race theory concerns my work as a feminist. I have always thought that feminism must involve men as much as women. Gender and sexist oppression do not impact just the lives of women, and so for feminist struggle to be successful, it needs to be a project for all people, not just "women's work." Especially when teaching feminist philosophy, I have been curious about men's relationships to feminist theory and practice. To imagine that relationship, I have tried to understand what it is like to be the one with relative privilege addressed (sometimes angrily, often critically) by those who suffer because of that privilege. Although not the only available route, the easiest way for me to do that was to think about my own position of privilege as a white person. While not assuming that race and gender operate in identical ways, I was initially motivated to think about white privilege by feminist concerns to better understand both ends of the oppressor-oppressed pole.

I found and often still find it easier to confront other people with the importance of struggling against oppression when talking about race, rather than sex and gender. This is not because, for example, my undergraduate students are more receptive to discussions of race than sex and gender. In fact, at the white-dominated university at which I teach, the opposite is generally the case. It is because I find such confrontation easier when it involves axes of oppression in which I am in a dominant position. In that case, I do not appear to be struggling on my own behalf. I am struggling on the behalf of other people, and any criticisms that I make are, at least implicitly, made of myself as much as anyone else.

Sex, gender, race, male, and white privilege transact in complex ways in my work in feminist and critical race theory. My being a woman and a feminist led me to focus on and (hopefully) better understand race and white privilege. But another way of explaining this shift in focus is to say that I began to concentrate on race and white privilege because of sexism. I did not want to be perceived as "complaining" about oppression, a perception that feminist but not antiracist struggle risked in my case. The

[11]

effects of male privilege on my gendered habits are clear. More comfortable being in the background with the focus on someone else, I am in this regard stereotypically feminine, and this femininity finds its expression, in part, in my turn to critical race theory.

But the story is even more complicated, in part because my gendered habits are middle-classed through and through. Struggling for others because "proper" women are not "supposed" to speak out on their own behalf is not just the result of sexism and male privilege. It also is a classed—and classic—means by which privileged white women have contributed to the oppression of people of color and the domination of colonized lands. With her self-sacrificing moral purity, the white, middle-to-upper class woman savior is able to speak out on the behalf of the helpless, under-class wretches who are too underdeveloped to understand or articulate their needs for themselves—or so the story goes. A product of male and class privilege, middle-class white women's self-abnegation is often an ideal tool for the furthering of white privilege, and she often takes pleasure in using it even if she cannot consciously admit that to herself. To the extent that my turn to critical race theory is fueled by such self-denial, it contributes to white privilege (with all its connections to class privilege) even though I do not intend that result.

My point in unraveling some of these complexities of gender, race, and class is not merely to analyze my own relationship to white privilege. It also is to suggest some of the particular struggles in which white women might have to engage in order to tackle the hidden workings of white privilege. Because of male privilege, white middle-class women tend to have gendered habits that lead them to downplay or even hide their own point of view. When a woman does this, it is not just her perspective as a woman that is hidden. Her perspective as a white and middle-class person also is made invisible. Her invisibility as a woman strengthens the invisibility of her classed white privilege, and the effect of male privilege on her gendered habits interferes with her ability to see or understand her raced and classed habits. These particular obstacles do not make it impossible for her to identify white privilege, as the trend of white women philosophers actively contributing to critical race theory happily attests. But they do create distinctive difficulties that white men generally do not have to confront. If they are effectively to combat white privilege, white, and especially middle-class, women must find ways to challenge the sexist imperative that they hide their (white, classed) voices. I have struggled not to hide myself in the chapters that follow, but I inevitably have failed to see all the ways that my particular perspective has influenced what I have written.[15] I can only hope that the instances of my retreat to invisibility will be telling in ways that illuminate white privilege, if also disturbing and disappointing to my readers.

*　　*　　*

The four chapters of part 1 of this book, "Unconscious Habit," develop the concept of unconscious habit in connection with white privilege. Beginning with the pragmatist concept of habit, I demonstrate why pragmatist philosophy needs to be supplemented with a psychoanalytic understanding of the unconscious. But not just any notion of the unconscious will do: a transactional conception of the unconscious is needed in place of the atomistic conception of it that tends to function in classical psychoanalytic theory. By combining a psychoanalytically modified pragmatism and a pragmatized psychoanalysis, I account for the formation of unconscious habits of white privilege in both their personally individual and their globally trans-individual operations.

The three chapters of part 2, "Possessive Geographies," focus on the proprietary relationship that unconscious habits of white privilege tend to have with non-white spaces and examine strategies for changing that relationship. Illuminating the connections between race, ontology, and geography, I show how habits of white privilege can be ontologically expansive and how their ontological expansiveness creates a dilemma for critical race theorists. Although indirect, environmental methods for changing unconscious habits are needed because direct methods inevitably fail, well-intentioned attempts to change racist environments can be just another expression of the white privileged habit of unconsciously thinking that and behaving as if all spaces were available for "proper" (= white) people to appropriate. I conclude by showing that although the dangers of reinforcing habits of white privilege through attempts to undercut them can never be entirely eliminated, sometimes those habits can be successfully used against themselves and other times they can be successfully blocked through the separatist efforts of people of color.

PART ONE

Unconscious Habit

ONE

Ignorance and Habit

It can be tempting to think that today most white people are racist primarily because of an inadvertent lack of knowledge about the cultures and lives of people of color. Many white people in the United States and other white privileged countries do not often personally interact with people of color, and when they do, such interactions often are of the trivial sort found in consumer exchanges. Given the de facto but persistent racial segregation of many cities, neighborhoods, and schools and the paucity of non-stereotypical portrayals of people of color on television and in Hollywood movies, white solipsism is a real problem. In many people's day-to-day lives, it can seem as if only white people exist. While the literal existence of people of color may be acknowledged, such acknowledgment often occurs on an abstract level that produces an ethical solipsism in which only white values, interests, and needs are considered important and worthy of attention. And this phenomenon can affect people of color directly, not just indirectly through white people's reactions and responses, since people of color often internalize messages about their alleged insignificance and inferiority. If only more accurate information about the lives, worlds, and values of people of color were available, so this line of thinking goes, everyone would know more about them and be able to see that they are not racially inferior to white people.

A similar temptation is to think that white people are racist because they lack accurate knowledge about the (alleged) scientific, biological basis for racial categories. This view of racism holds that many people fail to understand that there are no necessary and sufficient biological or genetic conditions for dividing the human population into distinct races. Because of this failure, they mistakenly think that race and racial hierarchies are real. Demonstrate the lack of scientific basis for race, so says this eliminativist view, and racism will disappear because the categories on which it is based—white, black, and so on—will have disappeared. Racial categories and the racism they support are like the emperor who wears no clothes. All one need do is honestly point out the emperor's nakedness, and the illusion of his clothing will disappear. Dismantling the biological theories of race upon which racism rests likewise requires merely the same straightforward good will to acknowledge the obvious: the lack of the scientific data to support racial categorization.[1]

White privileged ignorance, as I will call the ignorance that benefits and supports the domination of white people, does contribute to the racial privilege of white people. But what is misleading about the above accounts is their portrayal of white privileged ignorance as completely accidental and unintentional.[2] This naive view of ignorance posits it as a simple lack of knowledge, a gap that has not yet been filled but that easily could be. The racism that results from unfilled gaps in knowledge is not, on this view, the product of anything that anyone has done. It is the result of lack of activity and the absence of efforts to seek out information about non-white people and worlds. What is striking about these naive views is that they have the effect of excusing people for their racism—and white people in particular since they, and not people of color, are the beneficiaries of white privilege. Racism is not the product of anything that white people actually do, so the story goes. It is not something that they consciously intend. They might be chided a bit for not rectifying their ignorance of the lives of people of color and the latest scientific advances, but only if they are aware of their ignorance in the first place—for how can people be held responsible for something that they did not know about? Blithely wrapped up in a white world, white people often do not see their own ignorance and cannot be faulted for not addressing it, so it seems. Point it out to them, give them accurate information about science and non-white people, and white people will gladly fill in the gaps in their knowledge and eliminate their racism.

This view of ignorance problematically softens the ugly realities of white domination by presenting simultaneously a positive image of white people and an optimistic outlook on the prospects for eliminating racism. The only obstacle to the elimination of racism and white privilege, on this view, is the relatively manageable difficulty of generating and distributing accurate information about non-white people and worlds. Because of this positive image and optimistic outlook, a naive understanding of white privileged ignorance can be very tempting—and not just to white people, whom it flatters, but also to people of color, who often want or need to believe that problems of racism are solvable with straightforward hard work and persuasive rational argumentation. More than one contemporary critical race theorist has fallen victim to it, but they are not unique in this respect. Some of the greatest classical philosophers of race also were lured into thinking that white domination could be fought merely by eliminating naive ignorance of it. I focus for a moment on one of those greats, W. E. B. Du Bois, because his story both offers a "real life" example of the temptations of a naive view of ignorance and presents an important alternative to it. Introducing the concept of unconscious habit, Du Bois's work suggests a valuable model for understanding white privilege that deserves investigation and development.

In the early part of his career (roughly 1897–1910), Du Bois described himself as a scientist who was concerned about accuracy and the search for truth.[3] While much of his work during that time is located in the humanities, it is scientific in that it represents "a careful search for truth" that would "make the Truth clear" to all.[4] Du Bois's fiction, musical scores, and poetry share with his sociological descriptions and data the goal of lifting the veil that covers the black world, preventing the white world from seeing it as it truly is. His detailed studies counter the assessments of those who think that they can quickly understand the lives of black people as, for example, they drive by black laborers "irresponsibly" neglecting their work. To counter centuries of racism, much more careful and detailed scientific analyses are needed, including the "scientific" truths that the arts and humanities can provide. Du Bois's scientific work was not concerned with abstract and eternal laws (as, in his view, the research of most other social scientists of his day was), but rather focused on a concrete set of human beings—black people—who had been isolated from others due to race. By bringing scientific tools of investigation (broadly understood) to the issue of race, Du Bois hoped to transform the vague "Negro problem" into a collection of specific, context-sensitive facts. Du Bois largely fulfilled this goal, producing the first systematic studies of black mortality, crime, social betterment, churches, business, education, and health.

Du Bois's pursuit of truth worked hand in hand with what he called a "liberal" approach to the elimination of racism. Du Bois's liberalism naively posited human beings as always wishing to do good and as failing to do so only because they did not know what the good was. On this Socratic view of human nature, if human beings perform racist acts or hold racist beliefs, they do so only because they do not have accurate information about, for example, the black people that they discriminate against. Hence the need for sociological, artistic, and other work that shows the truth about black people. For the early Du Bois, one could assume, at their core white people were morally and personally good.[5] He thought that white ignorance of the lives of black people was the cause of racism, and he understood their ignorance to mean merely that white people were innocently oblivious of the details of black life and culture. In that case, the elimination of racial prejudice depended merely upon generating and distributing accurate depictions of and data about groups that are racially oppressed. Calling for white people to become more familiar with the lives and situations of black people, Du Bois put his faith in the basic goodness of white people. Their increased knowledge would reduce black people's (perceived) foreignness and eliminate the reason for white people's racist attitudes and behaviors toward them.

All this changed shortly after World War I. In 1920, Du Bois published *Darkwater,* which, as the title suggests, presents a much murkier picture of white people. In his biting essay "The Souls of White Folk," Du Bois describes himself as sitting high in a tower peering down into white people's souls, which sound remarkably similar to their unconscious: the "stripped,-ugly" insides or "entrails" of white people that usually are hidden away.[6] World War I led Du Bois to abandon his belief that the majority of white people were fundamentally good-hearted. He acknowledged that sometimes for the world's "salvation," the lie that white people are honest and can be trusted needs to be told, but he announced that he himself no longer believed it.[7] Du Bois came to realize that the ignorance manifested by white people was much more complex and sinister than he earlier had thought. Rather than an innocuous oversight, it was an active, deliberate achievement that was carefully (though not necessarily consciously) constructed, maintained, and protected. Du Bois eventually saw that to understand the white ignorance of non-white people, one has to hear the active verb "to ignore" at the root of the noun.[8] What had initially seemed to him like an innocent lack of knowledge on white people's part revealed itself to be a malicious production that masked the ugly Terrible of white exploitative ownership of non-white people and cultures. He recognized that the strategies for fighting racism most likely to be successful were the ones that addressed the "founding stones of race antagonisms," which

were "other and stronger and more threatening forces" than blithe ignorance or even deliberate malice.[9]

The strategy Du Bois turned to after abandoning liberalism confronted unconscious racist habits. Combining Freudian psychoanalysis
with a pragmatist understanding of habit, Du Bois began to believe that
much of human behavior is guided by irrational and unconscious habits.[10]
Criticizing his earlier liberal approach to racism, Du Bois states, "I was not
at the time sufficiently Freudian to understand how little human action is
based on reason."[11] While Du Bois never indicates which texts and how
much of Freud's work he read, he clearly credits Freud's "new psychology"
for changing his thinking about race. As Du Bois implies, his turn to Freud
did not constitute a break with the pragmatist side of his earlier thought,
but rather a deepened development of it:

> [Around 1930] the meaning and implications of the new psychology had
> begun slowly to penetrate my thought. My own study of psychology
> under William James had pre-dated the Freudian era, but it had pre-
> pared me for it. I now began to realize that in the fight against race
> prejudice, we were not facing simply the rational, conscious determina-
> tion of white folk to oppress us; we were facing age-long complexes sunk
> now largely to unconscious habit and irrational urge.[12]

Du Bois's use of the term "unconscious habit" suggests a return taken by
means of psychoanalysis to an element of pragmatism neglected in the
beginning of his career. Having been trained by James while an undergraduate at Harvard University, Du Bois must have been exposed to the
concept of habit found in James's *The Principles of Psychology,* yet it is
largely absent in Du Bois's early work.[13] Like other pragmatists such as
Charles Sanders Peirce and John Dewey, James operated with a "thick"
understanding of habit as deeply constitutive of who a person is and
therefore as difficult and slow (though not impossible) to change. By
contrast, the rare times Du Bois mentions habit prior to 1930, he dis-
missively uses a very thin, non-pragmatist version of it.[14] In 1920, for
example, he claims that "our modern contempt of Negroes rests upon no
scientific foundation worth a moment's attention. It is nothing more than
a vicious habit of mind. It could as easily be overthrown as our belief in
war, as our international hatreds, as our old conception of the status of
women, as our fear of educating the masses, and as our belief in the
necessity of poverty."[15] The comparisons made by Du Bois might make it
appear that his claim about the ease of overthrowing racism is meant
sarcastically—who today, after all, thinks that poverty and international
hatred can be easily eliminated? But Du Bois intends the comparisons to

have the opposite effect of reassuring his reader that racism, like other social ills, can be overcome if only we will it so. This is evident in the continuation of his remarks, in which he claims that "[w]e can, if we will, inaugurate on the Dark Continent a last great crusade for humanity."[16]

Although the early Du Bois either misunderstood or overlooked a key concept in James's psychology, he later declares that it was James's work that prepared him to accept Freud's concept of the unconscious. A circular influence appears to have operated in which James's psychology paved the way for Du Bois's appropriation of Freud's psychoanalysis, which in turn enabled Du Bois to appreciate James's thick understanding of habit.[17] Du Bois's concept of unconscious habit combines a Freudian idea of the unconscious with a pragmatist understanding of habit to posit an unconscious formed by socially inherited customs and attitudes that resists its transformation. As such, the concept broadens Freud's idea of the unconscious beyond its focus on the Oedipalized nuclear family and deepens pragmatism's concept of habit by connecting it with activities of repression and resistance to change that the psyche often employs. For Du Bois, a significant part of the constitution of unconscious habits involves active mechanisms and strategies for blocking access to them by conscious inquiry. That habits are dynamically constituted through transaction with the socio-cultural world rather than fixed by biology or psychology does not change the fact that transforming them will take a great deal of patience and time, in large part because of habit's ability to actively undermine its own transformation.[18]

Du Bois's insights into unconscious habits of white domination are fitting not only for the mid-twentieth century. They also remain extremely valuable today. While rational, conscious argumentation has a role to play in the fight against racism, antiracist struggle ultimately will not be successful if the unconscious operations of white privilege are ignored. White unconscious resistance to understanding racism as a problem must be tackled if inroads are to be made against specific problems of racism. Not only can white people not help challenge racism if they do not see it, but non-white people's attempts to combat racism cannot be maximally successful if white people's unconscious commitments thwart such work. Contemporary critical race theory cannot proceed effectively by assuming either that logical arguments against racism will convince racists to change their beliefs or that racism can be ended by conscious fiat. Even though logical arguments about race might lead a person to consciously decide to endorse non-racist ideas, such a decision does not necessarily have much, if any, impact on his or her unconscious habits. Here then is a place where consciously calculated judgments of praise and blame alone are insufficient. The unconscious, as Du Bois writes, is "an area where we must apply other remedies and judgments, . . . survey[ing] these vague and uncharted lands and measur[ing] their limits."[19]

It is such charting of unconscious habits that I pursue in this book. Du Bois suggests a powerful psychoanalytic-pragmatist model for surveying the unconscious operations of white domination, but it remains only a tantalizing suggestion in his work. With his model as inspiration, I develop an account of the seemingly invisible and yet actively productive unconscious habits of white privilege. Some of the uncharted lands to be surveyed are the body, the psyche, and the world in their co-constitutive transactions. Some of the limits to be measured include the mutual constitution of the psychical, geographical, and economic, especially in white consumption of non-white worlds, and relationships of race and space, including white habits of ontological expansiveness. And some of the remedies to be explored, in all their dangerous potential, involve turning away from a person's habits to the "external" environments that form them. But first these various chartings demand a more in-depth examination of habit in conjunction with race. What is habit and what is its significance for race and white privilege?

Understood pragmatically, habit is an organism's subconscious predisposition to transact with its physical, social, political, and natural worlds in particular ways. Habit is equivalent to neither routine nor a "bad habit," as the term is often used. Habits instead are that which constitute the self.[20] Most of them are not objects of conscious awareness; human beings enact them "without thinking," which means that a significant portion of the self is nonconscious. One could say that habits compose the style by which an organism engages with its world, as long as "style" is understood phenomenologically rather than epiphenomenally. Habits are not like clothing fashions that one can quickly pick up one day and then discard the next. They instead are manners of being and acting that constitute an organism's ongoing character. This does not mean that habit necessarily is fixed and rigid, although it can be. Habit is a stable yet somewhat malleable structure. It can be thought of as analogous to the structure of a house, as Dewey explains: "[a] house has a structure; in comparison with the disintegration and collapse that would occur without its presence, this structure is fixed. Yet it is not something external to which the changes involved in building and using the house have to submit. It is rather an arrangement of changing events such that properties which change slowly, limit and direct a series of quick changes and give them an order which they do not otherwise possess."[21] Like the structure of a house, habit is an arrangement of transformation relative to its context whose speed is governed by the sedimentation of its past.

The structured transformation that is habit is both physical and mental. The concept of habit, in other words, addresses the live organism in all its psychosomatic complexity. Functional distinctions can be made between mental habits, such as a female student's tendency to present her views in class apologetically, and physical or bodily habits, such as the same student's tendency to contract her body inward as she sits. But this distinction is not one between different mental and physical substances. Both types of habit involve a person's physiology and psychology and, as the example of my female student suggests, involve them not in additive ways but in their mutual and co-constitutive relationship. As is the case for many women, the student in my example has an inhibited style of engaging with the academic world that is inseparably psychical and bodily. Her transaction with a sexist world creates particular psychosomatic predispositions for engaging with it that cannot be chopped up into separate realms of body and mind.

As the example of my student also suggests, habits are simultaneously limiting and enabling. They provide the means by which one is able to act in the world, and in so doing they also exclude other possible styles of acting (at least until a change of habit occurs). Habit means that a person is not a blank slate, nor is she radically free to transact with the world in any way that she might consciously will. As the means by which a person can be effective in the world, habit is that which provides agency. Habit circumscribes the possibilities for one's action such that not all modes of engagement are available, but it also is an important means by which a person can act effectively in the world. A blank slate, if an organism could exist as one, would not be free, but rather powerless. In other words, freedom and limitation are not necessarily opposed. Freedom and power are found in and through the constitution of habits, not through their elimination.[22]

What then might a pragmatist concept of habit mean in the context of race and white privilege? Because habit is transactional, in a raced and racist world, the psychosomatic self necessarily will be racially and racistly constituted. Race is not a veneer lacquered over a nonracial core. It composes the very bodily and psychical beings that humans are and the particular ways by which humans engage the world. Like gender and sexism, sexuality and compulsory heterosexuality, disability and bias toward ability, class and class oppression, and other characteristics of contemporary human beings, race and white privilege are constitutive features of human existence and experience as they currently occur. Sometimes these habits are consciously felt, other times not, but in all cases they help make up who and what human beings are.

As an instance of habit, race often functions subconsciously, as a predisposition for acting in the world that is not consciously chosen or planned. Because raced predispositions often actively subvert efforts to understand or change them, making themselves inaccessible to conscious inquiry, race often functions unconsciously as well. Both the subconscious and unconscious aspects of habit can be either limiting or enabling—or both—depending on the particular situation. For example, to be a white person means that one tends to assume that all cultural and social spaces are potentially available for one to inhabit. The habit of ontological expansiveness enables white people to maximize the extent of the world in which they transact. But as an instance of white solipsism, it also severely limits their ability to treat others in respectful ways. Instead of acknowledging others' particular interests, needs, and projects, white people who are ontologically expansive tend to recognize only their own, and their expansiveness is at the same time a limitation. As this brief example suggests, being enabled by a habit may not always be a positive phenomenon. The meaning of the limitation and ability provided by habit can vary, and the power provided by white habits in particular often is oppressive to others. In the case of race, as in all other cases, it is important to ask: for what does a particular habit empower a person and from what does it limit her?

To demonstrate in more depth how habit can be used as a powerful tool for understanding the racial constitution of human life, I turn to Alexis de Tocqueville's racially attuned descriptions of the composition of the United States, reading them through a pragmatist lens of habit.[23] Tocqueville's work is valuable because it demonstrates how race and white domination can vary based on geographical and regional differences. In *Democracy in America,* the product of Tocqueville's nine-month tour of the United States in the early 1830s, Tocqueville notes that

> [t]he only means by which the ancients maintained slavery were fetters and death; the Americans of the South of the Union have discovered more intellectual securities for the duration of their power. They have employed their despotism and their violence against the human mind. In antiquity precautions were taken to prevent the slave from breaking his chains; at the present day measures are adapted to deprive him even of the desire for freedom.[24]

Understood as habit, slavery in the United States was not merely an external constraint imposed upon black people. It also constituted the slave's disposition to transact with the world as enslaved, as not needing or wanting freedom and as understanding his or her enslavement as appropriate and natural. Tocqueville calls this an "intellectual security" to distinguish it from the security provided by rope and chains, but this phrase should not be taken to mean that the effects of slavery were mental only. As habits, intellectual securities affected the slave's entire mode of being, as Tocqueville himself suggests when he describes slavery in terms of its influence on the slave's "manners." Tocqueville writes that "[t]he slave is a servant who never remonstrates and who submits to everything without complaint. He may sometimes assassinate his master, but he never withstands him."[25] The slave's submission could be seen in many of his or her habits—physical and emotional, as well as mental—which is to say that slavery contributed to the composition of the slave's self. Slaves tended not only to mentally accept their enslavement, but also to physically embody it through their bowed shoulders, their downcast eyes that would not look their master in the face, and their lack of overtly expressed anger to white people about their enslavement.[26]

Slavery affected the habits and the selves not just of black slaves, but also of white people. The white Southerner learned as an infant to be a "domestic dictator": "the first notion he acquires in life is that he is born to command, and the first habit which he contracts is that or ruling without resistance."[27] Tocqueville does not mention that this was truer for white men than women since white women in the United States were educated into a double consciousness in which they were to obey father and husband, but also to rule over the in-house slaves and other black people with whom they came into contact. In this way, the racial habits of white men and white women in the South tended to vary. Tocqueville's point nonetheless stands that, qua white, both male and female white Southerners were encouraged to develop overt habits of domination that Northerners were not. But this does not mean that white Northerners were not racist. They tended to develop racist habits of avoidance of, rather than explicit domination over, black people.

Tocqueville provocatively claimed that the abolition of slavery would increase, rather than decrease, the divisions and antagonisms between white and black people. He based his claim on the habits of white Northerners, who increasingly avoided intermingling with black people the more that legal barriers between them were removed.[28] In contrast, in the South, where legislation created significant formal separation between black and white people, "the habits of the [white] people are more tolerant and compassionate."[29] White masters could mix with black slaves during work and play to an extent because the hierarchy between them was firmly fixed and explicitly recognized. There was no danger that black slaves might be perceived or perceive themselves as similar to or equal with white people. But for Northerners, "the white no longer distinctly perceives the barrier that separates him from the degraded race, and he shuns the Negro with the more pertinacity since he fears lest they should some day be confounded together."[30] For this reason, Tocqueville remarks, "[i]f I were called upon to predict the future, I should say that the abolition of slavery in the South will, in the common course of things, increase the repugnance of the white population for the blacks."[31]

Tocqueville's prediction concerning the continuation of racism after the end of slavery in the United States was acutely accurate. Racism and white domination persist beyond slavery, and they do so in large degree because of the enduring force and subversive resistance of habit. Adapting Tocqueville's claims, one could say that the end of overt white supremacy, exemplified in slavery, does not set the slave free but merely transfers him to another master found in the covert habits of white privilege.[32] What Tocqueville suggested in 1835 and what needs more exploration today is the enduring legacy of slavery in personal, cultural, and institutional habits of white privilege. While the details of Tocqueville's account of the habits of white Southerners and Northerners are dated in some respects and there is reason to suspect that Tocqueville was influenced by pro-slavery propaganda of the time, Tocqueville's analyses are valuable because they evidence a contextual attunement to the racial composition of the self. Tocqueville is sensitive to the fact that habits might take a variety of different shapes in a raced and racist world even though his particular account of those shapes may be skewed. The general lesson that can be learned from reading Tocqueville through a pragmatist lens of habit is that attempts to change racist institutional and personal habits are likely to be ineffective unless they address the particular forms of habit that racism produces and the particular environments that encourage and discourage racism.

One of the most significant of those environments is the contemporary classroom.[33] Educational structures and practices are some of the most effective ways by which habits are formed and transformed, and for that reason, education is always simultaneously ontological and political. Racism in schools today generally is not as blatant as it was in, for example, Tocqueville's or Du Bois's day. While this is a positive development in many ways, it often has the paradoxical consequence of making racism more difficult to detect and combat. One of my black students recently remarked that he would almost rather be called a "nigger" to his face than deal with the liberal racism of the white person who espouses the abstraction that everyone is equal and cannot understand why black people feel discriminated against. The student felt that at least when fighting overt racism, he would not have also to fight the layers of mystification and charges of paranoia that tend to accompany liberal racism. Chicano/a students today may not be told explicitly that they have to choose between being a "legitimate" student and being a Chicano/a—although many still were through the early 1970s.[34] But the implicit privileging of standards of whiteness in current educational practices in the United States often can be equally effective in conveying the same message. These standards discourage the transactional remaking of white and non-white students alike and implicitly tell non-white students that they must abandon their racial and ethnic identities to enter the classroom.

One particular educational practice in which white privilege can be found is the habits of communication that college classrooms often enforce.[35] Modes of public expression in black and white communities can vary considerably, but only white, middle-to-upper-class modes of behavior tend to be utilized and viewed as appropriate in class discussions. To provide just one example, for middle-to-upper-class white people, turn-taking in discussion is to be authorized by someone other than the one who wants to speak: the instructor. The polite way to engage in discussion is to raise one's hand and make one's point in the order in which the instructor recognizes students. For another student to try to speak out of turn or before a prior speaker has finished making all her points is to interrupt and be rude. Also, a person does not have to have anything important or on topic to say in order to take a turn; white communities are "democratic" in allowing everyone to have a turn. Finally, middle-to-upper-class white people tend to think that in discussion their points should not be made in the form of a personal argument or in an impassioned manner. In their view, to argue effectively means to calmly, dispassionately, and objectively state a position without mixing it with personal opinions.

In contrast, in black communities, particularly those that are working class, people tend to value individual regulation of when turns are taken. In a classroom, this means that rather than wait on the instructor to call on people, a person who wants to take a turn should do so anytime after another makes a first point about which she has something relevant and valuable to say. For a speaker to continue making subsequent points and not let others into the discussion is to antagonize others by "hogging the floor." Also antagonizing is for someone to speak for the mere sake of speaking, when that person has nothing relevant or valuable to say. Likewise, silence on the part of others often is seen as disrespectful during discussion of a controversial topic since if someone disagrees with a view, she or he is obliged to speak up—this is because the pursuit of truth is seen as a community enterprise that requires everyone's assistance. Finally, black people, particularly those who are working class, tend to value contributions to discussion that are made in a more passionate and personal manner. While for middle-to-upper-class white people, truth is something intrinsic to the idea put forward itself and needs only a spokesperson, black people tend to take the role of advocate for an idea when they present it. Passionate belief in and feeling about an idea is not presumed by black people to interfere with discovering its truth.

I am aware of the danger of racially characterizing different habits of communication as black and white: doing so risks reinforcing common, racist stereotypes of black and white people. I am also aware of my descriptions' ability to mislead: certainly there are exceptions to the race- and class-based patterns sketched above, which are more complex in "real life" than any brief summary on paper can portray, and racial habits are not unchanging, eternal features of people of any color. But these dangers should not be used as an excuse to avoid the often difficult examination of the role that race plays in the classroom—a mistake to which white people can be particularly prone. I find it significant that a white person at an academic conference objected that my descriptions of race in the classroom stereotyped black people, while the black students in a class with whom I discussed the same issues agreed that similar racial patterns of communication existed and thought it important to acknowledge them. It is a mistake to think that any talk of racial habits necessarily is equivalent to malicious racial stereotyping, a mistake often made by white people who tend to think that the racial dynamics of a situation did not exist prior to someone's asking about them. The danger of operating with harmful stereotypes when talking about race is not negligible. But in a sociopolitical climate infused with de facto racism, it is more dangerous to avoid discussion of racial habits because such avoidance tends to leave their operation unexamined and likely misunderstood. Racial differences currently are real (although not essential), and their reality (as well as their historical contingency) needs to be recognized if racism is to be successfully fought.

My descriptions of racial habit should be read as an illustration of some of the ways by which habits of communication in the classroom racialize (and class) both the space of education and the habits of those being educated, a racing of educational space that must be confronted.[36] As bell hooks has explained,

[p]rofessors cannot empower students to embrace diversities of experience, standpoint, behavior, or style if our training has disempowered us, socialized us to cope effectively only with a single mode of interaction based on [white] middle-class values. Most progressive professors are more comfortable striving to challenge class [and race] biases through the material studied than they are with interrogating how class [and race] biases shape conduct in the classroom and transforming their pedagogical process.[37]

To the extent that turn-taking in class discussion is instructor-regulated, "democratically" allows the person holding the floor to talk until she decides she is finished, and prioritizes dispassionate calm on the part of speakers, the classroom is one in which middle-to-upper-class, white communication habits generally are rewarded and working-class and black communication habits generally are penalized. Black students who do not adopt white, middle-class habits of discussion will appear to fellow students and their instructor as rude and out of control. Their patterns of communication generally will not be welcomed as valid contributions to the transactional intermingling of habits. Black students who do not adopt white habits often will be silenced in and alienated from the class.[38]

Because of its emphasis on habit, my account of the implications of pragmatist philosophy for critical race theory differs significantly from one of the few contributions to the field that explicitly draws on pragmatist theory. In *Becoming a Cosmopolitan: What It Means to Be a Human Being in the New Millennium,* Jason Hill bases his attack on racism on Dewey's "metaphysics of becoming."[39] Hill's concern is that race and ethnicity often are understood as fixed aspects of the self, an understanding that locks people into a static manner of being, ignores the fluidity of the self, and labels as inauthentic anyone who attempts to change her racial or ethnic identity. Hill appeals to Dewey to combat this "tribalism." According to Hill, for Dewey "[b]ecoming is an inescapable feature of life."[40] As tribalists do, one can deny this pervasive aspect of existence and thereby arrest one's self-development, but this does not change the malleability of the self that makes it always an ongoing process.[41] In contrast to the tribalist, the cosmopolitan embraces the fluidity of the self and realizes that "[t]he self that we find ourselves in possession of at any moment need not be the self that we are saddled with for life."[42] Human beings are never fully determined by their present, according to Hill. More than just free, human beings are freedom itself.[43] Blending Jean-Paul Sartre's existentialism with Dewey's pragmatism, Hill defines becoming as a "radical freedom" that can liberate people from confining and oppressive racial and ethnic identities.[44]

Hill's concern to open up new possibilities for racial existence is well placed, and using the plasticity of the pragmatist self to argue for an antiracist future has the potential to be fruitful. But Hill misconstrues pragmatism in significant ways and in doing so blunts the distinctive contributions that the pragmatist concept of habit can make to critical race theory. Although Hill acknowledges briefly that "one can never divest oneself totally of the habits, values, and schema of the world of one's assimilated culture," he ultimately views habit as merely a restrictive burden placed on the self from sources external to it.[45] When he claims that "Dewey distinguishes between the old static and habitual self and the dynamic self" and that "[t]he old habitual self is encapsulated within the matrices of an unchanging frame of reference and thus assumes a standpoint of completion," it is clear that for Hill, habit is something categorically negative to be reduced as much as possible even if it unfortunately cannot be totally eliminated.[46]

One of the reasons for his misconception of the concept of habit is that Hill equates the constitutive with the permanent: if something is constitutive of the self, as tribalists take race and ethnicity to be, then it is something permanent and unchanging.[47] Another reason is that Hill assumes a dichotomy between the existence of subconsciously crafted aspects of our selves and the ability to transform our lives.[48] For Hill, racial and ethnic identities, which are largely learned in subconscious ways during childhood, interfere with the conscious choosing and re-choosing of one's self that is the mark of the cosmopolitan. But these are mistaken equations and false dichotomies. That habit is constitutive of the self and that habit is subconscious (or unconscious) does not mean that the self— or its habits—is incapable of change. Nor does it mean that a particular self has always and must always be constituted by means of its current habits. At minimum, this is because one of the particular habits that can be developed is that of openness to the reconfiguration of habit. As Dewey explains, habit formation can become subject "to the habit of recognizing that new modes of association will exact a new use of it. Thus habit is formed in view of possible future changes and does not harden so readily."[49] Even without this particular habit, transformation can occur. If and when it does, it tends to come gradually, is continuous with what came before, and often is difficult to achieve. A self constituted by means of raced habits can be changed, but the remaking of one's racial identity likely will be a slow-going and painstaking process with no guarantee of success.

Failing to allot sufficient weight to habit in a pragmatist concept of the self, Hill can claim, "Dewey's theory supports the idea that there is nothing *ontologically* binding in [his] status as a West Indian or Caribbean man."[50] My point here does not concern the details of Hill's identity in particular. It instead is that, due to the constitutive role of habit, in a raced and racist world one's race indeed has the status of ontology. My being a white person, for example, as well as a middle-class, well-educated, currently able-bodied, heterosexual woman from Texas, is part of the being that I am. These aspects of my being are not eternal, ahistorical, or acultural, nor do I have a felt awareness of all of them. But that does not mean that they are not ontological, for ontology is not composed of eternal and unchanging characteristics, nor is it reducible to conscious experience. Ontology is constituted instead by the historical, contextual, simultaneously malleable and stable, and only occasionally felt features of situated, located beings.

To deny that race is ontological is to imply that race is a sort of veneer laid over a nonraced human core.[51] But it is too simple to characterize race as imposed by a racist society upon a pre-racialized human being. Such an understanding of race inadequately acknowledges the ways in which the transactions between a raced world and those who live in it racially constitute the very being of those beings. It fails to appreciate that "the *source* of racializations, or at least one important source, is in the micro-processes of subjective existence" found in the ways that one both lives and resists one's race.[52] This does not mean that people immediately or always experience themselves as raced. A newborn does not live her bodily being as raced, and many people of color, in particular, experience a sudden shock upon realizing that they are raced, marking their passage into living race in a consciously aware way.[53] But the fact that people are not always consciously aware of the racial characteristics of their lived experience—or, in the case of many white people, never become consciously aware of their race—does not mean that human existence in a raced world is pre-racial or racially neutral. Nor does it mean that race has no effect on one's life or experience. In a racialized world, and particularly a racist one, race always already constitutes who and what individual human beings are. Even the newborn who has no conscious awareness of race is impacted by it in an ontologically constitutive way vis-à-vis the way that people treat her, the current and future opportunities that are available to her, and so on.

Because of its importance, let me repeat that the racial ontology I am developing by means of a pragmatist concept of habit is not racial biologism, which would hold that one's physiological or genetic makeup determines one's race. Nor is it a claim that human existence must always be raced. Race as currently constituted has not always existed. Race, including whiteness, takes different forms in different locales and situations, and at some time and place in the future, race may no longer exist. But today the world is raced in a variety of sometimes settled and sometimes shifting ways, which means that as composed of transactionally constituted habits, human beings, customs, and institutions are raced in a variety of settled and shifting ways as well. Race is not a fixed, unchanging structure, but its malleability does not mean that it is totally fluid. As a practical, habit-based reality, race has a durability that must be reckoned with rather than wished away.

I realize that to argue that race is ontological may sound rather conservative, especially in contrast to a use of pragmatism that promises freedom from race. It may seem rather suspicious for a white person to argue that the concept of habit entails that any possible transformation of race and elimination of racism will take a long time. But my goal in understanding race in terms of habit is not to urge patience with racism. In fact, just the opposite: it is to identify one of the main ways that personal and institutional racism operates so that it might be better fought. Declaring human beings to be radically free is not an effective strategy for combating racism, at least not at this point in history. The goal of freedom from racism—and freedom from race, if it is desired, although I do not think that such freedom is always desirable nor that it is necessary for the elimination of racism[54]—requires attending in detailed and contextual ways to the concrete means toward that end. If, as Dewey explains, "the thing which is closest to us, the means within our power, is . . . habit," then challenging racism requires attending to the complex ways that an organism's subconscious habits are formed through transaction with its environments.[55]

Hill's example is not the only or even the most problematic one of how to misuse a pragmatist concept of habit in a well-intentioned attempt to eliminate racism. One of the pillars of pragmatist philosophy, namely Dewey himself, provides several egregious ways of doing so. In "Racial Prejudice and Friction," Dewey persuasively argues that racial prejudice must be understood in terms of habit.[56] But he fails to understand the full significance of racial habits, largely reducing racial prejudice to an epiphenomenon of class and economic and political tensions and simultaneously portraying racial difference (read: non-white people) as a hostile threat. His reductivism is particularly clear in an essay he wrote ten years later, his 1932 "Address to the National Association for the Advancement of Colored People." Together these two essays demonstrate some of the ways that the recognition of habits as raced can go hand-in-hand with the implicit support of white privilege.[57]

In "Racial Prejudice and Friction," Dewey claims that in order to understand race prejudice, one must first understand the operations of prejudice in general. Prejudice is not a conscious judgment or belief. It is the subconscious desires, emotion, and perspectives that influence our judgments. Prejudice is the backdrop for judgment. It is a "spontaneous aversion" that preexists or precedes judgment, preventing some judgments and enabling others and "mak[ing] us see things in a particular light and giv[ing] a slant to all our beliefs."[58] In other words, prejudice is an instance of habit. It might be called "bias" as long as the word is not understood pejoratively. Human beings are always biased in that they are embodied, situated beings and not blank slates. Bias as such is not something bad to be eliminated, although, of course, particular biases might be judged as harmful and in need of change.[59]

One might expect Dewey to claim that racial prejudice is one of those harmful biases in need of elimination, but the story is more complicated than that. According to Dewey, as an instance of general prejudice, racial prejudice is "the instinctive aversion of mankind to what is new and unusual, to whatever is different from what we are used to, and which thus shocks our customary habits."[60] In a similar fashion, Dewey also characterizes racial prejudice as "the universal antipathy which is aroused by anything to which a tribe or social group is not adjusted in its past habits."[61] For Dewey, race prejudice is the subconscious antipathy to people with different skin color, manners of speech and dress, and so on, that shapes one's judgments about them. On Dewey's view, "the organic-psychological basis of racial prejudice is a native tendency that comes from being creatures of habit, namely, reacting against what is experienced as a threat to our habits."[62]

Race prejudice is not the same thing as racial friction, or what one today might call invidious racial discrimination. Dewey claims that left to itself, the aversion to the strange tends to disappear as people become familiar with what was once strange.[63] Race prejudice only becomes race friction when it is combined with other factors and encounters a catalyst of crisis. Physical, cultural, religious, and linguistic differences accentuate the felt strangeness of other groups, helping to consolidate the "native" prejudice felt against the unfamiliar. Political and economic tensions between groups, particularly nations, also exacerbate aversion to the strange other. These factors form the powder keg of racism that requires a crisis to ignite it. As Dewey explains, "[l]atent anti-foreign feeling is usually rendered acute by some crisis. . . . [L]et some untoward event happen, famine, plague, defeat in battle, death of some illustrious leader, and blame will be almost sure to fall upon the new-comers," in other words, those who seem strange.[64] With the advent of crisis, race prejudice, heightened by physical and cultural differences and political and economic tensions, can explode into full-blown race friction or discrimination.

This account of racial friction helps explain why Dewey claims that racial discrimination is not primarily about race. For Dewey, "[r]ace is a sign, a symbol, which bears much the same relation to the actual forces which cause friction that a national flag bears to the emotions and activities which it symbolizes, condensing them into visible and tangible form."[65] The actual forces causing friction are political and economic. Race prejudice, or the aversion to people who are of a race different than one's own, does not cause the friction in one's relationship with them. Race prejudice instead is the effect of that friction brought about by other causes.[66]

Dewey's account of racial prejudice is problematic in at least two significant ways. Let me begin with his claim that racial friction is not primarily racial. This claim is troubling not because Dewey is wrong that political and especially economic factors play a large role in racial friction and discrimination. It is troubling because Dewey's account of the relationship between race and political and economic factors is not sufficiently transactional. Not only do political and economic tensions help produce racial friction, but race also helps produce political and economic tensions. Dewey briefly recognizes this when he says that "[l]ike other social effects [race prejudice] becomes in turn a cause of further consequences; especially it intensifies and exasperates the other sources of friction [politics and economics]."[67] But then he proceeds to dismiss race as merely a symbol of friction that has other causes. One of the reasons he does so is to combat intellectualist psychology. Dewey rightly objects to such a notion because it disregards the role that social organization, bodily comportment, and other "external" factors play in the formation of one's mental habits. But in making his objection, Dewey errs too far the other direction, largely neglecting the way in which race plays a causal role in effecting racial friction and is not a mere epiphenomenon of other forces.[68]

While Dewey is right that race is always intertwined with political and economic factors, he wrongly—and uncharacteristically, a point to which I will return—takes a reductivist approach to race, collapsing it into politics and economics. Nowhere does Dewey do this more flagrantly than in his "Address to the National Association for the Advancement of Colored People." There he claims that the suffering that black Americans are undergoing during the depression is due to the same causes of the suffering of all other Americans. These causes are economic: "the real political issues of the day are economic, industrial and financial," not racial.[69] This is why Dewey tells his black audience, "the things that I should like to say to you tonight are the same sort of things that I would say to representatives of any white group that is also at a disadvantage economically, industrially, financially, and at a disadvantage politically in comparison with the privileged few."[70] Reducing race to class differences, Dewey treats the situation of black people and underprivileged white people as the same. But while it is true that class differences impacted black Americans negatively in the 1930s, it was not true that "the causes from which all are suffering are the same."[71] Failing to see this, Dewey makes the embarrassing case for the similar situation of disfranchised black and white voters. Speaking to black Americans, he claims:

> In many parts of the country your particular group is more definitely disfranchised than other groups. But if you stop to look over the field you will realize that there are large numbers of white groups that are voluntarily un-enfranchised if not disfranchised. The average vote in our national elections is about one-half, fifty percent, of those who might go to the polls and vote. That seems to me a very significant fact. Practically one-half the people who might vote voluntarily decline to do it; they disfranchise, un-enfranchise themselves. Why?[72]

Dewey's mystification is a result of his failure to see the particular impact of racial friction. While voter apathy undoubtedly was a real problem for many white people in 1932, the real problem for most black people was the violent efforts taken to prevent black people from going to the polls. Lynchings and cross burnings helped ensure that black American voices were not heard on voting day. White and black people may indeed both have been disfranchised, but the crucial difference was that white people disfranchised themselves, while black people often were violently disfranchised by others. The alleged similarity of suffering provided by disfranchisement is instead a large dissimilarity based on the reality of racial prejudice.

The second significant problem with Dewey's account of racial prejudice derives from his definition of it as an instinctive and universal reaction to what is new or unusual. Dewey suggests that on its own, there is nothing problematic about "instinctive dislike and dread of what is strange."[73] It is something that all human beings experience, and it tends to go away in time as people become accustomed to or familiar with what once seemed strange. This definition of racial prejudice implies that the nature of habit is such that it must be hostile to anything different from itself. As a result, Dewey's solution to the problem of racial prejudice calls for a transformation of the foreign into the familiar. More interaction and "mutual assimilation" between different cultures is needed to eliminate the racial prejudice that is at the base of racial friction. Eliminate the political and economic tensions, and racial friction also will disappear as people become familiar with what formerly seemed strange.

In his short essay on racial prejudice, Dewey construes habit as necessarily so resistant to change and difference that it must be hostile to the strange. But is that the only or primary account of habit available in pragmatist thought? Some of William James's remarks on habit tend to suggest that it is. He describes habit as a mechanism that keeps the various social classes in their place, protecting the status quo:

> Habit is the enormous fly-wheel of society, its most precious conservative influence. It alone is what keeps us within the bounds of ordinance, and saves the children of fortune from the uprisings of the poor. It alone prevents the hardest and most repulsive walks of life from being deserted by those brought up to tread therein. It . . . protects us from invasion by the natives of the desert and the frozen zone. . . . It keeps different social strata from mixing.[74]

It is unclear from this isolated passage whether James thinks that this is a praiseworthy feature of habit—although subsequent comments indicate that he does[75]—but it is unmistakable that he thinks that habit, though a result of the plasticity of organic matter, is first and foremost a conservative structure.

In major works such as *Human Nature and Conduct* and *Experience and Nature*, Dewey also presents habit as a structure that provides stability. But unlike James, he stresses that structure also and primarily is a process of change. To the earlier quote concerning the structure of a house as an arrangement of changing events, Dewey adds that "[s]tructure . . . cannot be discovered or defined except in some realized construction, construction being, of course, an evident order of changes. The isolation of structure from the changes whose stable ordering it is, [wrongly] renders it mysterious."[76] For Dewey and James alike, one cannot live in a world of total flux. Structure, such as that provided by habit, is necessary. But for Dewey, to claim this is not to oppose habit to flux, as if habit were entirely conservative or necessarily hardened with time and age. As a stable ordering of changing events, habit is composed of the organization of impulses. Or, better—since habit is not something apart from impulses directing their arrangement—habit just *is* the patterned flow of impulses, which can be disrupted by conflict with its changing environments. With this clash comes the need for a reorganization of habit, which—Dewey makes clear—includes the possibility of developing habits that might seek out and welcome future changes in habit. It is possible, Dewey says, "to subject habit-forming in a particular case to the habit of recognizing that new modes of association will exact a new use of it. Thus habit is formed in view of possible future changes and does not harden so readily."[77] Habit has a conservative side for Dewey, but it is not something that necessarily and always is adverse to the new and different. Ultimately, the main body of Dewey's work on habit is closer to that of Peirce than James when Peirce claims that " '[t]he highest quality of mind involves greatest readiness to take habits, and a great readiness to lose them.' "[78]

Given Dewey's general account of habit as capable of welcoming difference, it is odd that in his brief essay on racial prejudice he describes the habit of hostility toward the strange as universal to human existence. But perhaps this oddity is not so bewildering after all. Luce Irigaray describes her reading of Freud and major figures in Western philosophy as a process of listening carefully to their (sometimes overt, often covert) discussions of women's sexuality that, on their own logic, are inconsistent and contradictory. For Irigaray, the irrational leaps, elaborate contortions, and loud silences in their thought demonstrate that their so-called objective analyses of women's lack are fueled by unconscious anxieties, pleasures, and fears concerning the ongoing maintenance of phallocracy and continued support of women's bodies necessary to it.[79] In light of Irigaray's account, I cannot help but wonder if an unconscious anxiety about race is responsible for the strange inconsistencies that develop in Dewey's text as soon as he takes up questions of racial prejudice. Dewey's uncharacteristic description of habit as necessarily and universally hostile to difference, as well as his unusually reductive, non-transactional understanding of (raced) social phenomena, is less an objective account of the operations of racial habits than an unintentional report of what race looks like from the perspective of white privilege. An anxious unconscious speaks volumes about race in Dewey's works if only his readers can unclog their ears enough to hear it.[80]

Listening carefully to Dewey in "Racial Prejudice and Friction," one discovers that even before he moves to the specific topic of race in the essay, there is something amiss in his account of general prejudice that alerts his readers to the problems to come. In his explanation of prejudice as a subconscious bias that gives a slant to all beliefs, Dewey slips from a neutral to a negative sense of the term "bias" in the course of his descriptions of the concept. This slippage occurs when Dewey tucks in the word "aversion" to sum up his discussion of general prejudice as "a spontaneous aversion which influences and distorts subsequent judgments."[81] Presented as equivalent to his earlier, neutral accounts of bias, this definition allows Dewey to make an easy—even unavoidable—transition into defining racial prejudice as aversion. Dewey claims to define racial prejudice in terms of general prejudice, but in fact he appears to do just the opposite, beginning with his notion of racial prejudice as aversion to the strange and allowing that understanding to leak back into his general account of habit.

Aversion is one kind of bias, but it is only that. Many complex and varied forms of habit and bias exist, such as wonder, as Irigaray has pointed out. In her reading of Descartes's *The Passions of the Soul*, Irigaray praises wonder as the "first passion" felt in the presence of something new and different, a passion that might later give way to other "passions" that seek to categorize and judge but that itself does not do so.[82] Wonder is a kind of surprise felt in the face of the strange that lets its difference be without trying to assimilate it into something known, same, and familiar. For Irigaray, such wonder is necessary for any genuine ethical relationship to exist between two beings. When Dewey describes dread, dislike, and antipathy as universal in the face of the strange, Irigaray might say that he rushes past the possibility of wonder to a secondary or tertiary passion of "the anti-strange feeling."[83] If he were to recognize the possibility of wonder, different sorts of relationship between racial groups other than ones of aversion might be more likely.[84] One must be careful here that the passion of wonder does not camouflage a romantic orientalization of the other, a danger that Irigaray's work perhaps does not avoid. Her emphasis on wonder nonetheless helps reveal that antipathy toward the strange is not the only available option in the face of others different from oneself.[85]

Before I turn to Dewey's troubling solution to racial prejudice, I want to examine another problem that occurs with his description of it, which is that it implies that all people of all races see other people of other races as strange and unusual.[86] With his description of racial prejudice, Dewey universalizes his experience as a white Euro-American and, in doing so, assumes symmetry between white and non-white people that neglects the history and context of encounters between them. Let me be clear here that I am not claiming that, for example, black Africans did not find the light hair and skin of white Europeans to be unusual, even dreadful, when invading Europeans first showed up in Africa. Perhaps they did. My claim instead is that given the economic, political, historical, and nonreciprocal necessity for non-white people to work in and understand the world of white people, non-white people often have had to be very familiar with the lives and manners of white people in ways that white people have not had to be with non-whites. Both globally and locally, non-white slaves, migrant workers, and domestic help (just to name a few) have had to travel to the world of the white masters, bosses, and homes, and this world traveling has been and largely still is optional for most white people.[87] This establishes an asymmetry between white and non-white people that includes an inverse relationship of power and knowledge. The necessity of world traveling for many non-white people is a product of their relative lack of power, but it also is what tends to give them greater knowledge of white people's worlds. For black people, white people are not so much unusual or new as they are terrifyingly familiar. "All black people in the United States . . . live with the possibility that they will be terrorized by whiteness," explains bell hooks, and this phenomenon is nothing uncommon or strange.[88]

In his later work, Du Bois makes a similar point when he explains the intimate knowledge of white people that black people often have and have had. White people tend to think of themselves as clean, benevolent, and good while the black people that serve them see their other, more sordid sides. Speaking of the souls of white folk, Du Bois claims, "I see in and through them. . . . Not as a foreigner do I come, for I am native, not foreign, bone of their thought and flesh of their language. . . . I see these souls undressed and from the back and side. I see the working of their entrails. I know their thoughts and they know that I know. This knowledge makes them now embarrassed, now furious. . . . I see them ever stripped,— ugly, human."[89] Against Dewey and his own early liberalism, Du Bois's mature work suggests that it is intimacy and familiarity, not foreignness, that tends to produce anger and hostility toward others. On this point, Du Bois is closer to Freud's psychoanalysis than Dewey's pragmatism. Setting that issue aside, let me highlight Du Bois's challenge to Dewey's assumption that all races find people of other races foreign and unfamiliar. This assumption, which is the result of Dewey's projection of his own situation onto others, masks the particularity of whiteness and perpetuates its position of privilege.

Finally, and in addition to problems resulting from Dewey's definition of racial prejudice, I have significant concerns about his "solution" to it. Dewey claims that antipathy toward the strange tends to fade away: "In the main this feeling left to itself tends to disappear under normal conditions. People get used to what was strange and it is strange no longer."[90] According to Dewey, people become accustomed over time to what they once found strange and cease to feel the anti-strange feeling without really trying to, as it were. Put in more technical terms, Dewey's claim effectively is that after sedimented and change-fearing habits have been disrupted by something perceived as unusual, new patterns of impulses will come about that incorporate what was strange, eliminating its disturbing shock.

With Du Bois, Irigaray calls into question the idea that increased familiarity is a desirable solution to the "problem" of the disruptive strange, at least in the uncritical way that Dewey puts it forth. Her call for wonder in encounters with others is meant to prevent their incorporation into the same that familiarity threatens to bring about. But beyond that issue, my primary concern is that Dewey's solution of familiarity assumes an incredibly simplistic understanding of unconscious habits and naively underestimates the perversely complex operations of racism and white privilege.[91] Habits and their possible transformations involve imagination, fantasy, pleasure, and desire, all of which frequently operate on unconscious levels.[92] This is no truer anywhere than in the case of white privilege. Dewey neglects the irrationality and virility of racial power, especially in the tenacious hold it has on people's habits, apparently assuming that rational processes of inquiry will suffice to dismantle racism.[93]

Dewey makes the mistake of conflating ideologies of desire with ethnocentrism. Both are prejudices—in this case, racial prejudices—but ethnocentrism is a group-sustaining, ready-made approach in which one values one's own racial group over others, while ideologies of desire are tailor-made to create new racial groups on the basis of satisfying individuals' desires.[94] Ethnocentrism "is expressed in xenophobic assertions that have at least a tangential relation to the characteristics of real groups or subgroups, especially to those living separately," while ideologies of desire "are expressed in 'chimerias' [sic], or fantasies that have irrational reference to [allegedly] real, observable, or verifiable characteristics of a group or marks of difference."[95] Given the relatively rational basis for ethnocentrism and the relatively irrational basis for ideologies of desire, confusing the two undercuts effective understandings of and responses to racism. Assuming that all prejudices are ethnocentric leads to the mistaken view, held by Dewey and the early Du Bois, that all prejudice is born out of unfamiliarity with different groups. It also leads to the naive idea that integration of segregated groups will eliminate any kind of prejudice since increasing familiarity among groups will eliminate fear of and produce respect for the other. Although it may be helpful in the case of ethnocentric prejudice, this solution does not speak to "complexes of feelings and images of the 'Other' that are unconscious, as resistant to familiarity as the unconscious is to reasoned arguments or progressive social visions."[96] These complexes are indicative of ideologies of desire, which, as Du Bois but not Dewey eventually realized, are born out of intimacy and familiarity and demand different tactics and strategies for their elimination than ethnocentrism does.

In contrast to Dewey's naiveté, Cynthia Willett's analyses of racism demonstrate how habits of white privilege can operate by means of ideologies of desire located in the psychological pleasure that white people have taken in humiliating black people.[97] For example, one might think that the ultimate insult that a slaveholder could heap upon his or her slaves would be to view them solely as nonhuman brutes. From that perspective, for the slaveholder to see his or her slaves as a combination of the human and the subhuman would be relatively respectful (although, of course, still insulting and racist). Or, if not intended to convey respect, recognizing the human side of the slave would at least appear to have the purpose of alleviating the slaveholder's guilt, rather than that of inflicting additional injury upon the slave. But in fact, recognition of a slave's humanity can be used to increase her demoralization. Drawing from a scene in Toni Morrison's novel *Beloved* in which a slave woman overhears her master's teachings to white pupils about the differences between masters and slaves, Willett explains how racial hubris operates precisely by using the division of the African person into human and subhuman parts to produce maximal psychological pleasure for the white slaveholder. Seeing the slave as part human enabled the slaveholder to assault the slave even more ferociously than if the slave were assumed to be wholly animal. If the slave is part human, then using him or her like a brute is humiliating in a way that it could not be if the slave were fully nonhuman. The slaveholder in this case recognized a part of the slave that deserved dignity and respect only to ensure that the humiliating insult of slavery was felt that much more strongly.[98]

Because of the importance of unconscious racial fantasies and desires to the maintenance of many white people's sense of self, habits of racial prejudice tend to have a flexible tenacity that allows them to adjust to increased exposure to non-white others. But the point needs to be made even more strongly. It is not just that the roots of racial prejudice are so deep in the unconscious that mere increased familiarity over the passage of time will not be forceful or strong enough to yank them out. It is also that habits of white privilege can actively operate precisely so as to multiply and strengthen those roots and to thwart any attempts to eliminate them. Willett does not comment on whether the racial hubris in her example was conscious or unconscious, but in my view, there is no reason to hold that such hubristic machinations operate only on the level of conscious deliberation. Read as an account of the unconscious operations of white privilege, Morrison's *Beloved* not only shows the pleasure that white people have taken in racial domination, but also the active and devious effort that the white unconscious might engage in to produce and protect that pleasure.

Dewey demonstrates very little, if any, awareness of this. Admittedly, if read as a historically sensitive description of the white racist psyche, Dewey's essay on racial prejudice can be illuminating.[99] But nowhere in it does Dewey challenge, or even indicate awareness of, the white privileged perspective that operates within it. He drastically underestimates the obstacles to transformation that one's unconscious might erect, obstacles that are all the more effective because they are not the product of conscious deliberation. Habits can take the self-frustrating and self-defeating forms of repetition compulsion, projection, parapraxis, and other types of symptoms.[100] Habits, in other words, can often be defense mechanisms by which one protects oneself from perceived dangers and conflicts, the protection often including avoidance of conscious self-examination. Such habits are not the only kind that exists, but their potentially great influence on human behavior should be acknowledged. Unconscious habits of all varieties play a significant role in humans' psychosomatic lives in large part because of the way they disrupt habits of conscious self-examination.[101] In a racist world, habits of white privilege have a very important status in the unconscious life of most white people (including the well-intended, antiracist people that many white liberals take themselves to be) that Dewey's pragmatism has not yet begun to reckon with.

This is not to say that pragmatism is useless for such a project. Quite the opposite: I find a pragmatist understanding of habit crucial to understanding white privilege, only it must be developed in a more Du Boisian than Deweyan vein. Dewey's pragmatism does not constitute a Pollyannaish claim that virtually anything can happen. It is far too respectful of the past as embodied in institutional and personal habits to make outrageously optimistic predictions about the future.[102] But Dewey's account of subconscious habit tends to leave out the ugly hostility of human habits; it often seems to strike too genial a tone to grapple with the vicious realities of white privilege.[103] Dewey was quite right when he said that terms such as stranger, foreigner, alien, and outsider are just as psychological as they are geographical,[104] but he wrongly and dangerously claims that the prejudice often associated with them can be eliminated through mere increased familiarity of white with non-white people.

The concept of subconscious habit can account for certain forms of white-privileging ignorance of people of color. Subconscious habits of white privilege can explain both how white domination is enacted "without thinking" and how a person can be ignorant of her participation in white privilege. But the ignorance in question here is merely accidental. It is the naive ignorance that is inadvertent and unintended and that could be fairly easily eliminated if only it was brought to a person's attention. If white privileged habits are considered only as subconscious, the active verb "to ignore" at the root of ignorance tends to be neglected (or, more sinisterly, ignored). What often results in that case are the liberal strategies for fighting racism against which the later Du Bois rightly cautions.

To grapple with the twisted terrors and perverse pleasures of racism, a pragmatist concept of habit needs developing in connection with both an appreciation of imagination, fantasy, and desire and a psychoanalytic picture of the unconscious as often actively scheming against one's best efforts for change. This will require a pragmatized psychoanalysis. Thought as unconscious, the concept of habit demonstrates how habits often are deviously obstructionist, actively blocking the self's attempts to transform itself for the better. It suggests that habits often betray the self of which they are a part, complicating Dewey's claim that because they are closest to us, habits are the means within our power for change.[105] Habits of white privilege are both intimately close because they constitute the self, and elusively distant because of their ability to evade and obstruct conscious attention. They are both the means for change and that which actively interferes with it. Modified in this way, the concept of habit can be a powerful tool for understanding the operations of white privilege.

TWO

Engaging the Isolated Unconscious

Pragmatism and psychoanalysis: could there be a more unlikely pair? Pragmatism has a reputation for being levelheaded and down-to-earth, occupying itself with the practical and familiar, while psychoanalysis often is seen as more extravagant and excessive, dealing with the uncanny and unspeakable. While each of these pictures is something of a caricature, it is true that the two branches of philosophy tend to have very different temperaments and moods. And philosophers know, to borrow from William James and Friedrich Nietzsche, that a difference in style is a difference that makes a difference. It is interesting in this context to note that Sigmund Freud reportedly claimed, "John Dewey is one of the few men in the world . . . for whom I have a high regard."[1] Perhaps Freud saw possible connections between pragmatism and psychoanalysis that have been largely overlooked. Perhaps the two fields are not as alien to one another as they may seem.

I will not discuss here the large range of possible points of similarity and difference between pragmatism and psychoanalysis, nor address the issue of pragmatist versus psychoanalytic style. I am not so much interested in building complete bridges between pragmatism and psychoanalysis as I am in taking from each field theoretical tools that can help explain white privilege. Those tools, such as the pragmatist notion of habit and the psychoanalytic concept of the unconscious, often will need modification in light of each other. And occasionally significant obstacles to using those tools together must be addressed. One of those obstacles is Freud's atomism, which much of subsequent psychoanalysis has inherited. In my view, Freud's atomism creates the most significant clash between classical psychoanalysis and pragmatism and is the most problematic of the aspects of psychoanalytic philosophy that prevent it from making positive contributions to critical race theory.[2]

Dewey recognized this problem, although not in connection with race.[3] In one of his few positive comments about psychoanalysis, Dewey praises its insistence, against "the psychology of the conscious sensations," that much of human conduct, belief, and desire is not determined by consciousness.[4] But he then suggests that aside from this general point, many of the specifics of Freud's psychoanalysis betray that it operates with the problematic assumption of a psyche that is fundamentally separate from the body and "external" world. Beginning with an original individual psyche, one that is not formed in transactional relationship with the broader world, Freud's psychoanalysis develops elaborately artificial explanations of psychical problems.[5] In particular, Dewey charges that Freud grossly oversimplifies human impulses as sexual, manifesting themselves only in the Oedipal straitjacket of desire for one's mother. Rather than approach contemporary understandings of women, love, and sex in a historically attuned fashion, psychoanalysis appeals to a fixed, native, sexual instinct to explain them.[6] Most damaging in Dewey's view, perhaps, is Freud's (mis)taking what is the result of complex social interactions and situations as the psychical cause that alone is responsible for the result. This hypostatization leads psychoanalysis to focus on the mental, considered to be separate from its environing body and world, as the privileged site for effecting change. Dewey worries that rather than attending, for example, to the role that one's bodily comportment might play in one's mental habits, psychoanalysis tries to effect mental change by means of psychical manipulation only.[7]

Freud's psychoanalysis is more appreciative of the body than Dewey allows (and much more appreciative of it than Jacques Lacan's version of psychoanalytic theory). The symptom, after all, concerns the body's attempt to "speak" forbidden desires, albeit in indirect and misleading ways, that the mind is not allowed to consciously acknowledge. Dewey's criticisms of Freud nevertheless are largely on target. Classical psychoanalytic theory tends to assume that the unconscious is atomistic, an assumption that is extremely problematic. Especially in the case of racism and white privilege, thinking the unconscious as initially and primarily formed in relative isolation from its various social, political, material, and other environments risks the dangerous conclusion that the psychical operations of racism have not been internalized through processes of transaction with a racist world, but rather are innately present in the human unconscious.[8] This approach to racism effectively declares at the outset that attempts to eradicate white privilege are doomed to failure: the world necessarily is and will always be racist because the human beings who inhabit it are irrevocably racist. To the concern that racial prejudice not be thought of as universally necessary, classical psychoanalysis would seem to only add fuel to the fire. An atomistically conceived unconscious tends to support the notion of relatively fixed and unchanging instincts, and if some of those instincts are ones of hostility, then racial prejudice and friction seem inevitable.

Freud's analysis of group formation is particularly useful for generating fruitful hypotheses about white privilege and white supremacy. Yet, in the end, the power of Freud's thought to analyze white domination tends to be undercut by its atomistic assumption that problems of racism could be avoided if people could only resist forming groups—resist, in other words, becoming social beings. Freud's view that human beings ultimately cannot avoid entering the social world does not erase the atomistic assumption present in his work that in infancy, human life is sealed off from the larger social world that it inhabits. It is this assumption that must be examined and challenged if the notion of unconscious habit is to be productive for critical understandings of white privilege.

According to Freud, social groups exist by means of libidinal ties that bind individuals together.[9] Without the emotional "energy" of the erotic drives, a collection of individuals would be just that: an arbitrary assortment of unrelated individuals rather than a group whose members have significant connections with one another. As libidinal, groups are fueled by sexual drives, but this is not to say that group members necessarily pursue sexual unions. In many groups, sexual drives are diverted from this goal and express themselves in a less obviously sexual manner, such as that found in warm feelings toward group members, a desire to be near other group members, and a willingness to do things for group members, even to the point of sacrificing oneself in the process.

The libidinal tie among group members does not by itself explain a group. Or, rather, the libidinal tie does not come into existence among group members alone; merely collecting some individuals together does not guarantee the formation of a group. For Freud, the libidinal tie among group members depends upon their emotional ties to a leader. The leader is the "object" external to the individual with which the individual identifies. Identification provides a complex emotional relationship between the leader and each individual that binds the individuals together into a group and gives them an emotional connection with one another.

In many cases of identification, the external object takes the place of the individual's ego, but in the case of group formation the external object takes the place of each individual's ego ideal.[10] The ego ideal is "heir to the original narcissism," which is not a neurotic perversion but rather the emotional, loving attachment to one's self that is fundamental to the instinct of self-preservation.[11] As a child matures, demands external to the ego are made upon it that it cannot satisfy. The ego ideal, which embodies those demands, splits off from the ego and establishes an ambivalent relationship with it. Because it is an outgrowth of the ego even as it is functionally distinct from it, the ego ideal can be a source of great satisfaction to the ego when the two coincide. But due to its origins in the inadequacy of the ego, the ego ideal often conflicts with the ego. The ego ideal's functions are those of self-observation, moral conscience, dream censorship, and repression, and in that way, the ego ideal is like a parent whose role is to establish high standards for the ego, demand that it live up to them, and punish it when it does not do so.

When an external object, such as the group leader, replaces the ego ideal, the criticism and moral conscience provided by the ego ideal are suspended. The externalized object that has now been internalized can do no wrong, and nothing done for the sake of the object produces any qualms of conscience. The replacement of the ego ideal by an external object explains why Freud claims that there is a mental change forced by a group onto the individual and, more specifically, that this change is one in which the individual loses freedom, intellectual ability, restraint, independence, and originality. Individuality is surrendered in the group, and the group comes to rule the individual. The loss of the ego ideal means, in particular, that group members no longer have in place an agency to repress their unconscious instinctual impulses. Since the unconscious is that portion of the psyche in which the predisposition toward evil is contained, individuals' cruel and brutal drives are freed by group membership to find direct satisfaction, and group members will do things that they would not usually do as individuals.

Freud makes clear that a leader is essential to a group, properly considered, but he allows that an idea can substitute for a human leader. An abstract "leading idea" can do all that a flesh-and-blood leader can do, namely, provide the libidinal ties that hold a group together by replacing the ego ideals of group members. Like leaders, leading ideas can just as easily be negative as they can be positive. "[H]atred against a particular person or institution might operate in just the same unifying way, and might call up the same kind of emotional ties" as positive ideas, such as love, do.[12] It is here that Freud's account of group formation is instructive on white racist identity. White supremacy can be seen as functioning as a leading idea that replaces the ego ideals of some white people. This binds a mere assortment of people into a consciously raced group of white people who share a consciously held, deprecating belief about non-white people. The belief in question here could be characterized as either a positive or negative one since the positive and negative forms of it are the inverse of each other: either the positive form of loving white people since they are superior to non-white people, or the negative form of hating non-white people since they are inferior to white people. In both cases, the belief about white supremacy serves as the object to which the group members have an emotional tie, and their emotional connection with this leading idea provides the emotional bonds between them.

Because the leading idea of white supremacy replaces group members' ego ideals, white supremacists lose the ability to criticize both their devotion to the ideal and the activities done in the service of it. The predisposition to evil—in this case, racist evil—that Freud argues lurks within the unconscious is no longer fettered by the moral conscience that says racism is wrong. The hostility felt by white toward non-white people, upon which white individuals normally would not act, easily converts into cruel acts against non-white people for white supremacist groups.

Because white supremacy is a consciously held leading idea that forms extremist groups, this account of the formation of white groups may not seem particularly relevant to the lives of most white people today. But Freud's comments about the unconscious rightly suggest that an account of the operations of white domination must be broadened to include more than "fringe" groups of white supremacists. The evil that lurks as an unconscious predisposition dwells in the unconscious of all people, Freud tells us. According to him, there is no eradicating these evil tendencies, only controlling the circumstances that either keep them contained, such as peace, or lay them bare, such as war.[13] Virtually all emotional relationships between people include an element of hostility, though it may not always be openly expressed or consciously acknowledged. This means that racial hatred is far more widespread than most people would like to think. Even racial groups that are closely related, as are the English and the Scots, despise one another, and such repugnance only grows as the differences between racial groups does. Freud claims that once we understand that

[49]

hostility toward others is at the core of the human psyche, "we are no longer astonished that greater differences should lead to an almost insuperable repugnance, such as the Gallic people feel for the German, the Aryan for the Semite, and the white races for the coloured."[14]

Freud explains what many (and especially white) people like to ignore: racism is widespread, manifest in the lives and habits of "normal" people who are not extremists. In a world where racial differences exist, perceived racial differences translate into the disdain of one racial group for another. This disdain can and, Freud would add, should be repressed. In fact, for Freud, one sign of civilization is that no open hostility and aggression amongst different races exist.[15] But lack of open aggression does not mean that hostility toward other races has been eradicated from the unconscious. It instead means that "civilized" people have discovered ways of resolving hostile conflicts other than war, violence, and other forms of direct aggression.

Freud is right that unconscious racial hatred is much more common than often is supposed, but one need not follow him in coupling this insight with the problematic claim that racial differences inevitably translate into racial disdain. This claim is dangerous because its assertion of an ahistorical, psychological necessity for racial hatred and prejudice helps produce the very result that it claims to merely describe. If I believe that racial prejudice and hatred are unavoidable because of the fixed hard-wiring of the human psyche, then I am much less likely to try to devise ways to reduce, avoid, or eliminate them, which ensures that racism will persist. Unconscious racial hatred is more widespread than often acknowledged, but that does not mean that an a priori necessity predisposes unconscious habits to evil or that repression of disdain is the only possible alternative to overt hate-based aggression. To envision other alternatives, it is helpful to conceive of unconscious racial hatred as a habit that is the product of transaction between organism and world. Doing so offers no guarantee that racial hatred will be easy to eliminate, nor does it entail that the malleability of the human psyche is unlimited. What it does is avoid the hypostatization of racial hatred that negates all possibility for change.

While racial hatred is not inevitable, it is widespread because of the repression of once openly expressed attitudes of racial disdain. The so-called advances of civilization over the last century have produced the transformation of white supremacy into white privilege for many white people. As a result, the social, political, economic, psychological, and other benefits that continue to accrue to white people because they are white often are not seen by white people today. White people often work very hard to avoid consciously recognizing these benefits as benefits. Many times, those benefits are seen as part of the "natural," normal order of the world, as a way of living that includes no advantages that all other people do not have. When benefits of white privilege are viewed this way, it can be easy to think that if others do not have these "advantages," then it implicitly is because they have done something to forfeit them—it is their fault that they are disadvantaged. For example, as a white person, I do not usually worry about being tailed by store security guards who see me as a potential shoplifter; I generally enter stores psychologically and somatically comfortable and undisturbed. My being-at-ease might seem normal and natural, that is, as a psychosomatic state enjoyed by everyone or, at least, available to everyone and lacking only if one intends to shoplift. But the fact that many black people are assumed to be potential criminals and often are followed in or not admitted to stores reveals my comfort to be an instance of white privilege. It is a psychosomatic state *not* automatically available to everyone, but rather disproportionately available to white people because of their race.

Recognizing my privilege as privilege and not just the "natural" order of things, I am more likely to realize that black people are not responsible for ("guilty of") forfeiting their right to psychological and bodily comfort. This realization does not eliminate my racial privilege, nor does it automatically negate the ontological impact of white privilege on my habits. Security guards still view me as respectable and unworthy of suspicion, and I still walk in stores comfortably and "naturally." But it does change the felt component of that privilege such that I might be angry, rather than reassured, at the sight of a security guard tailing a person of color. Herein lies the possibility of building habits of resistance to white privilege even as I inevitably (in this day and age) benefit from it. A complaint about the security guard's behavior from an "upstanding" white person might make a store manager reconsider his or her security policies.

The unconscious operation of white privilege means that, while Freud does not make it in the context of group formation, a distinction can be made between conscious and unconscious leading ideas.[16] White supremacy is a leading idea that is consciously endorsed. The idea comes to replace the ego ideal by means of a deliberate choice of which a person is consciously aware. This is not to claim that the unconscious is totally uninvolved in white supremacy but instead that consciousness plays a larger role in white supremacy than it does in white privilege. In contrast to white supremacy, white privilege is an idea to which many white people are emotionally tied in ways of which they usually are not consciously aware. In the case of white privilegists, as they might be called, white privilege has come to replace the ego ideal, but the replacement is not consciously noticed.

I do not think that all people who are privileged because they are white necessarily have a leading idea of white privilege in place of their ego ideals. A white person can be racially privileged without supporting and while even rejecting the idea of racial hierarchy. But because of the unconscious operations of white privilege, I am suspicious of any white person's confident assurance that her ego ideal is intact. In principle it could be, but in practice it often is difficult to draw a clean line between "good" white people who are privileged without wanting to be so and "bad" white people who are racially privileged and also unconsciously endorse that privilege. Especially in the case of a white person who consciously opposes her racial privilege, it is psychologically and emotionally difficult for her to recognize when and how she is the beneficiary of it. That difficulty tends to make it easy for her to see her privilege as normal and even to view those who do not have it as abnormal or deficient. Viewing others in that way helps protect her self-image as good, hard-working, and fair: she is not the beneficiary of anything that she did not earn or deserve. The difficulty of self-recognition, in other words, makes it easy for white privilege to slip into place of her ego ideal, even though—or should I say, precisely because—she does not (consciously) desire her privilege.

Whether a person is consciously aware of her leading ideas has implications for her awareness of groups to which she belongs that are important for my analysis of white domination. Because the white supremacist consciously affirms white supremacy as her leading idea, she is consciously aware of her membership in a group of white supremacists. In contrast, it might sound strange to describe a person as unaware of what groups she belongs to, and Freud does not discuss this as a possibility. But people who are not consciously aware of their leading ideas often are not aware that they belong to a particular group and that the group's attitudes affect the way that they view and interact with the world. This certainly is true of many white people with regard to their membership in whiteness. The seeming naturalness and resulting invisibility of white privilege often prevents it from being recognized as a leading idea. Unaware that white privilege is one of their leading ideas, white people often do not recognize that they belong to a group of whites who are tied together by the privileges and ideals that they share as white. This lack of awareness of group membership is apparent, for example, in those white people who do not see whiteness as a race or who think that race is a topic that is relevant to non-white people only. It is also manifest in the attitude of the white, well-intentioned liberal who declares that she does not see people's races and sees only raceless individuals instead. These are examples of white privilege because it is a privilege of those who are not racially oppressed to see or treat race as optional. People who are discriminated against because of their race generally do not have a choice of whether to view race as relevant. It is relevant because it often is forced upon them by a racist world.[17]

But does it make sense to describe white people as unaware that they are members of a group when group membership is characterized primarily by emotional ties to the group's leading idea and to fellow group members? Can one have emotional ties to people and ideas without being consciously aware of them? On Freud's account, the answer is a qualified "yes." It might seem that emotions cannot be called unconscious since it is of the essence of emotion that it is something felt that enters consciousness. Strictly speaking, Freud tells us, this is true. But it is not inaccurate to call emotions unconscious because they can be misconstrued in the feeling or perceiving of them. Felt emotions are represented by ideas, according to Freud. The proper presentation of an emotion can be repressed, which forces the emotion to connect itself to another idea that is then interpreted by consciousness as the expression of the emotion. If the original presentation of the emotion is restored, the original emotion is appropriately called "unconscious" even though it was the presentation of the emotion and not the emotion itself that was repressed and unavailable to consciousness.[18]

Preferable to Freud's mentalist account of emotions in which feelings are re-presented by ideas is an account that acknowledges emotions as both unconscious and conscious. One often feels feelings without knowing either what they are or, in some sense, that one is feeling them. This is especially true when the feelings involve a sociopolitically difficult subject such as racism or sexism. White middle-class women, for example, often feel what usually is characterized as anger, but they do not know that they feel it because a sexist world has encouraged the development of habits that disallow the challenging of the status quo that anger enacts.[19] And it is not just that women often do not know what they feel. They also can actively work to unknow their emotions, to avoid recognition of their feelings as ones of anger because of the self-assertion involved in angry confrontation with others. Emotions are not always directly available to consciousness, as Freud claims, but not because they are hidden behind mental entities such as ideas. Like the body—indeed, as part of the body— emotions and the ties they create can exist without, and in fact in active opposition to, conscious awareness of them.

When an emotion is unconscious because it is considered morally or socially inappropriate to feel it, another emotion often takes it place. In the group membership of whites, the emotional attachments felt toward the leading idea of white privilege are such an example. More specifically, they might be something like distaste for or hatred of non-white people combined with fondness and respect for white people. Such an emotion currently is difficult to consciously acknowledge without causing considerable pain to the ego, so it is repressed or misconstrued as a different emotion, such as respect for all people regardless of race. A white person's felt comfort around white people can then be (mis)understood as merely an instance of the comfort felt around people in general, in other words, as *not* being part of an emotional tie toward white people in particular. In this way, white people could have a particular emotional connection with other white people as part of their membership in the same group without being consciously aware of it.

In contrast—and perhaps surprisingly—Freud's work suggests that white supremacists often repress affection for non-whites. White privilegists tend to repress their leading idea of the inferiority of non-whites and their emotions of cold hatred for non-whites. They find it more painful to consciously claim the inferiority of non-whites than to consciously endorse the opposite, their equality. White supremacists, on the other hand, tend to find it pleasurable to feel hatred toward non-whites and to consciously assert non-white people's inferiority, which suggests that what they find too painful to consciously acknowledge is again the opposite—their affection, often in the sense of sexual attraction, for non-whites. In both cases, the conscious beliefs and assertions of white people can be understood as reaction formations to their unconscious beliefs about non-white people. Whether the leading idea of the inferiority of non-white people is primarily conscious (white supremacy) or unconscious (white privilege) hinges on whether hatred of non-whites and a belief in their inferiority is accompanied by feelings of warmth and (sexual) attraction to them.[20]

White supremacists can be seen as hysterical racists, who need the racial other to exist as the site for all the racist's forbidden desires. A classical example of the hysterical racist is found in the nineteenth-century U.S. Southerner described by Tocqueville, who could allow him or herself to mingle (read: have sex with) the forbidden other precisely because the differences between them were explicitly and legally recognized. In contrast, white privilegists can be seen as obsessional racists, who fear the "contamination" of non-white people and often coldly and methodically work to avoid or even exterminate them (never, of course, in the name of extermination, but in the name of welfare reform, the war on drugs, and so on).[21] They are similar to the nineteenth-century U.S. Northerner described by Tocqueville, who lacks an overt, explicit barrier to "protect" him or her from non-white people and is much more anxious about interaction with them. While I do not claim that some forms of racism are better than others, I think that from this perspective white privilege is just as horrific as white supremacy. This is not to minimize the atrocities committed by extremist groups such as the Ku Klux Klan and Aryan Nation, but to suggest that rather than being a relatively benign form of white domination, white privilege is just as, if not more destructive than white supremacy, even if (or, perhaps, precisely because) it is not as spectacular.

Returning to white privilege in particular, how is the original emotion of hatred for non-whites repressed when the ego ideal has been replaced by the leading idea of white privilege? As the agency of censorship and the office of the moral conscience, the ego ideal is the primary influence in repression, and its replacement might seem to mean that censorship could not occur. Yet it does. For this reason, more accurate than saying, as Freud does, that "the functions allotted to the ego ideal entirely cease to operate" when the ego ideal is replaced by an external object, is to say that when the external object replaces the ego ideal, the object takes over the functions of the ego ideal.[22] On this point, Freud gives the example of someone who is in love and for whom the loved object replaces her ego ideal. When this happens, Freud explains, "in the blindness of love remorselessness is carried to the pitch of crime," and criticism carried out by the ego ideal, which primarily embodies the demands of parents (especially the father), ceases to function.[23] But in the blind love that is willing to commit crimes for the loved one, criticism per se has not ceased to function. While Freud may be right that criticism of the loved object disappears, the loved object certainly can and might criticize the lover for not doing what he asks, for seeming to put her interests above his, and so on. But ultimately, whether one says that the critical agency of the ego ideal has been eliminated or that it continues but with an allegiance to the loved one rather than to parents is not crucial to understanding love. In both cases, criticism in the service of the external object continues when the object replaces the ego ideal.

The situation is similar in the case of white privilege. When white privilege replaces the ego ideal, the ego ideal no longer functions to criticize the ego based on the internalized demands of one's parents. But criticism continues in the service of white privilege. White privilege maintains itself largely by seeming normal, natural, and unobjectionable. It functions best by remaining invisible, that is, unconscious. White privilege can be seen as functioning as a censor of all emotions or ideas that expose it to conscious examination. Any emotion that threatens white privilege must be transformed into a different emotion that does not conflict with it.

While Freud's concept of the ego ideal helps illuminate the formation of white racial identity and the unconscious operations of white domination, a strange implication of the above analysis of white privilege is that the ego ideal is not itself an instrument of it. If, in its establishment, white privilege displaces the ego ideal, then the implication is that the ego ideal is uninvolved in the psychological functioning of white privilege. Put another way, the analysis is strange because it implies that racism could be completely eliminated if people could only resist forming into groups, an implication that indicates Freud's individualism. As an individual prior to group membership, a person's ego ideal appears to be "pure" or neutral with regard to race. The critical institution of the conscience seems to take on racist overtones only, when in the process of joining a group, the raceless ego ideal is replaced by a raced leading idea.

Freud's account of the origin of the ego ideal, from which the superego is later derived, explains why it seems to be essentially unraced. The ego ideal is a product of the child's relationship with his father and—what amounts to the same thing—the child's resolution of his Oedipus complex.[24] As the first person the child identifies with, the father is the child's ideal. Loving his mother and wanting to be (like) his father, the child both admires his father as a model and feels hostility toward him as a competitor. To successfully resolve this conflict, the child must develop a superego. By repressing the child's conflict with his father and thereby shifting it from consciousness into the unconscious superego, the child avoids the pain involved with loving his mother and wanting to kill his father to replace him. But the child's ambivalent relationship with his father is not eliminated in this way. The father's unreachable standard lives on in the form of the superego's demands of the ego: you must be like your father and you are forbidden to be and incapable of being like your father.[25]

The superego gives "permanent expression to the influence of the parents."[26] While Freud acknowledges that the superego can be affected by subsequent influences, parental (= paternal) influence is primary and indelible.[27] One might think that this account could explain how sociohistorical factors, including race, contribute to the child's psychological development since parents are social beings and children learn many of their unconscious racial beliefs from their parents. But instead, this account tends to conceptually isolate the developing child from the social and political world because Freud's work portrays the family in an asocial manner as prior to the formation of groups. As French psychoanalyst Jean Laplanche provocatively puts the point, "what is it that makes Freud tick? . . . [I]t is not history."[28]

Let me elaborate this claim. A variation of atomistic individualism tends to be at work in Freud's theory that has the nuclear family, rather than the individual person, as its main focus. In standard atomistic individualism, as I will call it, it is the single individual who is conceptualized as fundamentally prior to and distinct from the world. While the individual's environments may affect parts of the individual, there remains an internal core of the "true" individual that is relatively untouched by the "external" world. In contrast, the individual person on Freud's account is fundamentally constituted by his or her relationships with his or her father and mother. Freud rightly challenges standard individualism in this regard. But he replaces it with a different kind of individualism— familialism[29]—in which the Oedipal triangle of father, mother, and child forms the core of who the child is and will become. On this model, the child likely will be impacted by his or her extra-familial interactions, but the familial core of his or her psyche remains distinct from (supposedly) extra-familial elements and primary in the psyche's constitution.

While in a loose sense, a family is a group because it is composed of more than one person, in the stricter sense defined in *Group Psychology and the Analysis of the Ego* it cannot be called a group during the child's first couple of years. This is because the replacement of the ego ideal by either a leader or a leading idea is fundamental to the formation of groups and the young child does not yet have an ego ideal to be replaced. In a more general sense of group in which a group is taken as a social entity, it also is difficult to think of the family as a group in the child's first several years. Again this is because the young child lacks an ego ideal, and as Freud claims, "[s]ocial feelings [which would bind individuals into a group] rest on identifications with other people, on the basis of having the same ego ideal."[30] While for Freud the relationships of a young child to his or her mother are the basis upon which the child will later join groups— including that of its own family once the child develops an ego ideal and if that ideal is shared with other family members—in the crucial years of Oedipally based psychic development, the family is not for the child a group.

Freud's analysis implies that "outside" influences such as those provided by work, church, political rallies, daycare, war, economic hardship, and so on are not substantially involved in the triangular relationship of father, mother, and child. To the extent that these factors play a role in family dynamics, they tend to be seen as manifestations of the family's

Oedipal relations and not as indicative of something primarily an- or extra-Oedipal. This familialist conception of the family creates a division between the individual and society, and, rather than bridging the gap as one might expect, the family is located on the side of the individual to support its atomism. While the adolescent or adult individual may come to be influenced by society on Freud's account, the essential core of the individual has already been formed by a childhood and family life that are conceived as Oedipally existing in a social vacuum. So when Freud claims that individual psychology is at the same time social psychology, he means only that individuals tend to join groups, not that the individual is originally constituted by its relations with the social (= extra-familial) world.[31] The social instinct is not irreducible, according to Freud. It can be dissected into something narrower, something a- or pre-social: the family.[32] Even in his account of the sociality of human beings, Freud "kept some part of character safe from society, restoring to the idea of human nature a hard core, not easily warped or reshaped by social experience."[33]

In combination with his familialism, Freud's account of the development of the superego through the resolution of one's relationship with one's parents explains why, on Freud's theory, the superego is relatively untouched by and irrelevant to social factors such as race. At its root, this position results from the dualism between individual and society implied by Freud. Freud clearly holds that "innate constitutional factors and influences from the real environment act in combination" and that "the relation of [that which is innate and that which is acquired through experience] to each other and to that portion of the instinctual life which remains untransformed is a very variable one."[34] But his affirmation of the interaction of an individual's innate constitutional factors and her social and other environments tends to dualistically posit two distinct realms initially formed apart from one another and coming into contact with one another only after this initial formation. Freud claims that even in the midst of such interaction, a portion of the individual's innate constitution will remain untransformed—an innate core (whatever its varying size) that is untouched by the environment, which in turn is conceived as capable of making only relatively superficial modifications to the individual. This is why Freud can say about the sexual drives that

> [o]ne gets an impression from civilized children that the construction of these dams [such as disgust and shame toward the sexual] is a product of education, and no doubt education has much to do with it. But in reality this development is organically determined and fixed by heredity, and it can occasionally occur without any help at all from education. Educa-

tion will not be trespassing beyond its appropriate domain if it limits itself to following the lines which have already been laid down organically and impressing them somewhat more clearly and deeply.[35]

For all of Freud's emphasis upon the cooperation of innate constitution with social and cultural environments in the constitution of a person's psyche, he continues to view them as substantially different even in their coincidence.

Freud's implied dualism between individual and societal environment is problematic because it cannot account for how social, political, physical, and other environments help constitute a person through transaction with her biological and psychological dispositions. On Freud's account, tendencies and possibilities that continually develop in cooperation and conflict with the environment often become construed as innate, relatively fixed elements of one's inborn constitution. It is the psychological equivalent of claiming that varicose veins are a result solely of the constitutional weakness of a person's vein walls, rather than also of working conditions in which a person must stand on her feet for hours a day.[36] Such a position tends to lead to positing the root cause of a psychological difficulty primarily or even solely in the individual, rather than in her environment. Locating the problem primarily in the individual means that few efforts to eliminate it will be focused where they also should be: in the social, political, and material world that helps constitute the individual.

The abstract question about the relationship of the individual and society has tremendous implications for the concrete situation of racism. In an anti-black world, for example, black people can easily develop feelings of inferiority by internalizing the ubiquitous societal messages about their worthlessness. What is needed is not an exclusive or even a primary focus on the individual with these feelings. Or, rather, the individual and environment should be seen as co-primary in that the individual's psychic condition is fundamentally connected with the world around her. On this model, the individual warrants attention in that she needs help becoming aware of her unconscious beliefs about the inferiority of black people, but her consciousness of internalized racism is for the purpose of enabling her to choose to act (or not) to change the racist world that fundamentally contributed to her neurosis.[37] It is a mistake for Freud's psychoanalysis to risk divorcing the individual from the society when difficulties created for the individual by society play a large role in the formation of psychological problems. It also is a mistake to normalize the environment, as Freud tends to, which suggests that in the conflict between a person and her environment, the goal of psychoanalysis should be to help the person adjust to the environment, rather than change it.[38] Time and again, as Franz Fanon claims, when examining cases of psychological difficulties, "we are driven from the individual back to the social structure. If there is a taint, it lies not in the 'soul' [or constitution] of the individual but rather in that of the environment."[39]

Social identification is not necessarily subsequent to other, supposedly more primary familial identifications. Questioning Freud's implicit dualism of the individual and society and the corresponding asocial conception of the family, one need not posit a "pure" ego ideal that is "uncontaminated" by racism until an individual associates with extra-familial groups of other people. Children learn about race and racism from their parents and society as their conscience develops and prior to any participation in a group on Freud's model of group formation. Or, put another way, group formation around extra-familial issues is not something that happens after a child develops an ego and superego and leaves the family to enter the larger world, as Freud's analysis seems to assume by reducing childhood to the development and resolution of the Oedipus complex. The formation of at least some groups, such as racial and racist groups, is concomitant with the formation of the individual's psyche. At a young age, societal, extra-familial forces can influence the child—sometimes by means of the family, sometimes not—in ways that help constitute the child's identity, including its superego. Gilles Deleuze and Felix Guattari make the point well: "the child does not wait until he is an adult before grasping—underneath father-mother—the economic, financial, social, and cultural problems that cross through a family: his belonging or his desire to belong to a superior or an inferior 'race,' the reactionary or revolutionary tenor of a familial group with which he is already preparing his ruptures and his conformities."[40] For this reason, it is misleading to think, as Freud's analysis tends to suggest, that the father's or parents' critical influence is *replaced by* white privilege. More accurate is to say that in many white families and also non-white families that have internalized racism, the father's or parents' critical influence is a crucial *vehicle for* white privilege. White privilege is less of an "external" leading idea that overtakes the ego ideal, and more of a leading idea, simultaneously "external" and "internal," that participates in the formation of the ego ideal itself.

Earlier I discussed the problem of Freud's hypostatization of racial hatred as psychologically inevitable. An additional problematic effect of the claim that racial difference necessarily translates into racial disdain is the erasure of an important distinction made by critical race theorists between raciation (using racial categories to differentiate racial groups) and racism (asserting the superiority of one race over another).[41] With the collapse of raciation into racism, to distinguish between races is automatically, if only implicitly, to declare the inferiority of some racial groups to others. In that case, the only way to eliminate racism is to eliminate racial distinctions altogether. This is the path championed by the contemporary liberal "anti-racist" strategy of colorblindness, which assumes the existence of a racially neutral individual. Racism, according to this viewpoint, occurs only because the raceless individual has been saddled with a group identity based on racial distinctions that have no ontological basis. The key then is to abolish racism by not seeing, or in other words abolishing, race. But given that whiteness often is not recognized as a race, colorblindness tends to become a de facto attempt to not see or abolish people of color, in particular, while white (= "raceless") people are recognized and allowed to thrive.

A complex relationship exists between white privileged attempts to eliminate people of color (as people of color), strategies of colorblindness, the allegedly neutral individual, the collapse of racialism and racism, and the claim that all racial distinctions inevitably result in racial hatred. All these problematic facets and implications of Freud's work are the result of its tendency toward atomistic individualism. Freud's hypostatization of racial hatred is an offshoot of his general suspicion and distrust of the social world. Seeking to distance the self from that world with an ahistorical, non-transactional account of ego formation, Freud tends to build a misanthropic isolation into the individual psyche. While the individual cannot be forever protected from the racial and other forms of discontent that social "civilization" inevitably brings, it at least can be said to have an original core that is untainted by the larger world. On Freud's account, if positing the necessity of racial hatred is the price of protecting that core, then so be it.

This is not a price that critical race theorists should pay. Yet concerns about Freud's tendency toward atomism do not rule out the need for a concept of the unconscious, as distinct from the merely nonconscious or subconscious. Instead of the atomistic unconscious suggested by Freud, a transactional unconscious is called for. This would be an unconscious that takes its starting point in habit. Thought transactionally, the unconscious is initially formed and constantly reformed (though often with the result of only strengthening the initial formation) in and through a dynamic, reciprocal relationship with its bodily, social, political, and other environments. This would also be a conception of the unconscious that does not underestimate the devious and manipulative ways in which habit can obstruct its own improvement—including hiding such obstruction from consciousness such that habit does not appear at all complicit in the blockage of its own transformation.

Conceived transactionally, the unconscious perhaps is better conceived as an adjective describing certain bodily and psychical habits than as a noun designating a thing or force inside one's head. "The unconscious" is found in unconscious habits, that is, in predispositions for transacting with the world that actively thwart their conscious examination and possible transformation. One might say that "the unconscious so conceived is as much (if not more) *between* ourselves and our world as it is behind or beneath the conscious regions of our own psychic life."[42] The unconscious exists, but not as an internal space set apart from the so-called external world. Whether used as a noun, adjective, or adverb, the term "unconscious" should be heard here in this dynamic sense of transactional in-betweenness. Reworked in this way, the concept of the unconscious becomes environmentally attuned and thereby capable of explaining the operations of white privilege.

THREE

Seductive Habits of White Privilege

White privilege is best understood as a constellation of psychical and somatic habits formed through transaction with a racist world. As such, it often functions as unconscious: seemingly invisible, even nonexistent, and actively resisting conscious efforts to know it. For these reasons, white privilege is best understood as unconscious habit, but how can transactional habit be thought as unconscious given Freud's legacies of atomism and an asocial notion of the unconscious? Freud's description of the infant's psyche as formed through relationships with its mother and (especially) father constitutes a minor break with atomistic individualism. But by sealing up the psyche in the nuclear family and isolating the family from the broader political world around it, Freud tends to promote a familialism that is just as atomistic, albeit on a larger scale, as traditional individualism. This familialism makes it difficult to understand, let alone combat, unconscious habits of white privilege. Either they cannot be explained, leading to the problematic denial of the existence of unconscious investments in white privilege, or they are explained as innate to the human psyche, leading to the equally problematic assertion of the permanence and inevitability of unconscious racism. Both horns of this dilemma are the result of the tendency toward atomism in Freud's depiction of the unconscious. To find a way out of the dilemma and to fully grasp habits of white privilege as unconscious, critical race theorists need a model of a transactional unconscious.

I develop such a model here, drawing primarily on the work of French psychoanalyst Jean Laplanche. Laplanche's theory of seduction presents the unconscious as initially and continually formed in relationship with concrete others in a sociopolitical world. As such, it provides a "radical metapsychological solution to the endless metaphysical debates over the question of inside and outside."[1] I read Laplanche's theory of seduction as a process of unconscious habit formation, showing how habits are developed as co-constitutively psychical and somatic in their unconscious operations. While Laplanche's version of psychoanalysis focuses on sexuality and tends to overemphasize the passivity of unconscious habits, I adapt his theory of seduction to include race and racism and to fully account for the active, productive aspects of transactional habit. The resulting account of unconscious habits of white privilege will shed light on the particular ways in which a racialized white psyche that is ignorant of its own racialized knowledge is formed—and might be re-formed differently.

Laplanche's theory of seduction explains the formation of the infant's unconscious by means of seduction by adults. But I immediately must clarify the term "seduction" since it does not mean that a sexually abusive act takes place between adult and infant. This was the central component of the seduction theory that Freud entertained early in his career to explain his patients' hysterical symptoms and then abandoned to develop his well-known theory of infant sexuality. Adult seduction of the infant is a real event, and in that sense, the early Freud was on to something that unfortunately was lost in his move away from the seduction theory. But what Freud did not see is that the event of seduction involves the transference of enigmatic messages about sexuality from adult to child, not a sexual act in the customary sense of the term.

The enigmatic message is a communication from the unconscious of an adult to the infant or child whose meaning is unknown to or hidden from both adult and child. This event of communication is the primal situation of seduction, which means that the creation of an unconscious via seduction is inevitable for human beings, not that the unconscious or id is inherited from ancient ancestors.[2] By means of bodily expressions such as gestures or grimaces—and also, though rarely for babies, by means of spoken words—the adult implants a message about sexuality in the child's body, at least a portion of which child cannot comprehend.[3] The child tries to understand the message, and indeed sometimes succeeds in part. The parts that she does not understand are repressed. These remainders of the attempted translation of the message form the child's unconscious.[4] The etymology of the verb "to seduce" (*seduire*) helps indicate why the process is seductive: in seduction, an adult draws an infant into the adult world in an irresistible fashion, captivating the child in ways that he or she does not know how to respond to.[5]

Toni Morrison's novel *The Bluest Eye* provides a helpful illustration of the process of seduction.[6] Morrison demonstrates how the narrator of the novel, a nine-year-old black girl named Claudia, and her older sister, Frieda, are tuned into the adult world around them, receiving its messages even though they do not fully understand them:

> Frieda and I are washing Mason jars. We do not hear their [the adults in the other room] words, but with grown-ups we listen to and watch out for their voices. . . . The edge, the curl, the thrust of their emotions is always clear to Frieda and me. We do not, cannot, know the meanings of all their words, for we are nine and ten years old. So we watch their faces, their hands, their feet, and listen for truth in timbre.[7]

Morrison reveals an adult world full of unintended bodily gestures and tones that communicates a great deal of enigmatic meaning to the children in it. From the sound of parents' and neighbors' voices, Claudia and Frieda know that something is up, but they do not fully understand the edgy mood that filters from the living room into the kitchen. The incomprehensible portions of the adults' message—which, in this case, involve the yearning and later angry revulsion generated by a newly arrived boarder in Claudia's home—will become part of each girl's unconscious.

Morrison's example demonstrates why the reality of seduction should be thought of as neither literal nor metaphorical. Or, rather, while it can be thought in these ways, doing so misses the main point of the phenomenon of seduction. Freud fell into this trap, which is why he abandoned the theory of seduction. Stuck within a literal-metaphorical dichotomy, he could understand seduction only in its most limited, obvious form—as a literal sexual assault—and had to reject his theory when he realized that not all the women he was treating had been seduced. But the way out of this trap is not to understand their seduction metaphorically because doing so makes the event of seduction a mere fantasy, something dreamed up by neurotic women that stands in place of the real issue in question. This attempted solution to Freud's dilemma is problematic because seduction is not a figurative representation of something else more important. It is an event that occurs between adults and infants that produces something very real: unconscious habits.

The literal-metaphorical dichotomy is inadequate to the event of seduction for at least three related reasons.[8] First, reducing reality to the literal, the dichotomy tends to render unreal the imaginative, unconscious, and desiring aspects of psychical life by opposing them to literal reality. Second, as relatively unreal, psychical life is then portrayed as relatively passive compared to non-psychical or material life. On this view, the psychical and material are sharply divorced, and psychical life is presented as mere image, myth, or metaphor, a second-rate citizen compared to material reality. Finally, having robbed psychical life of its productivity, the dichotomy conceives the activity of the psyche to be merely that of imitating or representing literal, material reality. What a metaphorical understanding of the contents of the unconscious assumes is a static world with passive spectators of it: a dead world with no becoming, a world devoid of the active and mutual transactions of organism and environment.

Undercutting the mind-body dualism implicit in literal-metaphorical dichotomies, Morrison's kitchen scene brings out the important role that the body plays in the transmission of enigmatic messages. Along with the timbre of voice—itself a bodily effect—it is the comportment of adults' faces, hands, and feet that communicate to the children. A tensely pursed mouth, an anxiously tapping foot, a worriedly wrung hand convey the gravity of their family's world to Claudia and Frieda even though they do not fully know why the situation is grave and cannot understand the words used by the adults to discuss it.

It is not just adult bodies that are involved in communicating enigmatic messages. The messages are implanted in the bodies of the children who receive them. As Laplanche explains, "the signifiers brought by the adult [to the child] are fixed, as onto a surface, in the psychophysiological 'skin' of a subject in which the unconscious agency is not yet differentiated."[9] A child is not born with an unconscious; such psychical complexity is not created until a later point in the process of seduction. Early in that process, in the moments of the initial creation of the unconscious, the enigmatic messages operate in and through the child's body. The body that receives these messages is not a mere lump of matter. Even prior to the formation of an unconscious, the body is already manifesting and being invested with meaning. Some areas of the body—primarily the mouth, genitals, and anus, but also the nose, ears, and hands—are receiving more intense attention from caregivers than others, due to the infant's feeding and excreting and its caregivers' cleaning up after both. This attention enables "the binding of component instincts to *determinate zones in the body,"* a binding that is not reductively biologistic since "there is no initial or natural opposition between the instinctual and the intersubjective, or between the instinctual and the cultural."[10] The "exterior" surface of the body is already becoming magnetized with cultural meanings prior to the development of an "interior" unconscious. It is this differentially charged, psychophysiological skin that receives the first enigmatic messages transmitted by adults.

Initially, the unconscious is not yet differentiated from the body. Or, rather, since the unconscious proper does not yet exist, the body serves as what will later become the unconscious, once the process of attempted translation has begun and produced untranslated remainders. While Laplanche does not elaborate the point, an implication of his claim about the body's role in seduction is that the differentially magnetized body continues to play an important role in the function of the unconscious once it is formed. Here Laplanche might be seen as reworking Freud's intriguing claim that "the ego is first and foremost a bodily ego; it is not merely a surface entity, but it itself the projection of a surface."[11] By this, Freud meant that the ego is formed out of bodily sensations that spring from the body's surface. In a similar fashion, Laplanche is interested in how the unconscious is first and foremost a bodily unconscious. The unconscious is a result of the body's influence on the psyche; it marks the primary site for psychophysiological investments and intensities that originate from the adult world.

It is at this point that the psychoanalytic term "the unconscious" becomes an obstacle to understanding the process of seduction. Because it tends to imply something psychical separate from, even if in connection with, the body, "the unconscious" interferes with an appreciation of seduction as a simultaneously somatic and psychical event. More helpful is to think "the unconscious" as unconscious habits that are inseparably bodily and psychical. Seduction is the process of the formation of unconscious habits involving the transference of enigmatic messages from adult to child via the adult's unconscious modes of transacting with the world, and especially the child. A child is not born with unconscious psychosomatic habits; this complexity is developed through transactional relationships with adults. Initially, enigmatic messages play along the child's body and become properly unconscious once attempts to understand them have failed. Unbeknownst to the child, these failed attempts at translation help shape her subsequent responses to the world and, through those transactions, constitute her self. Her unconscious habits are the result of the body's development of the psyche. They mark the psychosomatic site of the intensities that emerge from adult-child transactions.

The intimate relationship between body and unconscious habit means that, like the psyche, the body should be thought of as capable of unconscious resistance to the recognition and transformation of its habits. An example of this point that is relevant to habits of white privilege can be found in my reaction to the smell of cumin, a spice frequently used in Mexican and Tex-Mex food. I associate its smell with the (perceived) body odor of Mexicans. (Mexican-Americans, Chicano/as, and other Latino/a Americans were always called "Mexicans" in the West Texas town I grew up in, at least when racial slurs weren't used instead, and the olfactory association is very precise on this point.) Even though I now consciously know that the association is racist and I sincerely do not want to make it, I am not able to smell cumin without it occurring. It is as if behind or alongside my conscious knowledge, a much stronger olfactory un(conscious)knowledge exists, undermining my attempts to smell cumin as just plain cumin (if there is such a thing). This (un)knowledge is not a gap in my conscious knowledge about cumin or Mexican people, nor is it only a subconscious habit that repeats itself merely because of inertia. To capture the phenomenon in question, my olfactory (un)knowledge about cumin must be understood as the active, productive partner of my unconscious psyche, both of which seek to protect my white privileged sense of self. Mexicans are greasy and smelly, while I am clean and odor-free: this is what my nose assures me. This sense of self helps explain the anxiety I experienced when a former colleague once asked me if I ate garlic for breakfast. Apparently I smelled like garlic when I came to work each morning. But if this is true, then I am not as clean and odor-free as I thought, which means that I might not be fully white on the racial hierarchy established by my sense of smell. My reaction to cumin involves the racist process of identification through its projective disavowal. For my body to give up the olfactory association between cumin and (supposed) Mexican body odor would be to challenge the oppositional relationship between white and non-white people that helps guarantee my whiteness.

Racial and racist categorizations often operate by means of the bodily senses—and not just vision, which is often recognized, but smell and hearing in particular.[12] Given this modus operandi, the unconscious operations of white privilege must involve bodily habits if they are to sustain themselves. The seeds of raced and racist unconscious habits are initially planted in the body. As they begin to sprout, the result is unconscious psychical habits, which continue to be nourished by and provide nutrients to their somatic roots.

Given the origination of an infant's psychophysiological investments and intensities from the adult world, the bodily surface that becomes internalized in the formation of unconscious habits is not merely that of the infant. In some significant way, it also includes the bodily surface and habits of the adult other. Responding to Freud's comments on the bodily ego, Laplanche asks, "What is this surface that is projected within us? It is both our own corporeal envelope, and the surface of the other, the corporeal envelope of the human other."[13] The seduction that takes place between infant and adult, then, involves their bodies as much as their minds. Or, better put, the seductive relationship between infant and adult illustrates how body and mind are not sharply separated, just as the infant is not isolated from the adult environment. The bodies of infant and adult mingle in such a way that they both contribute to the formation of the infant's unconscious.

This means that my psychophysiological association of cumin and Mexicans should be understood as originating from the psychosomatic investments of my parents and other caregivers. Given that the same can be said about my parents' unconscious habits coming from their caregivers and so on, my psychosomatic unconscious habits must be seen as part of "a *multiply transgenerational* project."[14] For example, one of the enigmatic messages sent to me regarding race likely originated in the distasteful hiss of my grandmother's voice as she pronounced the word "Mexican." As an adult, I have trouble hearing or saying the word "Mexican" without anxiety because it sounds like a racial slur to me, and I do not seem able to discard that auditory habit. (The only exception is using the word in the phrase "Mexican food," which reflects my apparent racist comfort with the commodification of Mexican culture for the benefit of white society.) Here we can see how the unconscious is crowded with the bodily sounds and gestures of many generations of adult others. It is as if my grandmother's voice has been introjected into my ears and vocal cords, both immediately and through the likely mediation of my parent's bodily gestures, making those parts of my body (along with my nose) key sites for the operation of unconscious habits of white privilege.

Unconscious habits are always effecting and being effected by those of other people and impersonal institutions. They are a multiplicitous collectivity that cannot be reduced to a single voice.[15] For this reason, "at the very moment the subject is persuaded that he or she will be uttering the most individual of statements, he or she is deprived of all basis for [individualistic] enunciation," for the basis of enunciation is always transactionally collective.[16] My grandmother's voice speaks through me as I pronounce the word "Mexican." She, along with many others, must be considered a coauthor of all I write or say regarding Mexican people, life, food, and so on. The transactional multiplicity of unconscious habits reaches far beyond the triangle of the Oedipal family, and it involves even more than grandparents and other members of one's extended family. "Families are filled with gaps and transected by breaks that are not familial," as Deleuze and Guattari argue, "the rise of fascism, Stalinism, the Vietnam war, May '68, [September 11, one today could add, among other events]—all these things form complexes of the unconscious, more effective than everlasting Oedipus."[17] The transgenerational crowd that contributes to the formation of unconscious habit is as much composed of distant strangers, albeit in different ways and perhaps to different degrees, as it is of intimate relations that a person knows, loves, and/or hates.

To this point, I have focused on the child's inability to understand the message coming from the adult, but equally important is that the adult also does not understand the full meaning of the message communicated to the child. The message is enigmatic precisely because of its double-opacity. As Laplanche explains, "[t]hese signifiers are not rendered enigmatic by the simple fact that the infant does not possess the code that he will need to acquire. . . . The issue is rather that the adult world is entirely infiltrated with unconscious and sexual significations, of which *the adult too* does not possess the code."[18] An adult does not intentionally send enigmatic messages to a child. Intentional messages certainly exist. But it is the messages that the adult does not mean to send, does not realize that she is sending, and does not herself fully understand the meaning of, that are the material that is transformed into the infant's unconscious habits. These messages "are frequently ones of violence, savagery, castration, and anality," and they are conveyed by phenomena such as "a smile (in Leonardo), an angry gesture, a grimace of disgust, etc."[19] They can also be found in the tone of voice, the angle of a hand, and the positioning of the feet mentioned by Morrison's Claudia, and my grandmother's hissing of "Mexican." The adult world is sending unconscious messages to children all the time that they cannot fully understand, and it is these messages— not the more transparent, consciously intended ones—that have the greatest psychosomatic effect on children because they metabolize into unconscious remnants that have a potentially lifelong powerful impact on how children will interact with the world.

Clearly a person's environment is crucial to the formation of his or her unconscious. The other is at the core of who I am. And this other encompasses more than the mother and the father, the adult components of the Oedipal triangle that are so crucial to Freud's account of the development of the infant's psyche. This is why Freud's familialism is inadequate as a challenge to standard individualism. "The fact that a child is brought up by *parents,* or even by *its* parents, is, ultimately a *contingency.* . . . *Ulti-*

mately, and whatever distortions may result from the fact, it is possible to become a human being without having a family; it is not possible to do so without encountering an adult world."[20] The adult world is not a theoretical abstraction. It is a variety of concrete adult others: the entire array of the social, political, economic, aesthetic, material, and psychological adult world that helps compose adult unconscious habits. While it might be a contingent fact that much of this adult world comes to the infant through the messages of its parents or other primary caregivers, what is being transmitted is not just a familial meaning, but also a complex tangle of local and global significations.

In this vast web of meaning, Laplanche focuses on enigmatic messages concerning sexuality. His central example is the breast-feeding mother, whose own unconscious sexual pleasure and desire expressed through breast-feeding comprises a puzzling message that is passed on to the nursing child.[21] As Laplanche explains, the infant experiences the maternal breast as a question or demand: "what does it want of me? What does it want to tell me that it doesn't already know itself?"[22] But in his emphasis upon the nonfamilial adult world, Laplanche leaves open the possibility of focusing on different enigmatic messages, such as those concerning race and racism. As he claims when objecting to some psychoanalysts' pejorative use of the term "culturalism," "certain psychoanalytic parameters—all psychoanalytic parameters—may vary as a result of cultural differences."[23] The advantage of the theory of seduction is that its account of the formation of the unconscious "take[s] psychoanalytical account of a plurality of cultural scripts from the very beginning of the infant's life, . . . opening up a space for the mediation of psychoanalytical and socio-historical categories," such as race.[24] If an infant's unconscious habits are formed through its inevitably failed attempt (because of the infant's immaturity) to translate the enigmatic messages sent to it by the adult world, and given that the adult world historically has been and continues to be both structured by categories of race and riddled with white privilege, then an infant's unconscious habits inevitably will be formed by race and racism. An adult world that privileges whiteness helps produce a child's unconscious habits that also privilege whiteness by sending the child messages about race that often are opaque to both child and adult alike.

Morrison's novel again helps develop this point, demonstrating how the beauty ideals that support white privilege can be seductively communicated to black girls in particular. When Claudia receives a blue-eyed baby doll for Christmas, she reports that "[f]rom the clucking sounds of adults I knew that the doll represented what they thought was my fondest wish. . . . Adults, older girls, shops, magazines, newspapers, window signs—all the world had agreed that a blue-eyed, yellow-haired, pink-skinned doll was what every girl child treasured."[25] When Claudia dismembers the doll to try to find inside its beauty, which she does not see, the adults are saddened and outraged: "Tears threatened to erase the aloofness of their authority. The emotion of years of unfulfilled longing preened in their voices."[26] The adults' tears and tone of voice transmit an enigmatic message to Claudia about the importance and power of whiteness in the adult world. The message is unknown to the adults in that while they certainly are conscious of the existence of white racism against black people, they are not fully aware of how their intense desire to share in whiteness proudly swells in their voice as they speak of the blue-eyed doll. And the message is equally opaque to Claudia. She is able to translate the part of it that says that the doll is very precious, but she not able to translate its larger, more significant part, which is that whiteness is something desirable and that white standards of beauty are something that black females in particular should strive to achieve. This explains Claudia's dismembering of the doll, which can be understood as a physical manifestation of the psychological process of failed translation and subsequent repression that she is undergoing. Trying to understand why the doll is so valuable by tearing open its hidden inside, Claudia finds nothing and leaves herself only destroyed remains of something that she has failed to comprehend.

The physical remnants of the doll are refuse that can be quickly thrown away. But the psychological remnants of the message are not so easily discarded. They too are waste products, but they are retained rather than eliminated, forming part of Claudia's unconscious habits. These untranslated remnants of the enigmatic message of white privilege lead Claudia to hate and want to dismember blond white girls like Shirley Temple and light-skinned black girls like her schoolmate Maureen Peal. Morrison gestures toward these incompletely understood remnants when Claudia claims, "[a]nd all the time we knew that Maureen Peal was not the Enemy and not worthy of such intense hatred. The *Thing* to fear was the *Thing* that made *her* beautiful, and not us."[27] Here is a knowledge that is unknown, remainders that are unabsorbed: Claudia vaguely knows that the *Thing*, not a doll or a light-skinned girl, is the real issue, but she cannot understand at this point in her life what that *Thing* is. And so the *Thing* that is white privilege, and specifically white beauty ideals for black women, becomes a powerful influence on her unconscious habits. Claudia learns to self-destructively cope with it by loving the whiteness that she once hated: "It was a small step to Shirley Temple. I learned much later to worship her, just as I learned to delight in cleanliness, knowing, even as I learned, that the change was adjustment without improvement."[28]

The fact that the breast is an erogenous zone for many women helps make plausible Laplanche's claim that unconscious messages about sexuality and sexual pleasure are communicated from mother to child, including infants and babies who are much younger than Claudia. Less obvious is how enigmatic messages about white privilege could be transmitted to a child in its first few months. If messages about sexuality are somatically transmitted during the act of breast-feeding, what is the particular mechanism through which messages about race operate? With my cumin example, Morrison's reference to cleanliness suggests an answer to this question. Caring for a baby involves a great deal of cleaning its body: wiping off saliva, food, tears, urine, feces, among other things. These activities are a crucial site for the transmission of enigmatic signifiers about white privilege. At the same time that cleanliness attempts to ensure bodily hygiene, it conveys opaque messages about the meaning of hygiene in terms of white purity and black contamination.

Non-white people have long been associated with dirt, filth, and pollution by white people. On one level, this association speaks of the alleged lack of bodily cleanliness of those such as Jews, black people, Latino/as, and others. Their skin is seen as dark because unwashed, and they are perceived as having a particular "racial smell" that is borne of filth.[29] On another related level, their alleged dirtiness is a sign of a more intangible—though perceived as no less real—uncleanliness. Their inferiority to white people is found in their moral, spiritual, and mental impurity. These associations between non-white people and defilement took an extreme form in the genocidal murders of Jews, Roma, and others by Nazi Germany, which were produced by " 'the necessity to sweep clean the world.' "[30] But they also exist in the less spectacular form of unconscious habits of connecting whiteness with cleanliness and blackness with impurity and policing the boundaries between the two so as to maintain a strict separation. Blackness functions as the abject, which means not only that it is allegedly filthy but also that it threatens the boundaries between the clean and the dirty.[31] It must be kept at bay through acts of cleansing if the contamination of whiteness is to be prevented.

These racist associations are part of the adult world with which infants have transacted for hundreds of years. Just as messages about sexuality are transmitted to a baby through the process of breast-feeding, messages about race are transmitted to a baby through the process of cleaning it. An adult caregiver probably does not consciously think about the racial (and sexual) significance of cleanliness as she wipes up her dirty baby. In all likelihood, that idea is the furthest thing from her (conscious) mind. Yet messages about racial (and sexual) hygiene that she does not intend to transmit to the baby nonetheless can be implanted in its psycho-physiological skin. A baby of any race growing up in today's white privi-leged world often begins at an early age to introject messages about the purity of whiteness and the abjection of blackness. As in the case of Mor-rison's Claudia, she might not immediately delight in cleanliness, but the grounds for that perverse pleasure have been established in infancy. A baby of only a few months has already begun to develop unconscious habits of white privilege, even before she understands what it is.

The seductive mechanism of cleaning could be characterized as obses-sional because if operates out of a fear of contamination and strives to eliminate all impurities. Cleaning a baby does not always convey such messages. Seduction is always historically situated; it has no essential, timeless meanings to communicate unconsciously. But with a shift over time from the hysterical racism of white supremacy to the obsessional racism of white privilege, the act of cleaning came to convey particu-lar and especially intense messages about purity that had not previously existed, at least not as urgently.

If I am right that cleanliness is a crucial mechanism by which uncon-scious racial habits are formed, then the situation is even more complex than a simple comparison between breast-feeding and cleaning indicates. Given the alleged dirtiness and dangerousness of female genitalia, mes-sages concerning sexuality and gender also are likely transmitted through acts of cleaning. Female genitalia purportedly smell bad, as confirmed by the ubiquitous advertisements for products that eliminate "feminine odor." They also allegedly present a fearsome danger to men, wanting to voraciously consume male genitalia much as the female preying mantis eats her mate after copulation. The cultural anxieties surrounding female genitalia are great, and they tend to produce unconscious demands for female purity and cleanliness. These demands cannot be separated from anxieties about and demands for sexual purity, and both types of de-mands have a significant impact on the unconscious habits of both white and non-white females by teaching them the ideal of white, middle-class womanhood. To be sexually pure is to be racially pure, and vice versa. To become a proper woman, a white girl must not only guard her chastity but also avoid becoming racially contaminated. To smell like garlic and thereby slip over to the non-white side of an olfactory racial divide means not only jeopardizing one's status as white person but also possibly losing one's identity as a (proper) woman. A black girl such as Claudia, by contrast, can never fully reach the ideal of proper womanhood because her blackness marks her as impure. In theory, she could move a bit closer to proper womanhood if she is sexually chaste, but because her perceived racial impurity "necessarily" manifests itself in her sexual promiscuity, such movement is practically impossible. She is seen as doomed to both racial and sexual impurity, each because of the other.

I have deliberately referred to the leftover components of Claudia's attempt to understand the gift of the blue-eyed doll as remnants, rather than as enigmatic messages or signifiers. This is because there is no direct implantation of adult messages into the child's unconscious. A process of translation, which Laplanche often describes in terms of digestion and metabolism, always takes place and means that a disjunctive relationship between the adult's and the child's unconscious exists. Without such a disjunction, the adult's unconscious would be replicated identically in the child, and then in the child's child, over and over without end. There would not be any possible change or difference across generations in people's unconscious lives. This danger is why Laplanche cautions us not to "disregard the break, the profound reshaping, which occurs between the [adult and the child], and which may be likened to a metabolism that breaks down food into its constituent parts and reassembles them into a completely different entity."[32] The multiply transgenerational project of white privilege is not one of repetition without variation. Just as the waste products that result from digestion are both formed out of and greatly different from the food with which the process began, so too the remnants of Claudia's attempt to understand her family's gift of the doll are made up of and profoundly reshape their unconscious investments in white beauty ideals (evidenced in Claudia's later delight in cleanliness). The unconscious operations of white privilege are neither static nor monotonous. They transform themselves across time and generations even as their function of race-based oppression tends to persist.

In contrast with Freud, Laplanche argues that the unconscious is wholly created by repression. The infant is not born with an initial nub of an unconscious that is then later built up by means of subsequent acts of repression. Laplanche acknowledges that "this is the first point in my thought that would not be accepted by all psychoanalysts, many of whom would think that there is something biological and primary that is unconscious, which I don't believe because it would have to come from phylogenesis."[33] The effect of implicitly accepting an account of the unconscious as primary can be seen in psychoanalytic accounts of prejudice that claim that at least some unconscious racism is onto-psychologically hardwired and that attempts to eradicate it are pointless and naive.[34] In contrast to these accounts, Laplanche's conception of the unconscious as wholly formed by the repression of unmetabolized remnants of adult messages enables critical race theory to be psychoanalytically informed without endorsing an ahistorical and acontextual view of racism as natural and inevitable.

One of the reasons for Laplanche's rejection of phylogenesis is his refusal of what he calls "Robinson Crusoeism."[35] This account of the relationship between individuals and their world, common to much of philosophy as well as psychoanalysis, starts with the lone, isolated individual and then (tries to) build out from it to its surrounding physical, cultural, social and other environments. Inherent to Robinson Crusoeism, in other words, is both an atomistic conception of the individual and the positing of a dualistic relationship between "inside" and "outside." But as metaphors of bodily digestion already indicate, inside and outside cannot be sharply separated or contained. The food that is outside the organism enters inside it, both becoming part of the inside and being reconstituted by the inside into another form that will exit outside. And just as at the physiological level, inside and outside are always mixing such that each helps constitute the other, at the psychological level, insides and outsides also engage in a transactional relationship. From the beginning, as it were, the baby's outside that is its caregivers' unconscious is helping constitute the baby's psychical inside, and in turn, the baby's inner unconscious will have effects on the outside world as it guides the growing child's actions in it. Both psychologically and physiologically, there is no "solitary baby-Robinson."[36] When trying to understand the development of the child, "*the problem of becoming aware of or open to* [the outside world] *is a false problem.*"[37]

Freud's theory of phylogenesis is one of the misguided results of this false problem. It is "something like a theoretical symptom, a false synthesis, produced by the attempt to escape a conceptual impasse, the imprisoning either/or of the external event and the innate constitution."[38] If solitary baby-Robinson really exists, totally isolated from the world around her, then one is forced to posit innate structures and/or contents to explain the presence and development of the unconscious. But rejecting the dualism between inside and outside, one need not claim with Freud that the individual inherits memory traces of past events in the life of the species. "The idea of an organism initially closed upon itself, and only then opening itself to the object (or constructing it, even?) is one of the modalities of biological idealism or solipsism" that should be refused.[39]

One of the strengths of seduction theory is that it naturalizes the unconscious. As I use the term here, "naturalism" entails neither a reductive, biologistic elimination of the psychical nor an essentialist appeal to fixed natural kinds.[40] Naturalism instead explains how the psychical features of the world are grounded in the materiality and sociality of human experience. Rejecting Robinson Crusoeism, Laplanche is able to refute phylogenesis and other claims that the unconscious has a supernatural, transcendental origin, that is, one beyond the natural, material world. His account pragmatically suggests that the experiences of the human organism in transaction with its various environments are rich enough to account for the formation of the unconscious.

My use of the term "transaction" to describe the dynamic, co-constitutive relationship between the bio-psychical organism and its environments is deliberate even though Laplanche adamantly rejects the similar concept of interaction. As he explains, the communication between adult and infant "is not interaction. It is a one-way action. It is one-way only on the sexual [that is, the unconscious] level."[41] Laplanche does not deny that interaction (transaction) occurs on physiological levels, but he insists that the infant does not reciprocally contribute to the adult's unconscious as the adult does the child's. This, again, is because the infant has no unconscious prior to its receipt and attempted translation of the adult's enigmatic messages. And once the infant begins to metabolize an unconscious, it is still relatively passive in comparison to the adult because "the active one has more 'knowledge', more unconscious fantasies than the passive infant."[42] This is why, for Laplanche, the initial "communication situation" between them could never be described as an interaction because it "is neither bilateral, nor symmetrical."[43] Prioritizing the centripetal movement from the adult to the child does not mean that centrifugal and then reciprocal movements are impossible, but that the initial, inward-directed vector always guides those later movements.[44]

One of the reasons that Laplanche rejects interaction as a model for understanding the formation of the unconscious is that he suspects that it is just another way of denying that the other is the primary mechanism of the self. Ipsocentrism, as Laplanche calls it, "centers on the person."[45] In contrast to ipsocentrist operations such as projection and foreclosure, Laplanche prioritizes "mechanisms where it is the other who is the subject of the mechanisms," namely implantation.[46] Laplanche does not deny that, for example, projection takes place. His claim instead is that "at the bottom of projection, there is something that is not projection—that is, a question: what does [the other] want of me? . . . [U]nder this everyday projection there is . . . a question not about what I am introducing in the other, but that something comes from the other."[47] Laplanche attempts to shift psychoanalytic theory away from the first (and even the third) person to the other. The other, not the person herself (whether described as I or she), should be the focus of those who want to understand the person.[48] As Laplanche presents it, interaction smuggles back in the centrality of the person, making it co-primary with the other in the formation of the unconscious.

I do not disagree with Laplanche's description of the psychological asymmetry between adult and child, although I think it important to note that even at a child's young age, the relationship quickly becomes transactional—a claim that Laplanche sometimes seems to deny.[49] This is because while the child's psyche contains relatively few undigested remnants, the child is always already actively engaged in the world, and her budding unconscious very quickly begins to produce effects on her life and the life of those around her. Patricia Williams offers a striking example of this point in her recent lectures for the BBC, entitled *Seeing a Color-Blind Future*. At around the age of three, her son's nursery school teacher was concerned that the boy was colorblind because he could not identify colors. Yet a visit to the ophthalmologist quickly reassured Williams that her son's vision was perfect. What Williams eventually discovered was that when the children in the nursery argued over race-related issues—such as whether a black kid could play the good guy in their games—the teachers at the predominantly white school repeatedly told the children that color makes no difference at all. The result of William's son's mistranslation of this remark was that when he was asked what the color of the grass was, for example, he replied either that he did not know or, more cynically, that it made no difference.[50]

Here is an example of an enigmatic message about race forming the child's unconscious that in turn has an effect on the adult world around it. This message is not wholly enigmatic. There is a consciously intended message concerning colorblindness being sent verbally to the child from the adult: race and color should not matter when assigning roles in children's games. But with that conscious message is also an unconscious one generated by the white teacher's anxieties about race. The message sent to the child is not just about children's games, but about the (alleged) inappropriateness of race: of noticing race, of talking about race, of having a race, "as though it were an especially delicate category of social infirmity—so-called—like extreme obesity or disfigurement."[51] There is a message about silence contained in the adult's spoken words (and it is likely, as well, in the teacher's facial expressions and bodily comportment when she chides the squabbling children, but Williams does not discuss them). Although spoken language is used, a "silencing is passed from parent to child [that] is not only about the teaching of restraint; it is calculated to circumnavigate the question [of race] as though it had never been asked."[52]

This is the part of the message that likely was opaque to both Williams's son and his teacher. The children knew that race mattered; it already was deeply affecting the way that they divided up the world between good and evil. The enigmatic message sent to the children was that race matters so much that "we" (read: adult white people, which are posited as the standard of normality to which everyone else should aspire) dare not even discuss it. For her son, one can speculate that this means that a discomfort with racialized color has become part of his unconscious and shapes his everyday actions in the world even when they do not seem to involve race at all. And if his unconscious includes remnants of anxiety about racial color, then it is conceivable that in his gestures and bodily movements, he too will send enigmatic messages about race and color to others. I have in mind the opaque messages he might send to other children about the inappropriateness of race, messages that none of them are able to fully understand even as they begin to succumb to and perhaps also resist them.

I also have in mind the enigmatic message that the child probably sends back to Williams herself. Like the teacher's message to the boy, which had various components that were alternatively easy and difficult to digest, Williams's son's message to others is a multifaceted mixture of the transparent and opaque. The boy's overt remarks about the color of grass are fairly easily translatable by adults (or, at least, by Williams—the white teachers apparently were not able to understand them). But less so is the covert message they send about race as too dangerous a topic to consciously acknowledge. As Laplanche claims, "the adult-child relation is eminently suited to re-awaken the conflicts and desires coming from the unconscious" because it is a situation in which the early remnants that helped form the adult's unconscious tend to be reactivated.[53] He gives the example of a man's having his son circumcised, which can reactivate all sorts of untranslated unconscious remnants that remained after his own circumcision.[54] Likewise, a child's unconscious message about the "shameful" secret of race can reactivate and reinforce the early unconscious lessons that most adults—whether white, black, or another race—received as children about the inappropriateness of race from a white-privileged perspective. Once a child begins to develop unconscious habits, the reawakening of unconscious conflicts, tensions, and fantasies revolving around race can occur in either direction between adult and child. This does not mean that the relationship between adult and child is initially transactional—the chicken precedes any particular egg, after all—but it quickly becomes so even as it probably remains asymmetrical for many years. For these reasons, I do not place as heavy an emphasis on the child's psychical passivity as Laplanche does.

Another aspect of Laplanche's work that must be dealt with carefully when using it to understand unconscious habits of white privilege is its rejection of "trans-individual structures."[55] This rejection results from Laplanche's objection to Jacques Lacan's prioritization of language, which Laplanche believes neglects the concrete, particular, and individual adults that help form a child's unconscious. But in making this objection, Laplanche suggests that he considers problematic all appeals to sources of otherness beyond the level of the individual. This explains how Philippe Van Haute can claim that "[f]or Laplanche . . . the unconscious is essentially individual: your enigmatic signifiers are not mine."[56] In my view, Laplanche's emphasis on the concreteness of the other is well placed, but it should not and need not be understood as a rejection of social, political, and cultural forms of otherness that are larger, so to speak, than the individual. The implied opposition between the particular individual and the general culture is a false one that Laplanche's own position on Robinson Crusoeism cannot support. The sexual messages that are transmitted from an adult to a child, for example, are particular to that individual adult and formed out of the views on sexuality of the culture in which the adult participates. Likewise, the enigmatic messages about white privilege that an adult sends to a child are particular to that adult's specific background and experiences and are part of and created by general cultural attitudes toward race. Rephrasing Van Haute, one can say that your enigmatic signifiers both are and are not mine. Living in a racist world, you and I both operate with many of the same enigmatic messages about white privilege even though those messages also vary based on our potentially different races, genders, nationalities, sexualities, and personal experiences. This is a particularly important (though somewhat obvious) point for the purposes of a critical philosophy of race: the unconscious operations of white privilege cannot be properly understood if racism is individualized such that commonalities across individuals do not exist.

A final point in Laplanche's theory that merits caution is its emphasis upon the other's contribution to the self as utterly foreign or alien to the self. For Laplanche, "the unconscious [is] an alien inside me, and even one put inside me by an alien."[57] The alien unconscious is absolutely indigestible, "a foreign body hard as iron" or "an irreducible strangeness."[58] Laplanche insists on this alienness to prevent a return to ipsocentrism and the corresponding Robinson Crusoeism. He is concerned about the tendency, in Freud's work and elsewhere, to "re-assimilate and reintegrate the alien," which closes down "the path leading from the other thing in us to the other person who is its origin."[59] For Laplanche, softening the hard kernel of the unconscious into something that can be incorporated into the self narcissistically recenters the self as its own primary psychical mechanism and solipsistically isolates the self from anything or anyone other to it.

Laplanche presents a false dilemma on this point: either the self-centeredness of ipsocentrism or the irreducible alienness of the other. Both horns of this dilemma are complicit with—or, perhaps one might say, the result of—a lingering atomistic conception of the self. In both cases, the self is presented as originally and fundamentally separate from the other. Even the alien unconscious of the self, which originates from the other, is like a hermetically sealed bubble with an impermeable skin whose otherness never mixes with the self even though it is inside it. (I picture the alien other as a glass marble swallowed by a child and then, unlike the food eaten by her, passing through her body perfectly unchanged.) No wonder, then, that Laplanche's account of the other's intervention in the self has been described as "the effraction or breach of the organism or psychic entity from the outside . . . the breaching of a limit or a boundary, both in its initial impact and in its deposit, 'the internal foreign body.' "[60] That the other can—or, rather, must, if it is to have an influence—breach the limit of the self demonstrates how the self has been conceived of as fundamentally separate, as something initially self-contained that later can and must be broken into.

This false dilemma can be characterized as one between romantic and radical hermeneutics.[61] Psychoanalytic theory tends to operate with a romantic hermeneutics, which subordinates the other to the self. It ultimately thinks the relationship between self and other by merging them into each other, resulting in ipsocentrism. While Julia Kristeva does not soften the hard kernel of the other, for example, she nonetheless risks collapsing it into the self. When Kristeva argues that my recognizing the foreigner within me eliminates the foreigner because we are all foreign,[62] strangeness has been overfamiliarized in its absorption into the self. Kristeva's account of strangeness also too quickly transforms the exterior other into a mere component of the internal psyche.[63] Psychoanalytic theory is right to emphasize the connection between the unconscious and the strange other (including the fear and rejection of both that often occurs), but that connection does not mean that all strangeness is immanent to the psyche. While figures of alterity, such as strangers, gods, and monsters, signal fractures within the psyche, they also represent concrete others beyond us who are perceived as foreign, divine, and monstrous.

In contrast with Kristeva's psychoanalysis, deconstruction tends to be guilty of operating with a radical hermeneutics, which subordinates the self to the other. By positing the utter irreducibility of self and other, a radical hermeneutics produces their complete separation. Because of that separation, the self can only submit to the other, never possibly approach or understand it. Emmanuel Levinas's and Jacques Derrida's respective calls for infinite responsibility and absolute hospitality when encountering the other, for example, tend to subsume the self to the other such that the self has lost its ability to make distinctions and decisions. This ability is crucial for "not every other is innocent and not every self is an egoistic emperor."[64] Openness to the other is an important, perhaps even necessary, component of understanding strangeness, but it is not sufficient. A completely inaccessible other that one can only try to be open to cannot be addressed at all, which leaves the self powerless to make judgments about the other that attempt to promote justice. In addition to openness, "[o]ne must also be able to discern, in some provisional fashion at least, between good and evil. Without such discernment, it seems nigh impossible to take considered ethical action."[65]

Laplanche wants to avoid collapsing the other into the self, explicitly condemning accounts of the other "the essential point" of which is "to rediscover and recognize oneself in them."[66] Yet in his rejection of a romantic hermeneutics, he risks making the reverse error of endorsing a radical hermeneutics.[67] While a radical hermeneutics preserves the separate identity of the other, it does so by severing all connection with the self, making it difficult to understand how the other and self transact in the passage of enigmatic messages between them. By failing to conceive of how both connection and separation between the self and other are possible, a radical hermeneutics is no different than a romantic hermeneutics in effectively severing the relationship between them. If self and other either are fused into one or are irreducibly different, then no point of relation between them can exist.

Laplanche's radical position on the irreducible foreignness of the other is in tension with his naturalistic insistence that the problem of how to open the infant to the world is a false problem.[68] The open infant is permeable, always absorbing, such that boundaries between inside and outside cannot be conceived of as rigid—which is not to say that they completely disappear. Laplanche would agree insofar as this claim is restricted to a physiological level, but he tends to limit the infant's porous, fuzzy-edged relationship with the world when it comes to the psychical. On the one hand, Laplanche is very critical of body-mind dualisms that would separate the mental from the physical. As he claims, the human being is "a *bio-psychical being,* and the idea that an infant is a pure organism, a pure machine on to which a soul, a psyche or whatever else, has been grafted is an aberration."[69] And yet, he also claims that the initial relationship between adult and infant is "established on a twofold register:

we have both a vital, open and reciprocal relationship, which can truly be said to be interactive, and a relationship which is implicitly sexual, where there is no interaction because the two partners are not equal."[70] The first register is the physiological level of self-preservation, whereas the second is the psychical level of seduction—and Laplanche is very deliberate in his use of the language of "level" to suggest a hierarchy whose components are "sharply distinct" even as they are "clearly connected."[71] Laplanche's prioritization of the other, which in and of itself is not troubling, leads him to posit an absolute difference on the level of the psychical between other and self that problematically seals each off from the other.

And yet as his bodily metaphors for the process of seduction suggest, such hard lines between the physiological and psychical cannot be drawn. The waste product that is the unconscious is not a hard kernel or glass marble that passes through the body's digestive tract only to emerge from the process identical to how it began. As Laplanche himself has insisted, the psychical digestive process transforms the initial content, leaking away some aspects of it and soaking into it others, with an end-result that is neither wholly foreign nor completely familiar, that is new in such a way that it is constituted by elements of the old. The unconscious is transactional. This is not to deny the initial priority of the adult over the infant, but to claim that the other should not be thought of as atomistically separated from the self, and cannot be so thought with relapsing into solipsism and ipsocentrism.

For these reasons, the characterization of the formation of unconscious habits as a perversion of a child by a deviant adult—as seduction, in other words—also is problematic. Laplanche explains that "[i]n the primal situation we have, then, a child whose ability to adapt is real but limited, weak and waiting to be perverted, and a deviant adult. . . . Here, we have seducer and seduced, perverter and perverted. Someone is moving away from the straight and narrow; we have here . . . someone who has been led astray and 'seduced.' "[72] My primary concern here is not with the sexually loaded language of seduction and perversion, which Laplanche retains from Freud in order to demonstrate his debt to Freud's early seduction theory. I worry instead that even—or, I should say, precisely—in their more mundane senses of turning someone away from the path she is supposed to be on, "seduction," "perversion," and "deviance" imply that the unconscious engagement of adult and child is something odd, abnormal, or extraordinary—something that is not supposed to happen in the typical course of a child's life, as if there were a straight and narrow, atomistic path devoid of adult influence that an infant could follow as she matures. At times, Laplanche provides interpretations of "perverse" as "unknown" and "deviant" as "split," which combats his account's suggestion that seduction is atypical. The adult is perverse in that she herself does not know what unconscious messages she sends to others, and she is deviant in that she is split into the conscious or preconscious parts she knows and the unconscious part that she does not.[73] Helpful though these (infrequent) suggestions are, they do not entirely erase the atomistic implications of terms such as "perverse" and "deviant." While any particular transaction between a child and its world can be sexually or otherwise inappropriate, transactional engagement as such is not. It is the typical, fitting activity of any live organism, and for human organisms in particular, transaction is just as psychically as it is physically necessary for life to exist.

This is true throughout a human being's life. At times, Laplanche suggests that seduction happens in roughly the first year or two of infancy, after which the unconscious is fully formed and seduction ends. Translations and retranslations can and should take place after this point, according to Laplanche, but they are processes that rework the initial enigmatic messages absorbed in a person's first couple of years, not ones that contribute new messages to the unconscious. An unconscious core is created in the first twelve to twenty-four months of life whose formation does not continue into childhood and beyond.

Some scholars have argued that Laplanche draws the line at approximately the end of year one because an infant is more biologically dependent on caregivers during the first year than afterward. In Peter Osborne's words, the adult "cathects the infant in the course of the interactions which sustain it as a biological entity during the first year of its life." The message implanted in the infant "both demands translation and is untranslatable, since the child has no sense of desire beyond self-preservation, at this point."[74] Once the intense period of biological sustenance is (allegedly) complete—the implication here seems to be that the infant has been weaned at one year—enigmatic messages are no longer being sent from adult to child. With their termination, the child then enters a lifelong process of attempting to translate and retranslate the untranslatable bits of the messages that were metabolized into his or her unconscious.

For his part, Laplanche suggests that the infant's acquisition of language plays an important role in marking the end of seduction. As he remarks, "[t]he *primal situation* is one in which a new-born child, an infant in the etymological sense of the word (*in-fans:* speechless), is confronted with the adult world."[75] Criticizing Lacan, he adds, "if we identify the deepest stratum of man, namely the unconscious, with verbal language (or what we call language in the strict sense), we adopt an explicitly anti-

Freudian stance."[76] Seduction, then, takes place in the period of an infant's life prior to its ability to speak. The unconscious is not structured as a language or formed out of language, as Lacan claims. Just the opposite: the advent of language marks the end of the formation of unconscious habits via seduction. Although Laplanche objects to Lacan's particular emphasis upon language, he implicitly agrees that the ability to use it marks an extremely significant event in a child's life.

While twelve months is somewhat early for most infants to speak more than a couple of basic words, Osborne's explanation of the primal situation of seduction in terms of self-preservation complements Laplanche's language-based account.[77] The story presented by their collective remarks is thus: somewhere around one or two years old, an infant's biological dependency upon caregivers for self-preservation decreases (presumably due to weaning) and its ability to use language begins (and perhaps Laplanche here follows Lacan's view that this development also is related to the child's weaning from the mother). Leaving the maternal realm of bodily care and speechless existence, the infant breaks free of the adult's enigmatic messages and ends the seductive process of the formation of its unconscious habits.

On this account, the examples of Morrison's Claudia and Williams's son cannot count as situations of seduction because eight and three years of age, respectively, are beyond the cutoff point of twelve to twenty-four months. The children in these situations are no longer biologically dependent on caregivers in the way that a young infant is, and they understand and use language even if they do not always comprehend everything adults say. In their cases, unconscious habits must be presumed to already exist, and the puzzling (from their perspective) adult behavior that they try to translate has to be seen as a factor in the secondary process of retranslating the contents of their unconscious habits, not part of the primal process of seduction. The children must be understood as reworking the white privilege that is already present in their unconscious habits, not as continuing the process of forming them.

There are at least two reasons to question this account. First, Laplanche himself occasionally suggests that children beyond infancy are involved in processes of seduction. In yet another objection to Lacan about the role of language in the formation of the unconscious, Laplanche asks, "What maintains the alien-ness of the other? Can one affirm here, with Lacan, the priority of language? If, for my part, I speak rather of a 'message', this is for at least two well-defined reasons: *first,* the message can just as easily be non-verbal as verbal; for the baby it is principally non-verbal."[78] Laplanche's emphasis on the nonverbal nature of enigmatic messages sent to babies implies that human beings other than babies receive enigmatic messages too. Not all of those messages are verbal. Most likely, many of them are nonverbal, as they are primarily (but not necessarily exclusively) for babies. Singling out babies as a distinctive case of seduction suggests that there are other cases involving children who are no longer babies. While one could quibble over the exact age at which one stops being a baby, it is roughly when the child becomes a toddler, which occurs in the twelve- to twenty-four-month-old period when the child is walking, talking, and eating "adult" foods (that is, once the child is no longer breast-fed).[79]

My suggestion that the process of seduction extends beyond infancy is supported by Laplanche's remarks on Freud's analysis of fantasies of a child being beaten. Using "a conceptual arsenal . . . derived from the generalized seduction theory: message, translation and partial failure of translation," Laplanche appeals to the case of the beaten child to demonstrate (against Freud) that repression is not a process of memorization, but rather a function of the inevitable failure of the child's digestion of the other's enigmatic messages.[80] Laplanche uses the case to make a number of points about his theory of seduction, but what is relevant for my purposes here is that he considers it to be "exemplary in showing a process of repression [understood via seduction theory] at work."[81] For Laplanche, the people analyzed by Freud in this case developed unconscious (and then conscious) fantasies involving a beaten child because of the transmission of enigmatic messages from an adult when they were children.

Turning to the text of this "exemplary" case itself, one finds that Freud plainly states that the age of the children who developed sexual fantasies about another child's being beaten is between two and five years. In some broad remarks about the purpose of psychoanalysis, Freud explains that "analytic work deserves to be recognized as genuine psycho-analysis only when it has succeeded in removing the amnesia which conceals from the adult his knowledge of his childhood from its beginning (that is, from about the second to the fifth year)."[82] Freud adds that "[i]t is in the years of childhood between the ages of two and four or five that the congenital libidinal factors are first awakened by actual experiences and become attached to certain complexes," only after which do the fantasies manifest themselves.[83] While Laplanche never explicitly endorses this aspect of Freud's case, he also never objects to it—and this even though Laplanche's goal is to refute its problematic aspects (for example, its explanation of the beating fantasy in terms of amnesia surrounding an actual childhood experience). Laplanche's silence is significant. The fact that he describes Freud's case as exemplary for demonstrating many of the details of his seduction theory strongly suggests that on his account not just babies, but also older children, can be seduced.

But the most compelling reason to think that seduction extends into childhood and beyond is found in Laplanche's emphasis upon the openness of the human organism to its environments. Human beings are never atomistically closed off from the world. Their existence—psychical, as well as physical, for the two cannot be sharply divorced—necessarily is transactional. This means that human dependence upon others does not end once infancy is over. As feminists have long argued, the developmental story of a human's initial dependence upon caregivers that gives way to independence as an adult is deeply problematic.[84] Especially in its psychoanalytic versions, it associates dependence with the allegedly murky realm of the mother, in which distinct beings do not exist and from which the infant violently separates itself and is able to become an independent language-user thanks to the intrusion of the father into the maternal-infant dyad. In addition to its troubling support of patriarchy, such a story problematically assumes that the "normal" development of human beings involves eliminating (or, at least, greatly reducing) one's transactional interdependence upon others.

Laplanche emphasizes the role of dependency in seduction when he claims that "[t]he dependency of young human on adults, which is much more marked than in other species, fosters the delay that is at the origins of humanization, i.e., the early sexualisation of human beings."[85] I do not disagree that human babies are more dependent on adults for longer periods of time than the young of many other species or that the "delay" created by this marked dependency enables seduction. I also would agree that much of the formation of the unconscious probably occurs during early childhood. But given the ongoing transactional openness of the human organism to the world, I cannot agree that the formation of the unconscious stops once a child gains some independence from its caregivers. Human (inter)dependency on others never disappears, even though it takes different forms throughout a person's life and even though it is true that human babies are particularly dependent on adults for their survival. Given that human dependency on others for their psychical and physical well-being is what enables the process of seduction to take place and given the fact this dependency continues, with variation, throughout human life, seduction cannot be said to end after infancy.

Seduction theory manifests a classically psychoanalytic focus on early childhood in its account of the development of unconscious habits. But given its criticism of Robinson Crusoeism and ipsocentrism, this focus should not be understood as an implicit dismissal of adulthood as irrelevant to the "core" of the unconscious. Laplanche's claim that human beings are ontologically open to their environments is in tension with his claim that seduction, which is predicated on ontological openness, ends after early childhood. As I see it, this tension is best resolved by the position that seduction extends beyond infancy. One can continue to use the term "primal seduction" to refer to the earliest, and perhaps most intense, period of transmission of enigmatic messages from the adult world to the infant, but this term cannot be taken to imply a sharp break between the seductions that take place later in life. Attempts to (re)translate early enigmatic messages certainly occur in later childhood and adulthood, but they are accompanied by, and most likely closely related to, additional moments of seduction that continue the initial formation of the unconscious.

In that case, Morrison's Claudia and Williams's son can be understood as engaged in processes of seduction that are building unconscious habits of white privilege. Of course, it is extremely likely that at the ages of eight and three, the children already had received enigmatic messages about race and cleanliness whose unmetabolized remnants were part of their unconscious habits. In that case, the enigmatic situations described above likely tapped into those older messages. But as Morrison and Williams tell the children's stories, those older messages were not yet being reworked. The children were not yet able to understand the meaning of white privilege communicated to them by adults. Although not necessarily the same as the old, the new messages they received about race also were untranslatable and were producing undigested remnants that contributed to their unconscious habits.

One important reason to understand the unconscious as transactional is that doing so reveals how unconscious habits impact the world. This impact can be for better or worse, and viewing the unconscious as transactional does not guarantee that it will be for the better. But it does increase the chances that the impact will be positive because it allows us to understand unconscious habit as productive, rather than representational. The unconscious remnants of messages that children misunderstand do not mirror or copy the adult world from which they originated. That is not the role they play. Laplanche clearly agrees,[86] but his account so emphasizes the psychical passivity of the infant that the active side of its unconscious habits tends to be neglected in his account, which blocks the asking of important questions about what is being produced by unconscious habit and whether something different should be produced instead. Unconscious habits have powerful "external" effects. They help create the material, economic, social, political, psychical, and cultural world in which people live (just as it, in turn, helps create unconscious habits). Nowhere is this truer than in the case of racism and white privilege. Human beings historically have lived and currently live in a raced and racist world in significant part because of unconscious investments in and productions of that world.

Understanding seduction transactionally means looking at not just the receptivity of unconscious habits, but also their productive effects. This in turn means asking what a particular relationship of unconscious habits and the world does, not what it represents. There is no ultimate meaning that unconscious habits are supposed to convey and that human beings are supposed to decode. What is important about them is what the particular transaction between them and the world achieves. In that sense, habit can be thought of as a machine: a relatively stable, complex process of change that produces certain effects through its transactions with other machines.[87] To understand this claim, all one need do is consider any everyday machine: a personal computer, for example. I never ask of my computer what it means. Or while I could, such a question is impoverished and off the mark. What is relevant about my computer is what it can do (or not); what are its possibilities and limitations; what does it combine with in order to create (or sap) new powers? This last question is particular important because it reminds one of the connections and alliances that compose any particular machine. Machines are never isolated; they are always being plugged into and detached from other machines (for example, printers, modems, electric outlets, battery packs, etc.). To find out how any particular machine works, one has to ask of it, "what are the connections, what are the disjunctions, the conjunctions, what use is made of the syntheses" between it and other machines?[88]

These machinic questions apply equally well to organic as nonorganic structures. Asking about the effects of various conjunctions and disjunctions of organic habits, these questions cut across rather than uphold traditional divisions between "interior" psyche and "exterior" world. They entangle or blur the boundaries between things that are often seen as fundamentally or substantially separate from one another. Gilles Deleuze and Felix Guattari illustrate this point in "[t]he unforgettable associated world of the Tick," in which what the tick is are its connections with the branch on which it hangs, the passing human whose sweat it smells, and the skin onto which it latches to suck blood.[89] The tick is constituted by what it does with and to the world around it, just as the human onto which it drops is constituted in part by the tick-world in which it has entered. In the becoming-tick of the human and the becoming-human of the tick, there is an alliance of tick and human that is machinic in that it involves a nonrepresentational, dynamic transformation of each of them. The issue is never one of the tick coming to resemble a human or a human coming to resemble a tick, but instead is one of the relations and the degrees of those relations between the tick and human. For both the tick and the human, one can say that "[w]e know nothing about [it] until we know what it can do, in other words, what its affects are, how they can or cannot enter into composition with other affects, with the affects of another body, either to destroy that body or to be destroyed by it, either to exchange actions and passions with it or to join with it in composing a more powerful body."[90] Unconscious habit is not a theater of representations, but a psychosomatic machine that actively and directly produces and is produced by a social world invested with unconscious desire.

In the context of white privilege, my emphasis on the productivity of unconscious habit suggests not just the possibility of taking, but also the need to take, responsibility for racism. It demands that a person ask of herself: what kind of racial and/or racist world am I helping to produce? Characterizing white privilege as unconscious habit does not mean letting white (or other) people off the hook for their racist practices or their implicit and explicit acceptance of the benefits of white privilege.[91] If people cannot be held wholly responsible for their unconscious habits, they can be held accountable for their attempts (or lack thereof) to transform them. And given the transactional, productive relationship between the unconscious and its various environments, this is to say that they can be held at least partially accountable for habit's future development. All people, white people included, can and should "become answerable for what [they] learn how to see."[92] The point of this claim is not to increase white guilt about racism—which too often results in white people's narcissistic wallowing in their own suffering—but rather to demonstrate how action can be taken. While no one can easily, if ever, alter unconscious habits through direct attempts to change them, everyone can make at least some deliberate decisions about what sorts of environments they will inhabit and indirectly impact what sorts of psychic "food" will be taken in for attempted digestion and repression. As Laplanche emphasizes, the "binding schemata" for new translations of unconscious remnants are "not invented out of the blue: they are supplied . . . by an entire social and cultural environment."[93] This environment includes the people one is around, the books one reads, the films one sees, the political and other issues one seeks to learn about, and so on. The aim here, as Laplanche explains in a different context, is not to recreate an initial, "pure" stage of infancy prior to enigmatically racist messages. It instead is to de-translate, by both conscious and unconscious means, some of the initially misunderstood messages about race so that new translations might take place. In this process, some, although certainly nothing close to total, control can indirectly be exercised over what sorts of new translations might be produced.

I will say more in subsequent chapters about the dangers of appealing to the environment in attempts to transform unconscious habit. But a brief word of caution is in order at this point. Choosing to engage and inhabit environments that likely will challenge unconscious habits of white privilege is important for their possible transformation. In this way, environmental change might be thought of as the equivalent of psychotherapy for a transactional unconscious. But it is all too easy for this well-intended attempt to challenge white privilege to become merely another instance of it. This can occur when white people romantically appropriate non-white cultures, environments, and spaces as tools for the narcissistic transformation of their unconscious. I have in mind the example of many New Age attempts of privileged white people to take up Native American cultures and practices for the purpose of eliminating their Eurocentrism. Such attempts to leave "civilization" for the primitive "wildness" of non-white cultures tends to reinforce oppressive stereotypes about those cultures that sustain white privilege. In his biting criticism of the men's movement, Ward Churchill argues, "spiritual traditions cannot be used as some sort of Whitman's Sampler of ceremonial form, mixed and matched. . . . [T]o play at ritual potluck is to debase all spiritual traditions, voiding their internal coherence and leaving nothing usably sacrosanct as a cultural anchor for the peoples who conceived and developed them."[94] Deleuze and Guattari also come dangerously close to reinforcing white privilege in this way in their attempts to counter white racism.[95] But they then chastise themselves for "falling victim to a nostalgia for a return or regression" and caution their readers that opening the unconscious to the outside "is never a question of a return to . . ." something (allegedly) primitive.[96] This caution must be borne in mind in the case of all environments that often are considered other to the realm of the (white) human, especially the "wilderness" environments thought to be the natural home of Native American and tick alike. And read generously, perhaps Laplanche's emphasis upon passivity makes a similar point. Understood not as a rejection of transaction but as a tempering of pushy aggressiveness, the "passive" unconscious realizes that sometimes its activity can constitute an oppressive invasion of other people's cultural and physical space.

The danger of increasing white privilege through white people's engagements with non-white environments cannot be eliminated. But the response to that danger should not be for white people to solipsistically remain within white and white-privileged worlds. Given unconscious habit's resistance to its detection, its transformation must be approached indirectly through its various environments. To refuse to examine one's environments because of a fear of increasing racism is to relinquish one of the best possibilities that one has for gaining some influence over unconscious habits of white privilege. Again, this is not necessarily to suggest that human beings have unlimited access to and influence on the digestive remnants that compose unconscious habits. It is to question the traditional psychoanalytic view of the unconscious as necessarily hermetically sealed off from consciousness.

Laplanche argues that the unconscious is wholly created through an individual's engagements with her social and other environments. He then claims that parts of it can become so isolated that they are beyond societal reach. These parts are what Freud called the id, and they constitute the mute part of the psyche that is outside communication and signification.[97] As Laplanche insists, "part of the unconscious will never be recalled and brought back to consciousness, but can only be grasped within a network of constructions that attempts to approach it but which never reaches the thing itself."[98] The id "*does not talk,*" and to think otherwise, for Laplanche, is to deny "the most radical implications of the [psycho]analytic discovery: if the unconscious is no longer a separate register, or if it is simply the unknowable backdrop to our whole psyche, recognition of its existence is simply a pious gesture which has no serious practical implications."[99]

I agree that one should not blithely assume that the process of transforming the unconscious will be easy or completely successful. And I think that in any particular situation, one will always run up against limits beyond which transformation cannot occur. Certain aspects or strands of unconscious habits can be resistant enough to conscious intervention that they functionally lie beyond environmental influence. This most stubbornly impenetrable part of one's unconscious habits can be understood as Freud's id. But I cannot agree with the acontextual, substantive claim that there exists a segment of unconscious habit that necessarily lies beyond the influence of the "external" world. Such an a priori declaration both assumes that one already knows how much change unconscious habit is capable of and discourages the concrete attempts at change that are the very means by which the limits of those attempts might be discovered. At the same time that the distinction between (pre)consciousness and the unconscious should not be collapsed, it also should not be assumed to be absolute.[100] Rather than block efforts to discover the limits of the accessibility of unconscious habit, a psychoanalytically informed criti-cal race theory should encourage them by heuristically asking: what are the current possibilities for and limits of the transformation of uncon-scious habits built of remnants of white privilege? And it must insist that the answer to that question will only be given through the work of trans-formation itself.

FOUR

Global Habits, Collective Hauntings

As a process of unconscious habit formation, seduction accounts for the way that concrete others come to constitute the individual psychosomatic self. Not just parents, but other caregivers, loved ones, teachers, and friends send enigmatic messages about race and white domination that help make up one's unconscious life. An entire world of transgenerational others contributes to the undigested remnants of white privilege that are psychosomatically sedimented in one's self. A person's unconscious habits are woven out of the voices of many others. Sole authorship of one's unconscious life can never credibly be claimed.

Seduction theory reaches beyond the Oedipal triangle to include concrete others such as grandparents, neighbors, and even strangers in the formation of unconscious habits. But the expanse of habit formation must be understood as including more than just individuals. Laplanche rightly objects to the positing of trans-individual structures in the form of a transcendental language completely abstracted away from the concrete world of embodied, gestural beings. But he throws out the baby with the bathwater by disregarding the historical, temporal, trans-individual products of human life and activity. Rejection of transcendentalism does not necessitate rejection of all structures larger than the individual. Such rejection risks reinstating a form of individualism in which only individuals count as real, producing an anemic ontology in which non-individual structures, such as institutional forms of racism, colonialism, and white privilege, cannot be said to participate in the process of habit formation. Unconscious habit formation centers on concrete others, as Laplanche claims, but concrete others are not limited to individual people. Cultural and societal structures of white privilege are just as concrete and real as the individuals who participate in them. And those structures need not be geographically local or nearby. Habit formation can be a regional, national, and even global process that stretches across the world. Enigmatic messages about white privilege can be unconsciously communicated between portions of the world geographically quite distant from each other, which means that the national and geographical habits of various countries and areas of the world help form the unconscious raced habits of other peoples and nations.

Processes of habit formation must be understood as producing more than individual habits. Cultural or societal habits exist that are larger, so to speak, than any one individual. Cultures, societies, and groups can have distinctive styles, particular predispositions for transacting with others that distinguish them. Such cultural habits are not divorced from individual habits. On the contrary, cultural habits play a significant role in establishing individual habits, just as individual habits in turn impact the habits of the cultures and groups to which a person belongs. Habit formation includes the creation of cultural unconscious habits that can operate as concrete others who provide "food" for individual unconscious habits. Enigmatic messages can be unintentionally (as well as intentionally) sent to a culture, society, nation, or other trans-individual group that it cannot fully or adequately understand. The undigested remnants of those messages contribute to a culture's unconscious habits.

What I find particularly interesting about collective unconscious habits of white privilege is that, from the perspective of the individual, they both do and do not seem to exist. Often the impact of the collective unconscious on an individual is uneventful. No one has ever sat down and explicitly explained to me, for example, the (alleged) superiority of white people. There is no specific event to point to. Nothing seems to have happened, and no collective knowledge about white superiority seems to exist. Yet it does. A white privileged collective unconscious has slipped, undetected, into my individual habits. Because of this slippage, I unconsciously "know" that white people are superior to all others, and I manifest that knowledge in my psychosomatic engagement with the world.

In other cases, the collective unconscious involves specific events, but those events are so geographically or historically removed from a particular person that they do not appear to involve her at all. A culture's collective unconscious can include the remnants of events that no currently living individual underwent, and yet those remnants can compose some of the materials of her unconscious habits. For this reason, the reality of the impact of the collective unconscious on an individual is ill understood as either literal or metaphorical. Consider, for example, a contemporary African American—or a white person, to make a related point—who never actually experienced slavery and yet bears the psychosomatic effects of it. Those effects—embodiments of slavery and mastery, respectively—are real. This does not mean that contemporary black and white people in the United States literally are or have been slaves or masters. But neither does it mean that current patterns of racism and white privilege bear only a metaphoric relationship to historical occurrences of slavery and mastery. Slavery is a contemporary, not just historical, reality because of the real, lingering presence it has in the United States' collective unconscious. Its presence is a phantom, both there and not there, like a cloud that slips through one's hands when one tries to firmly grasp it.

Slippages and phantoms—these concepts describe a society's collective unconscious in its complex and fluid relationship with individual habits and capture the broad geographical and historical expanse of habit formation. I turn to them here, drawing on the work of Franz Fanon and complementing it with that of Toni Morrison and contemporary psychoanalysts Nicholas Abraham and Maria Torok.

One of the primary goals of Fanon's *Black Skin, White Masks* is to analyze the formation and effects of "the zebra striping of [the] mind" of black people like Fanon.[1] Fanon was a French citizen who grew up on Martinique, a former French colony, and who visited France for the first time as a young adult. More to the point, Fanon was a black Frenchman who grew up in a predominantly black world, never noticing that he was black—and, indeed, unconsciously thinking of himself as white—until he traveled to the predominantly white world of continental France. It was this world-traveling that zebra-striped Fanon's psyche.[2] His wholly white unconscious habits fractured into black and white, transforming a relatively peaceful, unified—which is not to say unproblematic—set of habits into a fragmented collection at war with itself.

A person does not have to physically relocate to engage in world-traveling. While Fanon's case did involve geographical travel, it more importantly exemplified what is central to the concept of world-traveling: the value-laden movement between different cultures, worldviews, and attitudes. Fanon grew up in a world that allowed a man with dark skin to be seen as a full person, and then he moved to a world in which a man with dark skin was thought of and treated as merely a subperson. The eventual internalization of these two worlds' perceptions of him produced the split "coloring" of Fanon's psyche, and it did so, as I will explain shortly, by violently impacting his lived bodily experience.

But first, how could a world such as the Antilles, predominantly populated by black bodies, produce inhabitants who unconsciously experienced themselves as white? The answer is that an ethical slippage (*un glissement éthique*) occurred in which the moral values of white France were transferred into black Martinique.[3] This slippage transmitted enigmatic messages about race to the collective Martinique psyche via Martiniquean bodies. The French/Western European value system transferred to Martinique dictated that black is bad, immoral, and sinful, while white is good, virtuous, and pure. To the extent that one sees herself as a morally upstanding person, one therefore must be white. As Fanon explains, "[i]f I order my life like that of a moral man, I simply am not a Negro."[4] When implanted into Martinique, the French/Western European value system deceptively did not (explicitly) biologize its values. This was part of their enigmatic force. "White" and "black" were understood by Antilleans as labels for virtues and flaws unrelated to skin color, which is why Fanon can retrospectively say from the perspective of his young self that racial "[c]olor is nothing, I do not even notice it, I know only one thing, which is the purity of my conscience and the whiteness of my soul."[5]

The slippage of white privileged values from France to Martinique created an Antillean collective unconscious. This is not the collective unconscious described by Carl Jung, which upholds the Freudian tradition of phylogenesis. Contra Jung, who claimed the collective unconscious was formed of universal and ahistorical images, the Fanonian collective unconscious is the summation of the unconscious attitudes and prejudices of a group. Jung's concept of the collective unconscious went astray because he confused habit with instinct, which is to say that he mistook the acquired for the innate or inborn. Jung was right that something larger than the individual unconscious is needed to explain the attitudes and values unconsciously held by an individual, but those attitudes and values must be understood as originating from his or her cultural environment, not from an allegedly unchanging psychical structure populated with permanent archetypes. The transfer of European valuations of black and white to Martinique constituted an infusion of color bias into the Antillean collective unconscious. The collective unconscious of "*homo occidentalis*" became that of the Martiniquean, and the Martiniquean also learned to distrust blackness as symbolizing everything sinful and evil.[6]

Fanon provides specific examples of some of the ways in which the Antillean collective unconscious is formed by ethical slippage. History textbooks, songs, and especially magazines and movies were the primary vehicles for the transference of white privileged values to Martinique. Black schoolchildren in the Antilles were explicitly taught to identify with "'our ancestors, the Gauls,'" which means that they were subtly taught to identify with a French "truth" that posits black people as savages in need of European enlightenment.[7] Movies such as the Tarzan series teach the same lesson and encourage black children to identify with the white conqueror over the black "savage." Magazines and comic books in which "the Wolf, the Devil, the Evil Spirit, the Bad Man, the Savage are always symbolized by Negroes or Indians" were particularly problematic. These publications were "put together by white men for little white men," and yet because they were distributed in the Antilles, they also impacted black boys and girls who came to see themselves as part of the intended white audience.[8]

Because the ethical slippage from France to Martinique operated by means of media images, it was difficult to detect and, as a result, especially effective. As Fanon comments, "[t]he black man among his own in the twentieth century does not know at what moment his inferiority comes into being through the other."[9] Magazines, comic books, movies: these generally are seen as frivolous and pleasurable, as mere entertainment, but their frivolity is what makes them so insidious. The values they convey slip into one's thinking subtly, smoothly, without much (if any) conscious attention or psychical disruption—this is what is conveyed by the particular term *un glissement éthique*. If this happened infrequently, it might not make much of an impact, but the constant onslaught of French/Western European values by means of these media make them a formidable conduit for those values into the Antillean unconscious.

While ethical slippage makes a great impact on individual unconscious habits, it can seem nonexistent because it often occurs apart from any specific event. Fanon explains this characteristic of ethical slippage when he analyzes the claim of Freud's 1909 Clark University lectures that all neuroses have their origins in specific lived experiences that are then repressed in the unconscious.[10] Fanon appears to misread Freud since Freud's point is to reject his earlier seduction theory.[11] But while Fanon misunderstands Freud's goal in these lectures, he does not take it as his own. Fanon's purpose is to use (his misreading of) Freud's seduction theory as a point of contrast for his own position. Like Laplanche, Fanon objects to Freud's claim in his seduction theory that psychical problems necessarily have their roots in actual traumatic events experienced in one's childhood. While Fanon values Freud's (alleged) emphasis on individual lived experience, he finds it simplistic because it overlooks the role that the collective unconscious plays in it. Freud's theory is not able to adequately account for the paradoxical ambiguity of the trauma of racism experienced by many black people. This paradox is revealed in the questions Fanon asks soon after his explication of Freud: "How is one to explain, for example, that a Negro who has passed his baccalaureate and has gone to the Sorbonne to study to become a teacher of philosophy is already on guard before any conflictual elements have coalesced around him? . . . Very often the Negro who becomes abnormal has never had any relations with whites."[12] If a black person has never been the victim of an actual racist event, then it seems that he could not feel personally traumatized by racism. Yet black people in that situation still do suffer from neuroses related to racism. Must we then posit an actual trauma in the person's childhood that has since been forgotten?

The answer is "no." The solution to the paradox is not to hold, for example, that the black child must have seen his father beaten or lynched by a white man and then repressed his or her memory of the violent event.[13] There often is no real experienced event in that sense. Yet the answer also is "yes," but not in the sense that (early) Freud would give to it. Fanon reworks the meaning of reality beyond the false opposition of literalism and metaphor and emphasizes the role of the unconscious in doing so. There is a reality to the black person's experience of racial trauma that is neither literal nor metaphorical/fictional. The key to understanding Fanon's account of reality is to interpret the terms "real" and "experience" in light of his analysis of ethical slippage and the collective unconscious. The ethical slippage of white values to a black world is not a specific, determinate event. In that sense, it is not real and is not consciously experienced as an actual occurrence by black people. But in the sense that this slippage has powerful, though largely hidden, effects on black people, it pervades their experience and is very real. Ethical slippage demonstrates that the concepts of the real and lived experience should not be understood as primarily or solely based on consciousness. There exists a reality that is the white collective unconscious of black people, and this reality undercuts black people's lived experiences of their bodies through its privileging of whiteness. The betrayal of black people by this reality cannot be summed up by any singular event, and it tends to go undetected unless and until black people travel to a white world. But this does not make this reality any less real.

As portrayed by Fanon, the ethical slippage from France to Martinique was so smooth that it appears to exactly replicate French values in the Antillean psyche. If the slippage is completely seamless, then there would seem to be little possibility for change or difference across generations in people's unconscious lives. But the process of *glissement éthique* also can be thought of as indirect and partial. In that case, the black person's "inferiority [that] comes into being through the other" can be seen as disjunctively created out of the incomplete translation of enigmatic messages contained in history textbooks, songs, and especially magazines, comic books, and movies. As those messages slide into the Antillean collective unconscious, they are partially digested, producing remnants that are both formed out of and profoundly reshape the French values from which they originated. Thinking of ethical slippage as indirect does not eliminate its destructive power. Race-based oppression can and does persist across its disjunctive communication. But it does emphasize the dynamic nature of white privilege, which makes it at least conceivable that it could be challenged.

Extending the time of the formation of the unconscious beyond the point of primary seduction, Fanon suggests that an ethical slippage from one world to another does its main damage in childhood and adolescence and that, by the age of twenty, the unconscious formed by it is quite deeply buried.[14] If not before, when he or she reaches adulthood, the young black man or woman living in Martinique fully identifies with whiteness and considers blackness as evil. Speaking as that young adult, Fanon exclaims, "I am a white man. For unconsciously I distrust what is black in me, that is the whole of my being. I am a Negro—but of course I do not know it, simply because I am one."[15] This existential situation might sound precarious, but Fanon suggests that it is quite stable since very little, if anything, in the Antilles challenged it. It is when the young black man travels to France, as Fanon himself did, that his self-understanding is disrupted. There, "the real white man is waiting for [him]," and recognition of his betrayal by the (white) values he holds dear begins to dawn.[16] Here one can see how a change in a person's environment can impact his or her unconscious habits, providing indirect access to them. The Antillean who travels to France realizes that "he is living an error"; he is black, not white, as the white man immediately makes clear to him.[17] The "peaceful violence" that the Antilles is steeped in becomes impossible to ignore and is transformed into overt conflict.[18]

Now the zebra striping begins: white unconscious habits are disrupted by the knowledge that one is black. Fanon's account reveals that merely being black with a white unconscious was not sufficient to produce this zebra striping, as one might have thought. A person has to know that she is black for her white unconscious to begin to change. Or, put another way, there is no such thing as *being* black in the way that a thing such as a chair is black. Being black is always a process of becoming that is constituted by both self-understanding and others' perceptions of one. But coming to know yourself as black through others' perceptions of you does not instantly change white privileging unconscious habits. They are far too resilient for such quick transformation to occur. Instead, the painful agony that is the striping/splitting of the unconscious begins: having fully endorsed France's white privilege, the black Antillean struggles to find a way to also affirm his or her newly discovered blackness. For such a person, traveling to a white world is not just a geographical relocation from the Antilles to the European continent. It simultaneously is a disruption of the place that he or she occupies within his or her ethical worldview. For the relocated black Antillean, "[m]oral consciousness [now] implies a kind of scission, a fracture of consciousness into a bright part and an opposing black part. In order to achieve morality, it is essential that the [newly discovered] black, the dark, the Negro vanish from consciousness [into the unconscious]. Hence a Negro is forever in combat with his own image."[19]

The trauma produced by racism and colonialism is not located in the mind considered apart from the body. France successfully colonized other peoples and countries by squeezing itself into native bodies, as well as psyches.[20] Revealing the intimate connections between psyche and soma, Fanon recounts the difficulties that the disruption of his psyche caused to his bodily schema when he moved to France. Drawing from the phenomenology of Maurice Merleau-Ponty, Fanon describes the bodily schema as the lived body by and through which one takes up the world. The body as lived is not the body as consciously reflected on; such reflection has already turned the body into an object for thought. As lived, a person's body is not consciously guided through its various activities and movements. Bodily life is instead the unthought means by which a person is an active agent in the world. As Fanon explains, "[a] slow composition of my *self* as a body in the middle of a spatial and temporal world—such seems to be the [bodily] schema. It does not impose itself upon me; it is, rather, a definitive structuring of the self and of the world—definitive because it creates a real dialectic between my body and the world."[21] This schema can be seen in the example of Fanon's desire to smoke.[22] When he reaches for matches and cigarettes, his movement toward the table and then the drawer are part of a lived situation that combines both body and world. Fanon does not think his arms and hands through the successive steps of opening the drawer, pulling out the matches, and lighting the cigarette. His body is composed of the implicit knowledge of how to accomplish this task by means of engagement with the socio-material objects of the world. This dialectic of body and world composes the socially situated, bodily self that Fanon is.

The lived, dialectical relationship of body and world also explains the origin of environing spatiality. A person's body is not an object in space, as, for example, Fanon's cigarette and matches are. Although a body's relationship to its spatial environment can be understood in this way, such an objective relationship is possible only because of bodily situatedness in the world.[23] It is lived, not objective space that is primary for human existence. This explains why environing space is neither empty nor neutral, but instead is always already imbued with direction and purpose. Because human existence is always bodily and situated, the world is always differentially charged or "magnetized" with meaning.[24]

The magnetization of environing space is significant for the concept of bodily schema. In Fanon's example above, the elements of the composition of the bodily schema are physical objects, such as tables and drawers, and bodily movements, such as reaching for a cigarette, that are racially neutral. But what if the world one engages is a racist world, and many of the compositional elements for the bodily schema are magnetized by a system of white domination? That type of situation—which is the actual situation in which Fanon lived and which many people today face— requires a much more complex account of the formation of the bodily schema through its lived spatiality. This more complex account would reveal the historico-racial schema that lurks behind the "normal" bodily schema. The historico-racial schema is composed of the stories and myths about the different races that give them their meaning. The historico-racial schema is, in other words, the somatic equivalent of the raced collective unconscious. Presenting whiteness as good and blackness as evil just as the racist collective unconscious does, the historico-racial schema associates the source of evil with physiology, tethering raced-based values to bodily features. It is this schema that leads the little child to exclaim, "Look, a Negro!" when she sees Fanon walking down the street. As Fanon remarks to himself in response to the situation, "I thought that what I had in hand was to construct a physiological self, to balance space, to localize sensations, and here I was called on for more."[25] What was demanded of him was that he incorporate white people's racist perceptions of him as a savage subperson into his corporeal schema.

Here one can appreciate in a fresh way phenomenological claims about spatial environment. What Fanon carefully reveals is the role that race and racism play in the bodily gearing of the subject onto the world

that originates environing space. The spatiality of situation that characterizes bodily existence includes more than racially neutral objects such as
ashtrays and paperweights. In a world infused with white privilege, a black
person's bodily comportment is always being constituted by the raced and
racist space in which he or she lives. In such a world, the lived space
that gives bodies their spatiality of situation is never neutral or empty,
but instead is always already shaped by social and political forces such
as racism.

Fanon tends to present the historico-racial schema as if it is something that only black or, more generally, other non-white people must
confront. And indeed, one of the privileges of whiteness is for it to seem to
a white person that no historico-racial schema is at play in the constitution
of her lived body. For a white person, *qua* white, the world presents no
barriers to her engagement with the world. She might trip over a crack in
the sidewalk or be blocked by other people in her way, but she generally
is not faced with frightened children who point out her whiteness and
thereby transform her from a lived subject into a static object. But the
lack of racialized obstacles to the formation of a white person's bodily
schema exists precisely because of the historico-racial schema that privileges whiteness. The same historico-racial schema described by Fanon
both disrupts the black person's and enables the white person's composition of their bodily schemas. As the somatic embodiment of the raced
collective unconscious, the historico-racial schema simultaneously supports the unconscious psyche's investments in white privilege and serves as
a site for racism's unconscious operations. The privileging of whiteness
imposed by a historico-racial schema impacts both white and black people, but this impact often remains invisible to the white person while it is
forced out of hiding in the case of the black person. Hence the black
person is "called on for more": she is explicitly called on to have a race
while the white person is allowed to (appear to) be raceless.

Because the historico-racial schema positions black and white people
differently, its effect on their bodily schemas also is quite different. For the
black person, the historico-racial schema causes the "normal" (= privileged) bodily schema to crumble and be replaced by a racial epidermal
schema.[26] Instead of having a lived body like the white person does, the
black person is forced to be aware of his or her body as an object. Even
worse, "it [is] no longer a question of being aware of [one's] body in the
third person [i.e., as an object] but in a triple person."[27] Instead of being
solely in the place of the immediately lived body, the black person's racial
epidermal schema means that she also is always in a second place outside
herself, reaching toward the white world for its approval. Because that

[103]

approval is not forthcoming, the third place that is no place is the result. If, following Hegel, recognition by the other is crucial to the constitution of the self, then to be denied that recognition is to be denied selfhood. Hence the nausea spoken of by Fanon because the substance and meaning of one's life is centered on an other who is evanescent.[28] This is why Fanon claims that a feeling of nonexistence, not that of inferiority, is the real problem afflicting black people.[29]

Given the importance of the social environment to the formation of individual psychosomatic habits, Fanon's use of Hegel's concept of recognition to explain the black person's racial epidermal schema is problematic. Explicating Hegel's *Phenomenology of Spirit,* Fanon claims, "Man is human only to the extent to which he tries to *impose* his existence on another man in order to be recognized by him. . . . It is on that other being, on recognition by that other being, that his own human worth and reality depend. It is that other being in whom the meaning of his life is condensed."[30] By characterizing the self as constituted through struggle with the other, Hegel's dialectical account of human relationships demonstrates the social basis of individuality. And yet, his account ultimately is not so different from the liberalism it attempts to challenge in that both support a narcissistic focus on the individual self. Different ways of accounting for the sociality of human subjectivity exist, some of which turn out to be rather asocial at their core. Hegel's notion of mutual recognition remains narcissistic by prioritizing the one who has the power to acknowledge—or ignore—the other.[31] In a world filled with asymmetrical relations of power, Hegelian recognition tends to maintain rather than challenge master-slave imbalances. Even as Hegel argues that the slave and not the master carries forward the development of consciousness, his sustained focus on the master's power in the dialectic between master and slave risks making their collective story a truncated tale about the master only.

A related problem with Hegel's dialectic is that in its assumption that mutual recognition is necessary for the achievement of freedom from oppression, it demands a synthesis of the perspectives of master and slave that requires the slave to see herself as the master does. A "Hegelian account of sociality . . . collapses the distinct points of view of the victim and agent of domination into a single perspective," that of the master.[32] But in the example of literal slavery, there was no freedom to be found for the African American slave who saw herself in the grotesque and humiliating ways that her master viewed her. A dialectic of mutual recognition only ensures a colonization of the slave's psyche that signals the total domination of the racial contract. If and when the racial contract establishing white domination over non-white people has succeeded in getting all its victims to happily sign on to its terms, that is precisely when white domination will have become completely victorious.³³

Fanon is right that recognition from others is an important component of human sociality and individual personhood. What a critical philosophy of race needs, therefore, is a non-Hegelian account of recognition that complements a transactional concern for the role that the environment plays in individuality. Such an account can be found in Cynthia Willett's work on social eros. Drawing from Toni Morrison's novel *Beloved,* Willett "represent[s] love as a way in which one person can lay claim to the self through the recognition bestowed by another."³⁴ Considered in isolation, this description of love and subjectivity could sound uncomfortably Hegelian. But Willett continues in a way that clearly distances her from Hegel's work: "Love moves the self outward. Its force is centrifugal."³⁵ This claim suggests that, just as there are different ways by which to conceive of human sociality, there are different types of recognition. Hegelian recognition could be described as centripetal; its driving force is inward, producing a narcissistic focus on the one self at the expense of the other. Centrifugal recognition, in contrast, moves the self outward. It establishes and nurtures social connections between and among people. Unlike the violent self-centeredness of centripetal recognition, centrifugal recognition stretches the self toward and into other people, nourishing human sociality rather than narcissistically starving it. The objectified black person whose bodily schema has been collapsed into a racial epidermal schema needs this loving recognition.

Even though black Antilleans were not afflicted with a racial epidermal schema before traveling to the white world of France, the processes that would give rise to that bodily transformation were set in motion in the black world of Martinique. The ethical slippage from France to the Antilles that so profoundly shaped the Martinique psyche was invisibly shaping the Martinique soma as well. Complementing Laplanche's remarks about the fixing of enigmatic messages on one's psychophysiological skin, Fanon explains that the internalization of black inferiority is better described as its "epidermalization."³⁶ Fanon further hints at the intimate relationship of psyche and soma when speaking of a similar situation in Madagascar, claiming that "[t]he arrival of the white man in Madagascar shattered not only its horizons but its psychological mechanisms."³⁷ I read this claim as a description of the twofold destruction of the black person's soma and psyche. The white man's arrival in a black world did not merely shatter black people's horizons in the sense of their futures; it also shattered their horizons that are their bodies. Or more accurately: black people's future horizons were shattered precisely in and through the shattering of their bodily horizons. Objects in the world have meaning only as figures that stand out against a background. The spatiality of the world, in other words, is fundamental to its ability to be meaningful, and crucial to the relationship between spatiality and meaning is human embodiment. As Merleau-Ponty explains, "[a]s far as spatiality is concerned . . . one's own body is the third term, always tacitly understood, in the figure-background structure, and every figure stands out against the double horizon of external and bodily space."[38] Human embodiment is part of the given background against which objects in the world take on meaning.

But it is more than a mere background. An adequate appreciation of unconscious habits suggests that one's body is not just a nonreflective backdrop to conscious awareness, but also sometimes an unconscious obstacle to it. To have one's bodily horizon shattered—understood as the disruption of both nonconscious and unconscious bodily habits—is to have one's ability to make meaning in the world severely damaged. Once shattered, the horizon of my body cannot serve as the hidden background to my activities and projects in the world. The shattering of my bodily horizons means that my body itself stands out as an object in the world. No longer out of the sight of consciousness, it is now concentrated upon, viewed as a thing rather than lived as a crucial component of my agency. Bodily horizons can be shattered by a number of situations, but what is common to them all is that once destroyed, a person's body is transformed into a thing to be manipulated rather than a means by and through which one lives.[39]

In *A Dying Colonialism*, Fanon provides a detailed example of one of those situations, which involved the fracturing effects of the French occupation of Algeria on the corporeal schema of Algerian women. Just as a woman's plumed hat, a person's car, and a blind man's cane form part of their bodily engagements with the world,[40] an Algerian woman's veil is not something foreign or external to her bodily schema. It is intrinsic to her lived body, crucial to the way in which she takes up her world. The attack of French occupational forces on Algerian culture by means of the unveiling of Algerian women was an attack on Algerian women's bodies. Newly unveiled, the Algerian woman's bodily schema was shattered; her body became an object to consciously operate rather than the lived means by which she actively engaged the world. The difficulty experienced by the unveiled woman can be found in something as simple as crossing the street: "Without the veil she has an impression of her body being cut up into bits, put adrift; the limbs seem to lengthen indefinitely. When the Algerian woman has to cross a street, for a long time she commits errors of judgment as to the exact distance to be negotiated."[41] Rather than be freed of something that most Western women would consider cumbersome, the unveiled Algerian woman is now burdened with the absence of her veil.

This absence distorts the Algerian woman's corporeal pattern, which is why "[s]he quickly has to invent new dimensions for her body, new means of muscular control. She has to create for herself an attitude of unveiled-woman-outside."[42] How quickly and smoothly this creation takes place is determined by both an Algerian woman's unconscious investments in her previous bodily comportment and her unconscious resistances to its replacement. Although the eventual composition of a new bodily schema does not erase or excuse the destructiveness of French colonialism, this destructiveness must be recognized as the condition for the possibility of a new somatic (and psychical) creation. The new creation for Algerian women was a bodily schema that often enabled them to more effectively fight the French occupation than the old bodily schema did. For example, Algerian women had to learn to comport themselves as "normal" either without the veil or with weapons and revolutionary documents hidden under their veils. While brought about through the violence of colonialism and always of ambiguous value, the new bodily schemas of Algerian women helped them liberate themselves from the very colonial powers that brutally transformed their bodies.

Fanon suggests that in contrast to Algerian women's new bodily comportment, the new corporeal schema that resulted for Antilleans who relocated to France was less positive. When the Antilleans' bodily schema was destroyed, an alternative schema that attributed an unchangeable biological essence to Antilleans replaced it. This alleged racial essence is the basis of a bodily schema built on Negritude, which embraces the white man's vision of the black person as irrational, emotional, simple, and freely communing with nature through the "tom-tom" of African music and dance.[43] While Fanon was initially attracted to Negritude after his discovery of the work of Amié Césaire and Léopold Senghor, he soon rejected it as reactionary because it posited blackness as immanent, static being.[44] For Fanon, Negritude might be a stage—perhaps even a necessary one—in the liberation of black people, but it needed to be overcome if black people were no longer to be considered inferior to white people. While it might occasionally have its antiracist uses, a body schema based on Negritude ultimately tends to backfire and only further white domination.[45]

Although similar in many respects, the corporeal shattering that occurred in Martinique ultimately took a different form than that in Algeria. Most likely because of the history of French slavery in Martinique, the Antilleans and not the Algerians were burdened with a racial epidermal schema, which was more debilitating than potentially liberating. This is

not to posit an extremely sharp distinction between the types of shattering that occurred in the Antilles and North Africa, nor to claim that
the French never saw Algerians as subpersons. It is to note that the particular results of the shattering of bodily horizons are shaped by the specific historical contexts in which the shattering takes place. The Algerians, who were in the midst of revolution at the time of Fanon's analysis,
were not seen as essentially raced things in the way that the Antilleans,
whose colonization by and struggle against France occurred much longer
ago, were.[46]

Fanon understands that racism and colonialism must be approached
in terms of the transactional relationship between specific environments,
psyches, and bodies. This is why racism and colonialism are matters of
sociogeny.[47] Sociogenetically put, the question of the alienation of black
people is one of how the social and political environment has produced
their psychosomatically internalized racism. To change a bodily schema
impacted by racism and colonialism, the environment must be addressed.
Fanon appreciates Freud's focus on the individual, which moved psychoanalysis away from phylogeny to ontogeny. But ontogeny is insufficient.
When taken on its own, ontogeny can be misleading because it can suggest
an atomistic understanding of the individual in which an innate constitution explains the individual's development. Here is where classical psychoanalysis tends to fail critical race theory. Some scholars have claimed that
one of Fanon's strengths is that he "constantly relates the psychological
predicament of the individual to his environment without losing sight of
the individual."[48] But I find it more important to emphasize the reverse: a
focus on the individual must never fall into Robinson Crusoeism.[49] One
must never lose sight of the significant role that the social environment
plays in the constitution of the individual. Those who critically investigate
racism are always "driven from the individual back to the social structure.
If there is a [neurotic] taint, it lies not in the "soul" of the individual but
rather in that of the environment."[50] Sociogenetically understood, the task
of psychoanalysis is to understand and untangle the relationship between
psyche, body, and world, not focus on the psyche at the expense of its
environment.[51]

This is not to dismiss the unconscious as a component of lived experience since part of the environment in question is the collective unconscious. Such a dismissal is characteristic of (at least) the early work of
Merleau-Ponty, who opposed the unconscious to the ambiguity of lived
experience in order to reject the former for the latter. Merleau-Ponty
attempts to demonstrate how "the pretended unconscious of the complex
is reduced to the ambivalence of immediate consciousness" and insists

that "[w]hat remains on the hither side of inner perception . . . is not an unconscious."[52] For him, the ambiguity of perception is "unconscious" only in the sense that it is not consciously focused upon—which is to say that it is not unconscious at all, but rather preconscious or subconscious.[53]

This is inadequate because the situation of black Antilleans cannot be understood apart from the collective unconscious that resulted from an ethical slippage from France to Martinique. Black Antilleans' somatic investments in white domination should not be thought of as a result of the inexactness of consciousness. The horizon of the lived body does not merely lie nearby conscious perception. The historico-racial schema that black Antilleans embody both is the product of and helps reproduce unconscious commitments to the white privileged values of France. Clearing up the ambivalence of immediate consciousness by noting the conflicting elements within it—found, for example, in the early Fanon's simultaneous insistence that color means nothing to him and that he knows that his soul is white[54]—will not, by itself, alter his conviction that white is good and black is evil. The black Antillean's unconscious psychosomatic commitments to French values must also be confronted if such change is to occur.

The ethical slippage of white values into black Martinique insidiously attacked both the psyche and the soma of black Antilleans in distinctive ways. Their collective unconscious was made white, and that transformation in turn began the process that would mutilate their corporeal schemas into an allegedly fixed racial essence. This is not to say that black people remaining in Martinique already had a racial epidermal schema, for it required a physical relocation to the white world for such a trauma to occur. It is to demonstrate that the production of the racial epidermal schema in France had its roots in the peacefully violent shattering of horizons that the ethical slippage effected. This is why Fanon claims that after a few weeks in France, "contact with Europe compels [black Antilleans] to face a certain number of problems that until their arrival had never touched them. And yet those problems were by no means invisible."[55] Even more accurate would be to say that problems of white privilege profoundly touched black Antilleans by shaping their psyches and bodies, but those problems were not visible until the Antilleans inhabited a different environment. On the one hand, prior to visiting France, racism never consciously troubled the black people in Martinique, and yet, on the other hand, it was there, unconsciously impacting them all along. Identifying as white, black Antilleans who had not visited France could easily accept a value system in which white represented goodness and black symbolized evil. But simultaneously the problems that this value system produces were already in operation, destroying black Antilleans' ability to have a distinctively black bodily horizon. Once in France, the inability of a black body to constitute a lived horizon could no longer be overlooked.

Ethical slippage describes the peacefully violent uneventfulness of the impact of a collective unconscious on individual psychosomatic habits and bodily schemas. Like fog slowly rolling in from the sea, values slipped from France to Martinique, creating an Antillean collective unconscious infused with French/Western values of white privilege. But subtle slippage is not the only way in which a collective unconscious is formed. It also can be built out of flagrantly violent events from a people's or nation's history. In that case, the collective unconscious is similar to what Nicolas Abraham and Maria Torok call a phantom: an unspeakable secret from previous generations that will not die, that has a murky but very real presence amongst the living.[56] The collective unconscious is a phantom not because it lacks materiality, but because it is composed of indigestible remnants for a culture that haunt its individual members even though they were not present at or involved in the actual traumatic event. The phantasmal collective unconscious explains how a contemporary individual can be psychosomatically traumatized, for example, by the historical events of the Middle Passage and U.S. slavery. U.S. slavery left much more than a legacy of economic racial inequality. It also left ghosts: horrific secrets from the United States' past involving actual, specific events that cannot be fully digested. These ghosts, which form a collective unconscious, are some of the concrete others that feed individual psychosomatic habits, which in turn feed back into the ghostly phantom. In that way, the phantasmal collective unconscious both is and is not part of individual experience. It includes remnants of experiences never directly undergone by a particular individual. In that the phantom helps structure the individual's psychosomatic life, the trauma it includes tends to be repeated, often in different forms and expressed through neurotic symptoms, in her own experience.

In her novel *Beloved*, Toni Morrison examines the phantom of the Middle Passage and U.S. slavery. Beloved is the daughter of Sethe, a runaway slave to Ohio who attempts to cut the throats of her four children so that her white master cannot take them back to slavery in the South. Beloved is the toddler whom Sethe succeeds in "protecting" with the knife. The other three children survive Sethe's murderous love, although the two boys flee the frightening presence of their mother as soon as they are old enough to do so. Nearly two decades after Beloved's death, Beloved appears on Sethe's front yard as the young woman she would have been if she had lived. Sethe, her surviving daughter Denver, and her lover Paul D take in Beloved, at first thinking that she is a slightly odd stranger but eventually realizing that she is the full-grown materialization of the invisible but rowdy ghost that had been haunting their house since it was a baby.

On one level, the phantom Beloved represents the traumatic killing of a child by its mother, a trauma that cannot be fully digested and so is absorbed into the unconscious of Sethe, Denver, and other family and community members. Beloved is part of their "submerged family secrets and traumatic tombs in which, for example, actual events are treated as if they had never occurred."57 Her return allows Sethe to treat her murder as if it had never happened. In an obsessive soliloquy on Beloved, Sethe proclaims, "I'll tend her as no mother ever tended a child, a daughter. . . . I'll plant carrots just so she can see them, and turnips. . . . We'll smell them together, Beloved. Beloved. Because you mine and I have to show you these things and teach you what a mother should."58 Now that her oldest daughter has returned, Sethe can do all the things with her that she would have done if she had never been killed. Yet her attempts to be a "normal" mother to her dead child do not erase the trauma. In fact, they only compound it through repetition, albeit repetition with a difference. After Sethe realizes who Beloved is, she cuts Denver out of the intimate mother-daughter circle that the three women initially had formed. To reclaim Beloved, Sethe metaphorically kills Denver and deprives her of a cherished sister for a second time. Sethe fully immerses herself in Beloved's needs and desires, and Beloved greedily absorbs all the maternal attention that she had missed after her death. But soon the loving intensity between Sethe and Beloved turns to arguments and fights. Sethe can never do enough for Beloved; Beloved is never satisfied. Having long ago stopped going to her job so that she could spend more time with Beloved, Sethe begins to waste away as she goes without food so that Beloved can have more. Denver too is at risk of starvation until finally she breaks the suffocating stranglehold of their home, leaving the house to get work to feed the family.

Not only does Sethe repeat the trauma of cutting one daughter by cutting (off) the other, but the killing of Beloved also is a repetition of a previous trauma inflicted upon Sethe. After Beloved's return, Sethe is able to gradually remember what she had forgotten about her own mother, who was brought to the Americas from Africa as part of the Middle Passage. A woman who was on the ship with Sethe's mother told the young girl Sethe how her mother had thrown away all her babies who were fathered by the ship's crew and other white men who raped her. She kept only Sethe, who was fathered by a black man.59 This angers Sethe for reasons she does not understand, and her anger is related to her anxiety over the likelihood that her mother later was hanged for trying to run away. Sethe knows that her mother's running meant that her mother was willing to abandon her child to obtain her freedom. Sethe muses to herself, "I wonder what they was doing when they was caught. Running, you think? No. Not that. Because she was my ma'am and nobody's ma'am would run off and leave her daughter, would she? Would she, now? Leave her in the yard with a one-armed woman? Even if she hadn't been able to suckle the daughter for more than a week or two and had to turn her over to another woman's tit that never had enough for all."[60] Because of the horrors of slavery, Sethe was never allowed to be the daughter that she wanted to be. To protect her daughters from a similar horror, she deprives them of the mother they desperately desire. Sethe tries to put a stop to the cycle of deathly violence in which her family is caught, but she does so by reenacting the very same violent acts. Beloved is the phantasmic embodiment of a secret about her grandmother that was her mother's psychic burden and that has been handed down through the generations.[61]

Beloved also is much more than a family phantom. She represents the "sixty million and more" to whom the novel is dedicated and who collectively haunt Sethe and other black American slaves, ex-slaves, and descendents of slaves. Beloved is the story of the Middle Passage and the cruel life for slaves on plantations that cannot be spoken. Denver knows only the "told story" of how Sethe ran away from the Sweet Home plantation while pregnant with her, walking on swollen feet until a white girl found her in the woods and helped her give birth in a canoe as they crossed the Ohio River into freedom.[62] Baby Suggs, Sethe's dead mother-in-law, found everything in Sethe's past life so painful or lost that it was unspeakable. Even with Paul D, with whom Sethe shares the story of her sexual assault and brutal whipping prior to fleeing Sweet Home, Sethe cannot tell everything. Only with Beloved present is Sethe able to share her unspeakable stories.

The telling that Beloved enables is more of an acting out or re-embodiment of previous trauma than a cathartic working through of it. As a phantom, Beloved embodies the traumatic stories of all who endured slavery, and she "is not a story to pass on."[63] Or, rather, she is a story that is communicable only as a collective symptom.[64] Beloved is a story that is both told and not told, that hovers above black Americans as a phantasmic presence, and that is simultaneously real and indigestible. Sethe evokes this looming presence when she describes Sweet Home as a place that would remain even if the plantation burned to the ground. When Denver asks if other people can see it, Sethe replies, "Oh, yes. Oh, yes, yes, yes. Someday you be walking down the road and you hear something or see something going on. So clear. And you think it's you thinking it up. A thought picture. But no. It's when you bump into a rememory that belongs to someone else. Where I was before I came here, that place is real. It's never going away." Denver remarks, "If it's still there, waiting, that must mean that nothing ever dies," to which Sethe responds, "Nothing ever does."[65] Beloved is Sweet Home, the event of slavery that lives on even after it has ended. Denver has never experienced it—she "who never was there"[66]—and yet it is there waiting for her, hovering around her just like her phantom sister. She encounters the event through the "rememory" of others who experienced it. In that way, "unsuspected, the dead continue to lead a devastating psychic half-life" in her.[67]

Denver is not unique in this regard. While Abraham and Torok tend to describe the phantom in familial terms, haunting can occur within and across entire communities and cultures. People living today can bump into the phantom of the Middle Passage and U.S. slavery. "The gap between Africa and Afro-America and the gap between the living and the dead and the gap between the past and the present does not exist," as Morrison explains.[68] The phantom is still there, waiting, even for those black Americans who have no (conscious) knowledge of distant relatives who were slaves, or perhaps do not even have distant relatives who were slaves. Granted, it does not materialize in the fantastically literal way that Beloved did. In that sense, "the dead do not return," except in novels.[69] But in another sense, the dead do return—or, rather, they often are not fully dead when one believes and hopes they are. They materialize, for example, whenever a black person is subtly (and sometimes, not so subtly) tailed by a white security officer in a tony boutique or stopped by a white police officer when driving a fancy car in an upscale neighborhood. While not literal, the materialization of the phantom in these examples also is not metaphorical. Nor does calling it a phantom mean that it is an illusion. The legacy of the Middle Passage and U.S. slavery tends to be unconsciously (and sometimes consciously) embodied in the psychosomatic habits of both the security and police officers and the black people being harassed, all of which are very real. Due to the phantom of the Middle Passage and U.S. slavery, a historico-racial schema impacts the bodily schema of each group of people. Both white officer and black "suspect" have incorporated white racist perceptions of black people as savage subpersons into their bodily schemas. The phantom does not affect white and black people in the exact same ways. It enables the "normal" bodily schema of white people that occludes the impact of the historico-racial schema, while it tends to shatter the bodily horizons of black people, situating them as raced objects rather than full persons. Nor does the presence of the phantom mean that black people (or white, for that matter) must accept the values imparted by a historico-racial schema. Those values can be challenged and fought. But they cannot be dismissed as if they did not exist. Difficult to pinpoint, they hover in the aisles of the boutique that separate shopper from security officer and in the space of the rolled-down car window where the officer leans in to ask for identification and peer around for anything "suspicious." The effects of the phantasmic historico-racial schema also are found in the tensely wary-but-trying-to-look-casual bodily comportment of the officers and the careful, slow movements of shopper and driver, designed to be easily seen by the officers and to minimize the chances of arrest or assault.

As these examples indicate, the phantom of the Middle Passage and U.S. slavery does not haunt only black people. It also haunts white people and communities, although they often are oblivious to the phantom's presence. I recently encountered the phantom of U.S. slavery when in Birmingham, Alabama, for a conference. Playing hooky one afternoon, I took the bus from the downtown station to a suburban mall. I was clearly out of place at the station: an overdressed professional in conference clothes, a middle-class white woman traveling alone in a sea of black people, a stranger from out of town who did not know how the Birmingham bus system worked, a person who did not ordinarily use the bus out of financial necessity. While waiting for the bus to arrive, I was befriended by a slightly down-and-out white man around fifty who confirmed that I was waiting at the correct bus stall. Extremely friendly in an entirely appropriate southern way, the gregarious man small-talked with me for four or five minutes until the bus appeared. After six or seven black people exited the bus, a black woman and two black men boarded. The white man—Charlie, as he later introduced himself—and I followed. I sat down next to the window in the second row, and Charlie sat down in the row behind me, in the seat to my left so that I would not have to crane to see him, clearly interested in continuing his nonstop chatter. Just after we sat down, several more black men began to board the bus, and Charlie said to me in a kind and generous voice as he left his seat for the one next to me, "I'll go ahead and move on up here so you won't be crowded in by someone you don't know."

And the phantom materialized.

A flood of thoughts and emotions hit me as he said this. I was a bit startled, but in an amused sort of way: how presumptive of him to think that he knew me. I was disappointed: I desperately had hoped that the bus ride would relieve me of his garrulous company and provide peace and quiet to gaze through bus windows at springtime in the south. And above all I was uncomfortable: without using the word "race," Charlie had announced to me and in front of everyone on the bus that he would sit next to me so that I was not "at risk" of having to sit next to a black person. As a true southern gentleman, he was protecting my white womanhood from the sexual and physical threat of black men. De jure segregation might have ended years ago, but he could do his small bit to ensure that the aims and values of U.S. slavery and Jim Crow lived on.

I do not know that this is what Charlie consciously thought when switching seats. He probably would be offended by my account of his actions. I would not know because I did not say anything to Charlie in response to his "generous" offer. I do know that as a good southern white woman, I was supposed to reply, with a slight drawl and appreciative smile, "That's mighty kind of you." But I froze up instead, silent and slightly stiff, neither welcoming nor protesting his move. No one else said a thing either. Though I was not able to see all the other passengers, Charlie's comment did not seem to register with them (perhaps I was wrong that everyone heard it?). The bus loaded with its eight or nine passengers, Charlie resumed his incessant chitchat and we took off for the mall.

The phantom hovered over our seats. It had been there in the bus station all along, but Charlie's comment gave it its full materialization. Yet even fully materialized, it was evanescent, hard to pinpoint. If I had confronted Charlie about the comment, he could have said, with a weird kind of plausibility, that he had not said anything about race or black people at all, that I was imagining the whole thing. And in a literal sense, part of this is true. But it was not just me thinking it up, to paraphrase Sethe. Ghosts are real, and not just as a product of thought.[70] I had run into the "re-memory" of someone else: of Charlie, of countless generations of white masters and black slaves in the south, of postbellum white men whose masculinity depended on a particular ideal of white womanhood as pure and defenseless. But this is also to say that I had run into my own "re-memory" because the collective unconscious of a white racist nation that Charlie's comment embodied is part of my personal unconscious habits as well.

My habits embody the phantom of the Middle Passage and U.S. slavery in particular ways due, in part, to the fact that I am a white, middle-class woman. It is no coincidence that I froze in a kind of "non-response" response to Charlie's comment. Uncomfortable with anger and confrontation, I was not able to devise an appropriate way to react. My discomfort with conflict trumped my discomfort with Charlie's racist remark. What should I have said or done? What would most effectively counter white racism and privilege in this situation? How should the phantom's presence have been handled?

Reflecting on the situation later that day, I first thought that I should have directly confronted Charlie, saying something that exposed and rejected his assumption that I did not want to sit next to black people. But then I wondered whether such a response would have been more of a self-indulgent project of working on my fear of confrontation than an effective blow against white racism. If much of Charlie's racism was unconscious, then my direct approach would not faze him at all, and if it was relatively conscious, then my response could put the black people on the bus in an uncomfortable and possibly dangerous situation. I still do not know how I should have responded, though it is possible that my silence was more effective than I thought. Given that I did not generously acknowledge or accept Charlie's "aid," perhaps a subtle message was sent after all.[71] About half an hour into the bus ride, after one or two black people had exited the bus freeing up a seat across the aisle, Charlie shifted to that seat, explaining kindly that it seemed he "might be crowding me a bit." It is likely that he was only responding to my weariness of his company, inadequately veiled (by southern standards) by my polite but lukewarm response to his chatter. But given that his use of the verb "crowd" echoed his earlier remark, I wonder if on some level he realized that I was offended by it. It is impossible to know with certainty, and it is all too easy to believe that my silence was effective since such a belief conveniently fits with my white, middle-class, and stereotypically feminine habits. My raced and gendered habits of avoiding of conflict are just as likely to buoy up racist phantoms as they are to tear them down.

In any case, the phantom did not disappear. It was present on the early evening trip back to downtown. Even though Charlie was gone and I was the only white person on the bus, the phantom could be found embodied within me. I sat in the same seat near the window on the return trip, and as I sat down I was careful not to tightly clench my arms around my purse and shopping bag toward my chest. I deliberately let my left arm and purse drape over the edge of my seat toward the seat next to me, indicating (I hoped) that I was relaxed and not worried about anyone (read: any of the black workers returning home from the mall) sitting next to me. But then I realized that my slight sprawl might appear to (and did in fact) block the seat next to me, effectively announcing that I did not want anyone to sit next to me. So I pulled my arm and purse back toward me, trying to figure out where to put them so that I did not enact the seated version of the white woman's protective march when alone after dark: face set on neutral, purse firmly clutched, purposefully striding as if bracing for a tackle.[72] I settled on keeping my purse and shopping bag in my lap, letting my arms "relax" at my sides, neither too far away from nor too close to the trunk of my body.

Obviously, I was not relaxed at all. I was carefully calculating my body's positions, treating it like an object rather than nonreflectively living it. The phantom's presence inside me ensured that nothing I did would feel "natural." My conscious intentions were in the right place, but I could not embody them. My psychosomatic habits actively resisted their trans-formation, and not merely because of the stubborn inertia of habit but also because of (I have to suspect) my unconscious, intense fear of giving up my race and class privilege. One might think that this is a case of the shattering of a white person's "normal" bodily schema into a racial-epidermal schema: I became white, not neutral, and my whiteness inter-fered with the smooth, nonreflective living of my body. But the difference between my and a black person's bodily shattering is that the historico-racial schema continues to uphold my bodily schema even in its disrup-tion. While it is true that my awareness of the phantom transformed my body into an object to manipulate, the historico-racial valuing of white-ness as good and blackness as evil was not disturbed. Although awkwardly comported, my objective body did not require the recognition and ap-proval of the black people on the bus. Even my disrupted bodily schema retained its white privilege. While unsure of how to live my body, I was never reduced to a subperson who faded into nonexistence. As the black mall workers chatted among themselves about what they would do after returning home, apparently unaware of my dilemma of how to send the right message to them with my bodily comportment, my personhood was never in question. I was still the overprivileged white middle-class woman returning to an upscale hotel with new blouses in hand.

Merely becoming aware of the phantom of the Middle Passage and U.S. slavery is not sufficient to dispel it. The same can be said for the ethical slippage of white privileged values. Whether peaceful or strikingly traumatic, the violence of white privilege and race-based oppression tends to operate unconsciously, and it does so at both collective and individual levels. The phantom of the Middle Passage and U.S. slavery connects my and other contemporary Americans' unconscious habits with each other and with events from other places and times. It is a crucial structure enabling subtle slippages of white privileged values from the United States to other parts of the world. But the connections between individuals and cultures provided by the slippages and phantoms of racial oppression are corrosive. They destructively connect people together by driving a racist wedge of white privilege between them.[73]

What then can be done about them? Are people today condemned to being haunted by the legacies of slavery and colonialism for eternity? I think it unlikely that the slippages and phantoms described by Fanon and Morrison will ever completely disappear—and that is a good thing, in that remembrance of the past is important to the possibility of justice in the present and future. But how the past is remembered is crucial. The key is to remember the horror in such a way that can be digested.[74] Such a remembering would minimize the ongoing destructiveness of the phantom of the Middle Passage and U.S. slavery without ignoring its presence. It would require taking responsibility for those past people and events that no one has taken responsibility for[75]—and not only the Africans who died somewhere in the Atlantic Ocean, whose names are lost and whose stories are not and cannot be told, but also the white masters, mistresses, and slave bosses who purchased the Africans who survived. This is a remembrance that must be not just individual but collective, and not just psychical but bodily—for collective memory, like the collective unconscious, is as somatic as it is psychical.[76] But it is also a remembrance built on what cannot be fully reclaimed, which means that practically speaking, it is a process without end. Past traumas always tend to exceed a culture's or individual's capacity for remembering them, and so a person can never be confident that she has remembered completely. As digestible as, for example, novels such as *Beloved* can make the Middle Passage—and by digestible, I do not mean palatable—indigestible remnants will tend to remain. They will make up a collective unconscious that will continue to haunt individual habits far into the future.

PART TWO

Possessive Geographies

FIVE

Appropriate Habits of White Privilege

W. E. B. Du Bois's realization that white people's unconscious habits were at the root of white racism was accompanied by his insight into the possessiveness of those habits.[1] In "The Souls of White Folk," Du Bois strips whiteness bare and then proceeds to display its ugly core as complete and total ownership. Revealing the white habit of propriety through an examination of World War I, Du Bois explains the war as a struggle between white nations over who will be allowed to exploit darker nations. Colonial expansion summarizes not just the war, but also the entire relationship of white European and Euro-aligned nations to the rest of the non-white world. "Bluntly put," Du Bois argues, the theory with which Euro-white nations operate is that "[i]t is the duty of white Europe to divide up the darker world and administer it for Europe's good."[2] If exploitation of others for their own gain is the fundamental principle of white nations, then the atrocities of World War I should come as no surprise. The judgment of the world's "darker men" about World War I is right on target: "this is not Europe gone mad, this is not aberration nor insanity; this *is* Europe; this seeming Terrible is the real soul of white culture—back of all culture—stripped and visible today . . . these dark and awful depths and not the shining and ineffable heights of which it boasted."[3]

I explore here the claim that "whiteness is the ownership of the earth," illuminating the possessiveness of unconscious habits of white privilege by examining white ownership of the contributions of black people to the development of the United States and the land depended on by Native American tribes.[4] Unconscious habits of white privilege manifest an "appropriate" relationship to the earth, including the people and things that are part of it. The appropriate relationship is one of appropriation: taking land, people, and the fruit of others' labor and creativity as one's own. Failure to embody this proper relationship with the world marks one as a subperson, as a quasi-thing that is then legitimately available for, even in need of, appropriation by full persons. Somewhat ironically, an inappropriate relationship to the earth renders one indistinguishable from it as a natural resource waiting to be put to proper use.

The claim that whiteness is ownership of the earth is as much an observation about ontology and psychology as it is about economics and geography. The economic reasons for white habits of ownership cannot be understood apart from the onto-psychological, just as the unconscious operations of white privilege cannot be understood apart from their economic and geographical commitments. Whiteness as possession describes not just the act of owning, but also the obsessive psychosomatic state of white owners. Commodifying non-white peoples and cultures, unconscious habits of white privilege tend to transform them into objects for white appropriation and use. The benefits accrued to white people through this process include not merely economic gain, but also increased ontological security and satisfaction of unconscious desires.

Du Bois charts the economic-ontological commitments of the white racist unconscious in *The Gift of Black Folk*.[5] Written in 1924, the book is positioned in the midst of the transformation in Du Bois's ideas about how to combat racism. It was written after he became disillusioned with white people and as his interest in communism and the Soviet Union was blossoming, and before he began to explicitly incorporate Freudian insights into his work. As such, it offers an interesting mixture of his old, liberal approach to racism and early signs of his new understanding of unconscious habits of white privilege. While neither Freud's name nor the concept of the unconscious is explicitly invoked in *The Gift of Black Folk*, the book indirectly addresses the role of the unconscious in racism and is implicitly concerned with the way that economic factors intertwine with the white psyche. Du Bois not only offers conscious arguments for the

recognition of black gifts to America but also subtly targets the unconscious sense of whiteness as ownership.[6]

Du Bois thought that African Americans had made and would continue to make distinct contributions to American culture, including black
exploration, black labor, black soldiers, the impetus to democracy, the
emphasis on freedom, the emancipation of women, the American folk
song, black art and literature, and the spiritual enrichment of religion. The
many gifts given by black folk illuminate some of the problems with
contemporary strategies of colorblindness for fighting racism. To abandon
the concept of race in attempt to eliminate racism would be to undercut
the ability of black Americans to make distinctive gifts to American culture that are recognized as the product of specifically black insight, experience, and creativity. Since the erasure of positive conceptions of blackness
occurs in American culture even without colorblindness, the last thing
needed in struggles against racism in Du Bois's day or today is a strategy
that reinforces this erasure. White Americans generally have failed to acknowledge the ample gifts that black Americans have made to American
culture. Seeing black Americans as incapable of contributing anything
positive to American society, white Americans could easily think that the
elimination of black identity through colorblindness is insignificant—or
significant only negatively, as a narrow, impoverishing constraint that has
been overcome. In the current racial context of the United States, colorblindness has little if any potential for changing white America's negative
conceptions of black people.

Du Bois implies that once white Americans realize what contributions
black Americans have made, they will recognize what a loss it would be to
abandon racial identity. Du Bois's line of thought here does not necessarily
hold that racial categories should be retained for all times. He vows in his
"Negro Academy Creed," "We believe it is the duty of Americans of Negro
descent, as a body, to maintain their race identity until this mission of the
Negro is accomplished, and the ideal of human brotherhood has become a
practical possibility."[7] The mission in question is for black Americans to
make the distinct contribution "to civilization and humanity, which no
other race can make."[8] Once black American gifts are recognized and
valued as the product of black experience and culture, "human brotherhood" between the people of different races can become a genuine possibility. While there could be a future in which distinct race identities no
longer need to be maintained, prior to that point they must be insisted
upon. Not to do so would amount to the cultural genocide of black
Americans.

But exactly how or why have the gifts of black Americans gone unrecognized as distinctively black gifts? Perhaps they have not been brought to the sufficient attention of white people? As Du Bois says in the prescript to the volume,

> Now that [America's] foundations are laid, deep but bare, there are those as always who would forget the humble builders . . . and picture America as the last reasoned blossom of mighty ancestors; of those great and glorious world builders and rulers who know and see and do all thing forever and ever, amen! How singular and blind! . . . We who know may not forget but must forever spread the splendid sordid truth that out of the most lowly and persecuted of men, Man made America.[9]

Du Bois explains that white Americans are blind to the truth of the crucial role that black people played in the formation of the United States. Or perhaps he might say that during the building of the foundation of the United States, white people saw the contributions that black people made, but now that that period is over, it is easy for them to overlook the gifts black people gave because those gifts are not immediately present to white consciousness. What is needed on this approach is to remind white Americans of what they once knew but have forgotten: that the America in which white people take pride could not exist without the enormous contributions of black folk. Once no longer blind to this truth, white people presumably will take a step closer to universal "human brotherhood" by valuing the distinctive abilities and products of black culture and experience.

Considered apart from other strategies, this approach problematically assumes that white privilege operates primarily or even solely on the level of conscious belief and that a correction of false beliefs will result in nonracist actions. It allows white people's ignorance of black people and culture to be seen as passive and innocent. But even in 1924, Du Bois's strategy for changing white people's treatment of black people was more complex than this liberal position. At the same time that Du Bois pointed out that white people had forgotten the gifts made by black people, he understood that their forgetting was deliberate and malicious, rather than accidental and innocent. One indication of the complexity of Du Bois's analysis of white forgetting is his frequent criticism of white people's treatment of black people as property. If black folk are pieces of real estate owned by white people, then contributions made by black folk to America are the contributions of white people instead. By treating black folk as property to be bought and sold, white people are able to graft the contributions of black people onto themselves, transforming, by means of a racist alchemy, black contributions into white contributions.[10]

Fifty years before Gilles Deleuze and Felix Guattari criticized capitalism's appropriation of the unconscious to further political oppression, Du Bois sounded a similar alarm.[11] He alerts contemporary readers to capitalism's role in the white arrogation (both conscious and unconscious) of black gifts, and his warning is perhaps even more needed today than in 1924. It might seem that a type of equality between black and white people recently has been achieved through capitalism's increasing inclusion of black people as potential consumers. But to argue, as some scholars do, that capitalism has produced "the greatest contemporary advances in racial justice" oversimplifies the damaging complexity of capitalism's relationship to non-white people.[12] The belief that material goods and consumer choice function as a racial equalizer is an instance of the capitalist appropriation of the psyche for its own ends.[13] And given the investment of capitalism in selling racial images of the "exotic other," this belief simultaneously functions for racist ends.[14] More helpful is an analysis of racism that recognizes the support it gives to and the benefits it receives from capitalism:

> White racist capitalism involved racialized theft: the severance of racially-developed gifts from their givers, and racialized reductio[n] of gifts and givers as objects for commodity exchange. Whites participated in the treatment of African Americans and their gifts either as valuable extensions of themselves or expressions of their own culture, or as property over which whites held (explicit and implicit) arbitrary sway.[15]

Yet from the perspective of black folk as property, the grafting of black contributions onto white people as an extension of themselves is not theft. There is no gift stolen by white people if there is no agent to do the giving and therefore no gift. Likewise, there is no theft from black folk if white people themselves make the contribution in question through the efforts of an alleged extension of themselves. Understood as people and not property, black folk are robbed by the grafting of their contributions to white people. From this perspective, the language of "gift," rather than the more neutral "contribution," can and should be used. Black folk are not a piece of real estate possessed by white owners but a people with agency who can and do offer distinct gifts to American culture. Only by denying the status of black folk as property can black people's contributions be recognized as the gifts they are.

Severing the gift from its giver goes hand-in-hand with the reduction of both the gift and giver to pieces of real estate. Commodified in this way, both black folk and black contributions are made available for white exchange, profit, and—it should be added—pleasure. Black people may be more included today than in the past as potential consumers, but "blackness" simultaneously is increasingly being packaged for white middle-class consumers who long for the novel and exotic. (In a similar fashion, *latinidad* is increasingly being marketed to those who long for something "spicy" to liven up a bland life.[16]) Inclusion in (white) society as an object of consumption does not necessarily challenge racist perceptions of black people as primitive and animal-like. In fact, precisely the opposite tends to occur in the United States today. In the name of a multicultural pluralism that consciously welcomes other cultures, unconscious fantasies and fears surrounding the "black savage" (and "spicy Latino/a," for example) often circulate unimpeded. Forbidden longings for contact with the non-white other that are generated out of habits of white domination paradoxically receive an expression that renders them invisible because they are consciously experienced as a wholesome desire for diversity.

Nowhere is the racist pattern of non-white commodification more prevalent than in the contemporary phenomenon of urban gentrification: "In the context of gentrification or redevelopment, mainstream white consumer culture's exoticization of the city has meant the development of 'white pleasure spaces,' places where mainstream whites, in what were once poor black neighborhoods, indulge in the exotic consumerism of black music, dance, sports, and fashion, with the security of police and electronic surveillance to guard against the dangerous blacks."[17] Black cultural gifts are sanitized through their commodification, retaining just enough "dangerousness" to be of interest to (white) consumers but detached from the political and social contexts that give them a meaning and an effect beyond that of consumption. Decontextualizing non-white cultures, "consumer cannibalism" tends to eradicate any of their differences that are not pleasurable to white people, especially differences related to history, community, and political struggle.[18]

The alleged danger of black urban zones plays a double role. It is perceived as seductive and alluring even as—or, rather, precisely because— it is perceived as risky and unsafe. Dangerous urban (read: black) spaces can attract at the same time that they repulse because the white person who enters them has the power to leave at any time she pleases. Whatever the perceived risk, there is no danger that the white person will have to remain on the "urban frontier." Blackness is construed as something to dabble with to spice up an otherwise "vanilla" existence, but it never truly threatens white people. If and when it does, then blackness loses its desirability and becomes something merely to avoid or, more sinisterly, eliminate. The capitalist strategy of planned obsolescence is at work here as elsewhere. If and when blackness no longer brings pleasure to white people, it will be cast aside so that new desires can be manufactured and desired. (Salsa, anyone?) This means that the black people and culture that produce the materials for the capitalist production of blackness also will be cast aside, revealing the racial justice achieved by the inclusion of black people in capitalism to be a sham.

White racist capitalism depends upon the treatment of black people and gifts as property not only to provide products for consumption, profit, and pleasure, but also to protect the white psyche. If black folk are a piece of real estate that is incapable of offering gifts and is available for exchange on the market, then white people's racist treatment of black folk need not trouble their conscience. But if black folk are people, then treating them as property and stealing their gifts likely would produce extreme guilt on the part of those who steal from them. The interdependent onto-psychological and economic aspects of white domination are clear: "Without the sanctity of property, the whole defensive structure would break down: [black] things would become people again, and [black] people would make [white people] guilty, or even fight back."[19] White people can see themselves as good only if black people remain property-like things. The end of discrimination and prejudice against black people entails a significant transformation of the white psyche, not just the white pocket-book, which likely is one reason why so many white people fight against it.

Colorblindness is not simply a new strategy in this fight, enabling the ongoing theft of black gifts in the name of antiracism. It also operates as an unconscious defensive device that allows white people to avoid recognition of themselves as non-white people often see them: as "sheer malevolence."[20] Appeals to multiculturalism and diversity likewise can operate as a related mechanism for protecting the white "soul." If those who are (allegedly) colorblind have gone beyond race, then it is easy for them to think that racism no longer exists. In that case, the unequal power relations evoked by the language of race are flattened out into a mere multiplicity of diverse cultures to be celebrated and affirmed. Such a power-flattened multiculturalism erases the images of terror that white people have evoked in black people for hundreds of years. This erasure makes it easy for white people to both forget and further their malevolent history. "The eagerness with which contemporary society does away with racism, replacing this recognition with evocations of pluralism and diversity that further mask reality, is a response to the terror [of whiteness]. It has also become a way to perpetuate the terror by providing a cover, a hiding place."[21]

One of the hiding places of the terror of whiteness is white people's blithe ignorance of race and racism. "The habit of ignoring race is understood [by white people] to be a graceful, even generous, liberal gesture," but behind that "generosity" often lurks a very self-serving desire.[22] Far from being merely innocent, ignorance can operate as a shield that protects a person from realizing her complicity in an oppressive situation. Patricia Williams captures the operation of this defense mechanism as she recounts a situation in which a white colleague profusely apologized to a black person for not noticing an instance of racism. Explaining her weariness with white people's ongoing obliviousness to race, Williams argues that even though the white colleague's apologies were sincere and heartfelt, they manifested "a profoundly invested disingenuousness, an innocence that amount[ed] to the transgressive refusal to know."[23] White people often are strongly invested in not knowing much about whiteness, especially its emphasis on ownership, because such knowledge would reveal their treatment of non-white people as things, which would disrupt their sense of themselves as morally good. Given this investment, eventually "a suspicion sets in of the wistful giftiness with which non-knowing is offered" by white to non-white people.[24] White people's naive ignorance of race and racism has become the gift they offer non-white people in place of their recognition of non-white gifts to the world. Its wistfulness is composed not only of the regretful apology that white people are (allegedly) unable to notice race, but also of a yearning desire that non-white people accept the gift and thereby absolve white people of any responsibility to learn to see race and racial injustice. This defense mechanism allows white people to think that non-white people can and will forget hundreds of years of racial oppression and the ongoing effects of white domination because they themselves have easily managed to do so.

These criticisms of white people's treatment of the gifts of black people operate with an ontology of whiteness that reworks the traditional meaning of ontology as static. Race cannot be dismissed as accidental or irrelevant to what it currently is to be a human being. But the alternative to such dismissal does not have to be an appeal to fixed racial essences. Acknowledging that the desire "to minimize and deny the realities of racial difference" is understandable, Du Bois forces his readers to face "the fact of a white world which is today dominating human culture and working for the continued subordination of the colored races."[25] Racial categories are historically, socially, economically, and psychologically constructed— and are nonetheless real for being so. A reconfiguration of ontology as historical and malleable allows one to acknowledge the tremendous constitutive impact of race and racism on human life without treating them as eternal and immutable. The being of white people qua white, for example, often is malicious, possessive, and destructive. These characteristics are fundamental to what it is today to be white, although this fact of the white world need not always be the case in the future.

This portrayal of the ontology of whiteness is a difficult gift for many white people to accept. While white people sometimes use conscious strategies to reject it, many of their strategies are unconscious. As Du Bois explains, "[t]he present attitude and action of the white world is not based solely on rational, deliberate intent. It is a matter of conditioned reflexes; of long followed habits, customs and folkways; of subconscious trains of reasoning and unconscious nervous reflexes."[26] Recalling Freud's characterization of repression as a kind of forgetting, I read Du Bois's emphasis upon the unconscious as including repressive forgetting. Unlike nonrepressive forgetting, repressive forgetting conceals something too painful to be consciously acknowledged. In the case of white forgetting of black gifts, what is repressed is that black contributions are indeed gifts and that black folks are indeed givers, that is, people and not things. What also is repressed is the guilt white people might feel as they dimly understand, perhaps consciously as well as unconsciously, that black people are not extensions of themselves. Recognizing the unconscious level of white privilege, Du Bois rightly urges that "[t]o attack and better all this calls for more than appeal and argument."[27] Among other things such as economic struggle, it calls for psychological warfare at the level of the unconscious: "not sudden assault but long siege [i]s indicated; careful planning and subtle campaign with the education of growing generations."[28]

The Gift of Black Folk operates on both the level of conscious argument and that of unconscious attack. In that it overtly instructs its readers about the role that black people have played in American history, it is an explicit appeal to white people to recognize the value of blackness. But more important is that by calling black contributions "gifts," *The Gift of Black Folk* also is a covert reclamation of black property and personhood and an implicit confrontation with white repression and guilt. It thereby subtly engages in antiracist transformation of the white "soul." By operating on this second level in particular, Du Bois helps chart the current limits and possible transformations of white unconscious habits of ownership.

The intertwining geo-economic, ontological, and psychological aspects of white habits of possession also are found in white America's response to Native American relationships to land. For most Native American tribes, the land is part of a religious view of the world that locates human beings in kinship relations with the natural world. Native American origin stories speak of alliances, friendships, and even marriages between human and nonhuman animals. Relationships also exist with trees, rivers, mountains, and other parts of the natural world, which can respond to human dance and song. Perhaps most importantly, the land holds the bodies of Indian ancestors, human and nonhuman alike. As Chief Seattle explained to the governor of the Washington Territory in 1855, "[e]very part of this soil is sacred in the estimation of my people. Every hillside, every valley, every plain and grove has been hallowed by some sad or happy event in days long vanished. Even the rocks which seem to be dumb and dead . . . thrill with memories of stirring events connected with the lives of my people, and the very dust upon which you now stand responds more lovingly to their footsteps than to yours because it is rich with the dust of our ancestors."[29]

From an Indian perspective, land is not a piece of property to be bought and sold. Native relationships with it generally are not ones of possession and ownership, but rather ones of identity and continuity of life.[30] As an anonymous Indian chief asks when the "good White Chief" in Washington sends word that he wishes to buy Indian lands, "How can one buy or sell the air, the warmth of the land? That is difficult for us to imagine. If we don't own the sweet air and the bubbling water, how can you buy it from us?"[31] Attempting to own the land, the white people do not see the earth and sky as kin, but as enemies to conquer and merchandize.

From a colonizing Euro-American perspective, in contrast, Native Americans have an inappropriate relationship to the land precisely because they do not treat it as property.[32] Even worse, tribal systems of land use and occupation violate the concept of individuality of property, which to white people demonstrates the persistently uncivilized nature of Native Americans. The U.S. Commissioner of Indian Affairs said in 1838, "At the foundation of the whole social system lies individuality of property. . . . [I]t has produced the energy, industry, and enterprise that distinguish the civilized world, and contributes more largely to the good morals of men than those are willing to acknowledge who have not looked somewhat closely at their fellow-beings."[33] The U.S. Secretary of the Interior confirmed in 1877 that "the enjoyment and pride of the individual ownership of property is one of the most effective civilizing agencies."[34] The impropriety of Native Americans simultaneously was found in their (im)moral and geographical habits. Failing to properly own the land, Native Americans were seen as lazy, indolent, and wasteful. To transcend their geo-ethical "wild" state, Native Americans would have to learn Euro-American standards of virtue, thrift, and individuality.

Given the reciprocal relationship between civilization and proper land use, nineteenth-century politicians in the United States puzzled over whether allotting individual parcels of land on reservations to Native Americans should be a means by which to assimilate Native Americans into civilization or a reward for those Native Americans who had already done so. Indians "would never cease to adhere to the tribal system until they ceased to be Indians," but how to get them to cease being Indians?[35] Ultimately, the decision was made that private property was the point of entry into the circle: "Unless some system is worked out by which there shall be a separate allotment of land to each individual, . . . you will look in vain for any general casting-off of savagism. Common property and civilization cannot co-exist."[36] The Dawes Act of 1887 allotted 160 acres to each Native American head of a family and each single person over eighteen years of age. The so-called surplus land in a tribe's territory that remained after the allotment process was purchased by the U.S. government and opened up to Euro-American settlers.[37] Civilizing the Indians by changing the way they inhabited the land had the simultaneous geo-economic "benefit" of providing the white citizens of the United States with room to expand.

To change Indian relations with the land was to attempt simultaneously to change Indian ontology. At no time was this clearer than in the ceremonies conducted in the early 1900s to award "competent" Native Americans with fee patents for their land allotments. Created for the purported purposes of eliminating U.S. paternalism toward Native Americans, fee patents eliminated the ward relationship between the U.S. and certain Native Americans, allowing them to own the title to their land and sell it if they so desired. During the fee patent ceremony, each Indian receiving a title and simultaneous U.S. citizenship "stepped from a tepee and shot an arrow to signify that he was leaving behind his Indian way of life. He placed his hands on a plow to show that he had chosen to live the farming life of a white man, with sweat and hard work. The secretary of the interior then handed the Indian a purse as a reminder that he must save what he earned."[38] Everything associated with "savagery" was to be left behind in this ceremony. The Indian was to become a white person, prizing white values of sedentary agriculture, private property, and hard work.

The fee patent system was unsuccessful on several levels. Because title-owning Native Americans had to pay taxes on land, many soon became impoverished and were forced to sell their allotment. The sale of Indian land meant that the fee patent system was extremely successful in another respect: it further decreased the amount of land in Native American control. But attempts to transform Indians into white people through manipulation of their relationship with the land largely failed, and this is so even though the United States overtook much of Native American land through treaties, sales, and military battle. Indians' core religious beliefs about the land remained intact. This is well illustrated by the Nez Percés' response to the Dawes Act. When forced to choose an allotment of land on the Nez Percés territory in (now) Idaho, instead of selecting the fertile prairies, each Indian chose the allotment that was closest to the place he or she was born, which tended to be in the rocky areas next to the creeks and streams.[39] From a white perspective, the Indians' selections merely demonstrated Native Americans' incorrigible wildness: either they did not know how to choose land on which to farm or they lazily avoided choosing the land that would require hard agricultural work, but in either case their uncivilized state continued to reassert itself. But from an Indian perspective, parcels of land were never interchangeable squares of dirt with more or less capacity for generating wealth. One's spiritual relationship to the land was of prime importance, and choices for allotments were made on that basis.

From white America's perspective, given that Native Americans did not know how to or lazily refused to work the land properly, it was appropriate that white Americans took it over. Such appropriation was not seen as theft, and not only because the United States sometimes paid Native American tribes for the land. More importantly, it was not theft because the lands were seen as vacant. Utilizing the environment by regularly moving from one place to another, Native American agricultural methods were not sedentary and were not recognized by Euro-Americans as signs of Indian occupancy of land. With the rhetoric of *vacuum domicilium*, Euro-Americans declared these supposedly unoccupied, vacant lands as available for settlement.[40] If Native Americans would not properly settle the land, then nothing prevented white Americans from doing so. Moreover, the Christian God, who was on the side of progress and civilization, required that Euro-Americans conquer the wilderness if Native Americans would not or could not do so.

Euro-American appropriation of Native American land also was not seen as an instance of theft because there were no full persons from which to steal. Native Americans were merely subpersons because of their inappropriate relationship with the land. Even worse (from a Euro-American perspective), Native Americans' refusal to individuate themselves through land ownership meant that they were virtually indistinguishable from the land and the "wild" nature of which it was a part. In other words, white Americans recognized Native American kinship with the land only insofar as such recognition worked in favor of white America's interests in ownership. On the one hand, white Americans often impatiently dismissed Native Americans' claims that the land was their kin and it should not be sold or farmed in Euro-American ways. As General Oliver Otis Howard responded to the Nez Percé chief Toohoolhoolzote while in negotiations with him, "Twenty times over you repeat that the earth is your mother. . . . Let us hear it no more, but come to business at once."[41] Native American kinship with the land was seen as irrelevant to the question of how and by whom the land would be used. On the other hand, Native American kinship with the land was extremely relevant to this question because it revealed the (alleged) inadequacy of Indian ontology. Native Americans were not people but part of the wilderness that was not (yet) under the control of "man."[42] Native American kinship with the land was cruelly used against Indian tribes, promoting rather than hindering U.S. appropriation of Indian territory.

As part of the land in need of appropriation, Native American people became pieces of property to be owned and exploited by those (white) individuals who could bring wilderness under control. They could be moved around at the pleasure of white America, which demanded more and more land as the British colony and then new republic grew. Social evolution, the growth of nationalism, and the development of American political institutions were all seen as dependent upon the western movement of the frontier between civilization and savagery.[43] Americans were seen as embodying "an expansive power which [was] inherent in them" and which produced their "universal disposition . . . to enlarge their dominion over inanimate nature."[44] Native Americans were merely one component of "inanimate" nature in need of such domination. Forcibly moved westward and then restricted to discretely bounded reservations, Native Americans were the targets of a Euro-American geo-spatial agenda that both relied upon and reinforced a white ontology of ownership.

As the frontier began to close—officially its end was declared in 1890, when all the territory occupied by the United States had at least two people per square mile—white America began to romanticize nature, including the life of the "savages" who were part of it. Put in their proper place through the conquering of the wilderness, Native Americans now could be appreciated for their closeness with nature. The "primitive" setting of the uncivilized wilderness was seen as offering a needed antidote to the immorality, conflict, and materialism of the increasingly large urban centers of the United States. The wildness of nature would help ensure that white Americans' refinement did not make them too soft. It also served as a cultural resource that proved the superiority of the United States to Europe, which was seen as artificial and inauthentic because overcivilized, and thus unnatural.[45] But the shift from a pioneer to a romantic attitude toward Native Americans did not lessen white America's appropriation of them. Native Americans were and generally still are considered as pieces of property owned by white America to do with what they please, only now this "knowledge" of Native Americans by white people ·is much more unconscious than conscious. White habits of ownership of Native Americans generally have not been eliminated; they have only changed the form of their expression. Rather than something wild to consciously set out to conquer, Native Americans—especially their religious traditions and rituals—tend to be unconsciously appropriated as exotic objects for Euro-American use, pleasure, and consumption.

One flagrant example of this unconscious appropriation involves the "museumification" of Native American sacred objects. These objects include pipes, feathers, drums, and other items for use in religious ceremonies. They also include the skeletal remains of dead Native Americans who were removed from burial grounds for archeological and scientific study. Displaying these items in museums made it possible for mass numbers of Euro-Americans to learn more about Native American rituals and peoples, but it also prevented many tribes from practicing their religions due to the removal of irreplaceable sacred objects. Even worse, the placement of religious objects in museums was and is a sacrilege from a Native American perspective since their artificial preservation prevented them from decay through use, which is seen as their natural end. Given the role of dead ancestors in Native American cosmology, the desecration of Native American graves for the advancement of Western knowledge was particularly offensive. In an attempt to preserve "dying" Native American traditions for the benefit of future (white) peoples, Euro-American appropriation of Native American artifacts made their death more likely. Beneath conscious attempts to help Native American cultures and peoples, unconscious habits of white privilege reasserted the white "right" to ownership of all things non-white.[46]

Given the difficulty Native Americans often have practicing their own religions due to lack of access to sacred lands and ceremonial objects, it is cruelly ironic that middle-class Euro-Americans are increasingly adopting Native American spiritual traditions as their own. Sweat lodges, vision quests, drum beating, and incense burning are just some of the religious practices that have been appropriated by New Age Euro-America, often in the attempt to get in touch with the so-called authentically primitive. Treated as a repository for all things natural and simple, Native American traditions often are valued for their alleged ability to help Euro-Americans escape from the rampant consumerism and hyper-materialization of the United States. And so the "solution" to the problem of contemporary (white) society is to purchase Native American artifacts and pay New Age gurus large sums of money to lead spiritual excursions into the "wild." Just

as it was elite, urban literati who began the late-nineteenth-century romantic transformation of "threatening" Indians into ideal "primitives," it
is relatively affluent Euro-Americans who tend to fuel the contemporary
commodification of Native American cultures and peoples.

Little if any of this is done out of a conscious sense of disrespect. Just
the opposite: learning about and practicing Native American traditions
often are seen as ways of honoring them that contrasts with previous
decades' shameful attempts to eliminate them. They are ways that Euro-
Americans show their appreciation for ethnic and cultural diversity. Yet
the conscious intent to honor and appreciation of diversity often is simultaneously a vehicle for white unconscious habits of ownership. Euro-
American attempts to reconnect with nature, authenticity, and the primitive are grounded, in the words of one New Age leader, in "the rights of all
men to transcend cultural boundaries in redeeming their warrior souls."[47]
Native American traditions, like all other traditions and cultures, are seen
as available for appropriation by anyone who wishes to engage in them.
Ironically, given the gutting of the American Indian Religious Freedom
Act in the 1980s in the interests of tourism and logging, the First Amend-
ment sometimes is invoked in defense of the "right" of Euro-Americans to
engage in Indian religious practices.[48] The Constitution that was established to protect persecuted religious minorities is used to ensure that
white Americans are free to appropriate whatever religious culture they
please.

My claim is not that Euro-Americans should never learn about or
engage Native American or other traditions different from their own. It is
that the particular ways that Euro-Americans often engage these traditions
tend to be an extension of rather than a break with past attempts to
dominate and control Native Americans for white pleasure and profit.
Conscious attempts to honor Native traditions do not automatically erase
unconscious habits of domination and control that denigrate the very
cultures and peoples that they are supposed to support. Euro-American
appropriation of Native American religions tends to divorce them from
actual Native Americans, including the particular social and political circumstances of their lives. Native Americans suffer from far higher rates
of poverty, alcoholism, and ill health than other and especially white
Americans—facts that are directly related to Euro-American treatment of
them over the centuries—yet this part of "authentic" Indian life is conveniently left out of Euro-American appropriation of it. If Euro-American
appropriation of Native American life is a "charade by which [white peo-
ple] cloak themselves in the identity of their victims," then this identity is
very selectively constructed to include only the elements that do not chal-

lenge Euro-Americans to examine their habits of white privilege.[49] Just as "Mexican food . . . is a more palatable ethnic gift than Mexican agricultural stoop labor, although in its concrete expression of social inequality and physical distance, it is the latter that defines whatever authenticity one might find in tortillas and frijoles," Indian struggles to reclaim their land and religious traditions are just as authentic as, if not more so than, the Indian jewelry and woven rugs that Euro-American tourists like to purchase.[50] But since Euro-America's relationship to Native America continues to be one of ownership, Native American identity as conceived by Euro-America continues to be reduced to an object that can be manipulated, bought, and sold by white people.

In *Wretched of the Earth,* Franz Fanon claims that what is of greatest importance to an occupied people is the land.[51] His emphasis upon violent revolution in this work is sometimes taken as evidence of a shift away from the more theoretical terrain of psychology to the more practical region of activism.[52] But what his remark reveals is the intertwining of psychology, ontology, and geography in political, practical struggles to end domination. Since the occupation of land tends to result in the occupation of psyches, psychical space is just as important an issue in oppressive situations as is geographical space.[53] Or, rather, the two types of space are implicated in each other, and to move to revolutionary activism is not necessarily to abandon concerns about the psyche of the oppressed. Just as unconscious habits of white privilege are about ownership, "[r]evolution is about territory: political, economic, geographic, ideological, and cultural."[54] For non-white people to reclaim the geographic territory of land, the economic territory of money, and the cultural territory of religious practice is to make possible the reclamation of Native American, African American, and other non-white onto-psychological territories from colonization by white people. Likewise, their reclamation of a non-white psyche and ontology improves the chances of their reclamation of geographical, economic, religious, and other material and cultural terrain.

The intertwining of psychology, ontology, geography, and political struggle to end domination takes very concrete form in the hotly debated contemporary question of whether the United States government should pay reparations to African Americans for slavery and return land to Native American tribes. Du Bois's strategy of targeting not just consciousness, but also unconscious habits in the fight against white privilege both illuminates and strengthens the approach taken by proponents of reparation. On one level, reparations proponents are attempting the significant, but still straightforward, task of getting the United States to pay for its past practice of enslaving black people.[55] This task tends to operate on a conscious level of argumentation and includes the possibility of legal action against the U.S. government.[56] It involves providing information about the psychological, bodily, and economic injury that slavery inflicted and that its legacy continues to inflict upon African Americans, and claiming on the basis of that data that reparations are owed.

But on another level, proponents of reparation simultaneously have a subtler, more subversive goal in mind (which is not to dismiss the powerful effects that the first task would have if accomplished). That goal is to use economic demands to modify the psyches of black folk by transforming them into beings who see themselves as justified in claiming their due. This would be for black people to see themselves as full persons rather than as the subpersons they often have been told and believed that they are.[57] As Randall Robinson says, "how blacks respond to the challenge surrounding the simple demand for restitution will say a lot more about us *and do a lot more for us* than the demand itself would suggest."[58] What it will do is reclaim black personhood for African Americans, and it can accomplish that goal whether or not reparations are ever actually made.

This is so even though the demand for reparations inevitably operates within a white capitalist context. Given that unconscious habits of white privilege tend to be ones of ownership, one might think that struggle against them should not take the form of claiming a right to monetary restitution. If asserting rightful ownership to the forty acres and a mule (or its monetary equivalent) promised to freed slaves merely duplicates white habits of ownership, then the struggle for reparations would appear to be evidence of black internationalization of white racist habits rather than a disruption of them. How does black ownership challenge white habits of possession and appropriation?

Du Bois wrestled with this issue in his fight against white racism. He was sympathetic to communism from the time of the 1917 Russian Revolution and joined the Communist party in 1961, and communism both promotes the abolition of private property and would eliminate the exchange of commodities that gave birth to the concept of money. So it might seem that Du Bois's appreciation of Marxist communism would entail his rejection of the idea of black people's accepting property and/or money as compensation for slavery. But Du Bois makes clear that since black people are not divided into opposed classes of capitalists and laborers, Marx's analysis of capitalism will have to be modified when applied to the United States, and especially to the situation of African Americans.[59] The capitalist exploitation of black people "comes not from a black capitalist class [though Du Bois recognized that such a class existed] but from the white capitalists and equally from the white proletariat."[60] The response to capitalism can never be as simple as calling for black people to fight it en bloc.

More specifically, Du Bois raises the example of black people living in tenement houses in Harlem and paying exorbitant rents to the white capitalists who knew that their black tenants had no choice but to pay since white laborers would not allow them to move into their neighborhoods.[61] In this case, there is only one thing for black people to do: "buy Harlem."[62] Granted, "the buying of real estate calls for capital and credit, and the institutions that deal in capital and credit are capitalistic institutions."[63] But a distinction must be made between "capital as represented by white big real estate interests" and "the accumulating capital in [the black person's] own group."[64] The former must be fought. In contrast, the latter is crucial to the possibility of rectifying the exploitative situation of black people in Harlem and elsewhere, and to fight it is for the black person to "sla[p] himself in his own face."[65] With this example, Du Bois makes clear that black people should not oppose capital as such. This is not to abandon criticism of capitalism's exploitation of black people and culture, but to argue that in some cases, black people need to wield the tools of capitalism in order to undermine (white) capitalism itself.[66] The award of reparations for slavery is precisely one of those cases. In a strikingly fitting challenge to white capitalism's appropriation of the gifts of black folk, the payment of reparations would grant ownership of land and/or money to those who have been regarded as incapable of it because they themselves were seen as marketable pieces of property.

The reclamation of tribal lands by Native Americans is another such case. For Native Americans to reclaim their land would be for them to challenge the Euro-American belief that because of their kinship with the land, Native Americans are not full persons and are incapable of determining how the land should be treated. And such challenges are well underway. Native Americans are wielding the tools of Euro-American economic and legal systems to regain tribal lands, and rather than reinforce white habits of ownership, such actions limit the extent to which Euro-America can treat Native Americans as commodities to buy, sell, and consume. Some tribes have pressed old claims, legally forcing the United States government to live up to its nineteenth-century recognition of Native American sovereignty over particular portions of land.[67] Other tribes have taken advantage of the Euro-American idea that land is an object to be sold by buying back land that was previously purchased or taken from them.[68] Some of these legal and economic efforts were made possible by financial settlements with the United States government, but increasingly the money to hire lawyers and purchase land is provided by Native American private enterprise, namely gambling and, to a lesser extent, the sale of tax-free cigarettes. By accumulating Native American capital, Indians have been able to fight white capital's appropriation of them.[69]

Casinos also have paid off in terms of psychological benefits for Native Americans. In the 1990s, for example, families from a Cherokee reservation in North Carolina who lived below the poverty line suddenly experienced a quick rise in income thanks to casino payments. Once families were pushed above the poverty line, many of the psychiatric problems of children from these families dropped to the same levels found among children of families that had never been poor. The key was not the money in and of itself; it was the extra time to spend with their children that the money bought the parents. Strengthening Indian families, the development of Native American capital in casinos produced not just positive material but also beneficial psychological effects. The overall well being of the families was improved, which reduced the children's conduct and oppositional defiant disorders.[70]

Native American casinos and cigarette shops are not wholly unproblematic. Increases in crime, for example, sometimes occur in their vicinity, and not all Native Americans are happy about encouraging addictive activities such as gambling and smoking. But, interestingly, it often is Euro-Americans who most strongly object to Native American casinos because of how "tacky" and "garish" they look against the natural backdrop of desert sage and watermelon colored mountains in, for example, northern New Mexico. Casinos do not fit into the romantic Euro-American vision of Native American reservations as a primitive place divorced from markers of contemporary civilization. White Americans wish to see on Native American land adobe hogans (sacred houses) and earth-colored hornos (outdoor ovens for baking traditional breads), not concrete and metal square buildings with flashing neon lights. But if Native Americans have control of their land, then they also have some control over their identity and can refuse to be the site for Euro-America's redemption from its perceived artificiality.

What Fanon says about capital in the context of the decolonialization of Africa is just as applicable in the case of the "decolonialization" of African and Native America. After colonial powers are forced out of a colonized state, it can seem to a newly freed people as if everything should be done differently than the colonizers did. The colonial regime established certain economic patterns of developing (= exploiting) and exporting native resources, and rejection of those patterns seems to call for "chang[ing] the nature of the country's export, and not simply their destination, [re-examining] the soil and mineral resources, the rivers, and—why not?—the sun's productivity."[71] But starting from scratch in this way would require tremendous amounts of capital, capital that the exploited and dominated country does not have. "The truth is," Fanon claims, "we ought not to accept these conditions. We should flatly refuse the situation to which the Western countries wish to condemn us. Colonialism and imperialism have not paid their score when they withdraw their flags and their police forces from our territories."[72] There is no way to start from scratch, as if the withdrawal of dominating powers created a blank slate that erased all previous exploitation. This desire to call everything even once overt exploitation has ended is the colonialist equivalent to the cultural fantasy of colorblindness: act as if economic, ontological, and other differences generated by white domination do not exist, and they magically will vanish. Revealing this desire to be yet another expression of colonialism, Fanon argues that prior economic patterns can and should be used to build up a newly freed people, and the people who dominated them owe them reparations to compensate for the impoverished and "underdeveloped" conditions that they created. Precisely because "the spectacular flight of capital is one of the most constant phenomena of decolonization," the return of capital must be insisted upon—not to uphold previous patterns of exploitation, but to hold white capital accountable for meliorating the problems it created.[73]

Fanon's argument suggests that even capitalist processes of commodification and consumption can be used against capitalism itself to decolonize non-white America. The commodification of black, Native American, Latino (or even white) people is not going end in the United States anytime soon. While criticism of commodification is important, critical race theorists should not assume that it is the only way to fight capitalism's racism. Other ways, such as non-white ownership of marketing and advertising firms, also can be effective. The marketing of images of blackness to white audiences by black executives, or images of *latinidad* by Latino/a companies, can be complicit with white domination. Often the white corporate clients of Latino/a advertising firms, for example, insist on using stereotypical images of Latin Americans to sell their products.[74] Yet having some control over the process by which images of blackness, Indianness, and *latinidad* are manufactured and distributed means that the commodification of black, Native American, and Latino/a people could be way of preserving non-white language, cultures, and traditions, not just a means of marginalizing them through white consumption.[75] The problem might be not so much that non-white cultures are commodified per se, but that they are only partially commodified as the exotic, wild, and spicy objects that white America believes and wants them to be.[76] If black, Native American, Latino/a, and other non-white people can (at least partially) control the way images of them are produced, a less racist picture of non-white cultures and people might begin to emerge.

Ward Churchill makes clear that the creation of Native American capital that produces Native American sovereignty is not necessarily a reenactment of white habits of ownership. Responding to white American fears of dispossession of homes, farms, and ranches upon return of tribal lands to Native Americans, Churchill retorts, "I mean, what *are* people worried about here? Do y'all really foresee Indians standing out on the piers of Boston and New York City, issuing sets of waterwings to long lines of non-Indians so they can all swim back to the Old World? Gimme a break."[77] Most instances of Indian reclamation of lands involve national forests, state parks, and military reservations—land owned not by individuals but by state or federal government. And in cases where Native Americans demand jurisdiction of lands occupied by non-native individual homeowners, dispossession or eviction is never mentioned.[78] The idea behind "Indian Country" is not the Euro-American vision of exclusive ownership, which involves kicking off the people who were already there. Indian ownership of the land instead would mean establishing relationships of collaboration and cooperation between nations and between the land and the people living on (with) it. Anyone who wanted to remain on Native American land could do so, as long as the carrying capacity of the land was respected. Giving Native Americans a say in how to treat the land means giving the land a say as well. And the land has limits in terms of how much water and power it can supply and how large a population it can support.[79]

Finally and in addition to the positive economic and psychological impact of the reclamation of land by Native Americans and the demand for reparations by black people, another important end is posited by the demand for land and monetary reparations. The reclamation of black and Native American personhood made possible by the demand for land and reparations has not only the power to affect Indian and black psyches, but the ability to transform the white psyche as well. If Indian and black people conceive of themselves as full persons who are owed land and/or monetary reparations, then it will be more difficult for white people to ignore their repressed guilt about and complicity in the aftereffects of Native American genocide and African American slavery. This does not mean that once Native American and black people demand reparations, white people will instantly become antiracist. It means instead that a significant source of the power of non-white demands for reparations is

[141]

that it is as much a confrontation with unconscious habits of white privilege as it is an argument for economic and racial justice.

The fact that the demand for reparations confronts white people's unconscious habits of ownership is one of the reasons why white people often so vehemently oppose it. This confrontation perhaps explains why some conservatives have claimed that the debt that exists between black Americans and the United States is from the former to the latter, instead of the other way around.[80] It is the combination of onto-psychological and economic factors, rather than the issue of money and property alone, that produces strong negative reaction to the topic of reparations on the part of many white people. This combination is one of the reasons that white privilege is so difficult to uproot.

The land that became the continental United States has been called "the land which has no history."[81] But if history is the way different people are implicated in each other's traumas, then the vision of North American land as vacant before European settlement is a refusal to acknowledge how white people are implicated in Native Americans' and African American' traumatic experiences of forced evacuation from their homelands.[82] White habits of ownership have refused to know this knowledge, stubbornly viewing black gifts and Indian land as unclaimed pieces of property merely awaiting, and even demanding, their possession by white people. Given that these habits are held up as the appropriate standard for white and non-white people alike, we all have "got an awful lot to unlearn, and an awful lot to relearn, [and] not much time in which we can afford the luxury of avoidance."[83]

SIX

Race, Space, and Place

Far from being a neutral, empty arena in which people of various races are located, space both constitutes and is constituted by white privilege. Many spaces that might seem free of the impact of race and racism often subtly and invisibly privilege white over non-white people. Just as ontology can be affected by the type of relationship one has with land, personhood often correlatès with the way that one is forced or allowed to live in relationship to space and place. Space, race, and place are constituted transactionally such that space is raced and that bodies become raced through their lived spatiality. This means that the idea of space as racially neutral often is complicit with white privilege, that spatiality can contribute to the racial and racist division of a civilized "we" from a wild "them," and that systems of white domination respectively tend to allow and constrain white and non-white people to live their spatiality in different ways.

This last point is of particular interest to me. Lived spatiality both contributes to the formation of racist habits and can play a key role in their transformation. Given the difficulty, if not impossibility, of gaining direct access to unconscious habits of white privilege, the choice to change the space(s) one inhabits is an important, perhaps the primary, way to indirectly modify them. But that choice also presents many dangers. Because it is not equally available to everyone, the decision to alter one's relationship with space can just as easily further white privilege as it can challenge it. While non-white people often are compelled to live their space in restricted ways, white people tend to manifest a habit of lived spatiality that I call ontological expansiveness. As ontologically expansive, white people consider all spaces as rightfully available for their inhabitation of them. A white person's choice to change her environment in order to challenge her unconscious habits of white privilege can be just another instance of ontological expansiveness. This problem leads to the question of whether white people can attempt to change their unconscious habits and simultaneously live space in antiracist ways. While the danger of ontological expansiveness cannot be entirely eliminated, the answer to this question sometimes can be "yes."

Patricia Williams examines the connection between race and space by means of a number of racially charged incidents, two of which I will focus on here.[1] In *The Alchemy of Race and Rights,* Williams explains that while shopping one Saturday afternoon before Christmas in New York, she was denied entrance into a Benetton clothing boutique.[2] As Williams recounts, many small stores and boutiques in New York installed buzzers in the mid-1980s to reduce the incidence of robbery. "Legitimate" customers could be admitted into the shop, and those who looked undesirable could be prevented from entering the store at all. After pressing a buzzer to request that the door be unlocked so that she might be admitted, Williams peered into the store to see a white teenage employee stare at her a few seconds and then mouth that the store was closed, even though several white patrons clearly were shopping inside.[3]

The Benetton incident demonstrates how desirability and how who was seen as properly inhabiting the space of the Benetton boutique are racially constituted, as well as how the very racial demarcation of space often is not seen. Space often is thought of as neutral and uniform, a conception that overlooks how the racially magnetized whiteness of space is precisely what allows the conception of space as lacking such magnetization. When it was a matter of admitting white customers into Benetton, it could easily appear that no distinction between the spaces of "inside" the store and "outside" on the sidewalk existed. People seemed to flow smoothly from the sidewalk to the interior of the store and back to the sidewalk, as if space were a neutral arena that is not oriented toward some and against other particular bodies. The races of bodies might have seemed to be irrelevant to people's living of space, to their taking up and inhabiting space in the pursuit of their goals and projects. But the spaces inside and outside Benetton were racially constituted and lived (although not necessarily consciously experienced) as racially magnetized by the people that inhabited them. Once a non-white person tried to pass over the threshold from outside to inside, the demarcation of outside and inside, as well as the racing of those bodies and spaces, became more apparent.

Because bodies are part of the horizon against which objects and situations stand forth, the spaces of "inside Benetton" and "outside on the sidewalk" were not neutral, uniform spaces. They were magnetized with meaning. In this case, they racially and racistly demarcated an "inside" from the "outside" and an "us" from a "them." Black and white bodies disclosed objects in these spaces, such as the Benetton store and the teenage clerk, in different ways. The horizons of black and white bodies made relatively visible and invisible, respectively, the coloring and separation of spaces. The apparent racial neutrality of the spaces inside and outside Benetton was itself a product of the racialization of bodies. Space appeared as an empty, unconstituted void when only white people populated both inside and outside, an appearance that can be attributed to what one might call the "whitewashing" of space. When non-white people also populated the space outside Benetton's doors, some of the illusion of non-raced space in this situation was dispelled.

I say that only some of the illusion was dispelled because a black person's presence outside of Benetton is not enough to bring to full consciousness all the operations of raced space in this situation. A purely phenomenological reading of Williams's experience does not capture all of its complexity. While the horizons of black and white bodies raced the spaces of inside and outside Benetton, those bodily horizons tend to be just as unconscious as they are subconscious. They operate in league with an epidermalized collective unconscious, which obscures insight into the machinations of white privilege. This means that it is not the case that the raced spaces of inside and outside Benetton merely happened to go unnoticed before Williams stood at the store's threshold. Many unconscious habits were at work actively seeking to ensure that those raced spaces remained unnoticed since their continued invisibility was—and is—crucial to the smooth, uninterrupted operations of white privilege. One example of those unconscious habits can be found in the clerk's conscious—and, in all likelihood, sincere—belief that Williams's "threatening" appearance legitimately barred her entry into Benetton. Other examples might be found in the habits of the white patrons inside the store to not question the clerk's behavior since it is unseemly for a white middle-class person to make a disruptive scene in a public place.

In addition to illustrating how space is racialized, the Benetton episode demonstrates how white and black people often inhabit space differently due to the different ways they are situated in a racist society. The polarizing of space into inside and outside that racism produces curtails black people's inhabiting of space. White existence tends to be allowed an expansiveness when transacting with its world that is not equally available to non-white people. In contrast with white people, black people generally are not allowed to direct their transactions with the world in significant ways. Instead, they often are compelled merely to accept the form of transaction forced upon them. One can see the different ways in which transaction occurs in the different treatment that black and white customers received from the Benetton clerk. The clerk's allowing admission to white but not black people meant that Williams was not free to take up and live her space in the same way that the white people inside the store were. The expansiveness of Williams's lived space was curtailed by the racial demarcation of space. While white patrons were allowed to complete the familiar, habitual activity of freely transacting with the world by moving to enter a store, Williams was made painfully aware of her active, bodily assumption of space through the interference of it occasioned by the clerk. Williams's bodily horizons were shattered, transforming her body from a subconscious and unconscious background to her shopping activities into a thing-like object of conscious awareness and manipulation. A historico-racial schema forced a racial epidermal schema upon Williams.

The Benetton example illustrates not only the way that space is racialized through bodily existence, but also the way in which spatiality helps constitute the race of those bodies. In a significant sense, their position inside or outside the store composed the raciality of the people who wanted to enter it. Because white but not black people were allowed into the store, those who gained admittance were constituted in part as white and those who were denied admittance became black. This is not to claim that before attempting to enter Benetton, Williams and other would-be patrons were racially neutral. Nor is it to assume that the race of the white and black people was unproblematically given prior to their attempt to enter the store. It instead is to indicate the way in which race exists by means of a transactional relationship between bodies and world in which neither can be considered wholly primary or foundational. In a raced world, the race of bodies helps effect the race of spaces, which effects the race of bodies who inhabit those spaces, and so on. This is most clear in cases of mixed or ambiguous race, when a person can "pass" as either white or black. For such a person to be admitted to a white space such as Benetton is in a significant sense for her to be white, in the dynamic sense of being as becoming. Likewise, for her to be denied admittance to white space is for her to become black. And this is true for all people in a raced world, whether of mixed race or not. Because race is dynamic and con-textual, the race that one is and that constitutes one's lived experience is composed in part by the spaces to which one is admitted, just as the race that one is and that constitutes one's experience helps reciprocally "color" those spaces in turn.

The racialization of lived space, as well as the bodies who inhabit those spaces, can also be seen in another incident that occurred in New York. In 1986, three black men were assaulted after their car broke down near the virtually all-white neighborhood of Howard Beach. After their car stalled in Queens, the three men walked to Howard Beach, stopped in a pizzeria, and ate pizza. An anonymous caller reported "black trouble-makers" to the police, but the police found no trouble upon their arrival and so left. After the men ate, immediately upon their leaving the restau-rant eight to ten white teenagers surrounded the men and taunted them with racial epithets. The teenagers chased the men for up to three miles, beating them severely enough to permanently blind one man in one eye and contributing to the death of another as he was hit by a car when trying to flee across a highway.[4]

In the aftermath that followed the Howard Beach incident, it was said many times that three black men could have no legitimate reason for being in an all-white area of town, and so they had to be "up to no good." An implication of this claim is that the white teenagers' actions should be seen as either preventative of the trouble that the men were about to start or punitive of the already guilty men for starting the alleged trouble. In either case, this claim asserts that the beatings were justifiable because the sheer act of entering the neighborhood of Howard Beach made the men guilty of a crime against its inhabitants. The victims of the beatings were in some sense responsible for or deserved their suffering because they initially "victimized" Howard Beach residents by intruding into "their" space.

"Their" space was not neutral space, nor was it the space that was "theirs" because they lived there. "Their" space was racially, not merely geographically, bounded.[5] It was white space, to be understood as and kept separate from the black space of, for example, the nearby town of Jamaica in Queens. The bodies of the black men and of the white Howard Beach residents made up the racial horizons that helped constitute the geographical spaces of inside and outside Howard Beach. When the black men crossed over from Queens to Howard Beach looking for help, they violated the boundaries between black and white space, messing up the compartmentalization of distinct, racialized spaces by injecting a black presence into white space. What might have seemed to be "natural," as yet racially unconstituted spaces in the Howard Beach episode were racially demarcated. When a black man tried to cross over from one space to the other, from Queens to Howard Beach, the apparently unconstituted space of Howard Beach showed itself to be a racially composed white space.

Like the Benetton case, the Howard Beach incident demonstrates the way in which the racialization of geographical space is inextricably linked to the racialization of lived space by both black and white people. The Howard Beach case reveals society's assumption that black, but not white, people "need documented reasons for excursioning into neighborhoods where they do not live, for venturing beyond the bounds of the zones to which they are supposedly confined."[6] Black and white bodily existence differentially licenses people to inhabit space in unequal, non-reciprocal ways. White people may freely transact beyond their immediately inhabited spaces. The whiteness of their space is expansive and enables, rather than inhibits, their transactions.

This often is not true in precisely the same ways for white men and white women; the former generally live space more expansively than do the latter. For example, some young middle- to upper-class white men view "slumming" in lower-class non-white communities as a rite of passage by which they rebel against their parents.[7] In contrast, white middle- to upper-class women are more likely to avoid entering those neighborhoods out of fear of being sexually attacked—which is not to say that such avoidance is less racist than the intrusive attitude of some young white men toward non-white communities. But even though white women may not transact as freely as do men in some situations, qua white both white women and white men tend to live their space as a corporeal entitlement to spatiality. While their gender complicates and often limits the degree to which they expansively live their spatiality, white women's whiteness provides them a racial license to unencumbered spatial existence.

Black people, on the other hand, are not supposed to transact in such an expansive way. Their existence is confined due to the racialization of space. This generally is true for black people in white racist societies even though the degree to and the ways in which black women and black men are allowed to live their spatiality may differ. For example, in the Howard Beach incident, it is significant that the "troublemakers" were black men. Since women—black, white, or any other race—usually are not taken to be

RACE, SPACE, AND PLACE

implicitly hostile or aggressive in the way that men and black men in particular are, black women entering Howard Beach would not be as likely as black men to be perceived as violent criminals. (Williams's Benetton experience, however, demonstrates the limitations of this generalization.) Black women's spatial existence nonetheless is constrained in a way that white women's is not. A black woman might be allowed to enter Howard Beach without hassle or hostility if she were perceived as a domestic worker but probably not if she wished to engage in a recreational activity like eating at a pizzeria. While they are not criminalized by a white racist society to the same degree or in the same manner as black men, black women, like black men, generally are allowed into white spaces under very restrictive circumstances that are delineated by white people, rather than themselves.

The fact that white people sometimes feel uncomfortable and even fearful when in predominantly black spaces, such as black neighborhoods, does not necessarily indicate that white existence is constrained in a similar way that black existence is. Unlike black people, white people are seen by a white racist society as having the right or authority to enter freely any public space they wish. That they cannot do so comfortably in, for example, prominently black neighborhoods tends to be seen as a violation of the "natural" order of things, as an "unjust" limitation. White people do not tend to see similar limitations on black existence as unjust or as violating any sort of "natural" order. Black people generally are not understood as having the reciprocal right or authority to inhabit whatever space or neighborhood they like. Given the non-reciprocal habitation of space by black and white people, I suggest that the three men beaten in Howard Beach were punished not only for "threatening" white people by coming into "their" space. They also were beaten for presuming to live their bodily existence as a white person does, by inhabiting space as if it was theirs in which to transact freely and expansively.

This particular motivation probably was not conscious. Like the Benetton clerk, the teenagers who attacked the black men probably saw themselves as legitimately rebuffing a genuine threat to their community. The white privilege of ontological expansiveness nonetheless was being (unconsciously) protected by means of these beatings. To allow black men from Queens into Howard Beach would help break down sharp boundaries—psychological, as much as geographical—between black and white existence by permitting black people to live space as only white people (allegedly) should.

By their entering white space as if they had a right to be there, the race of the three men shifted somewhat to include whiteness. Allowing the men to remain in Howard Beach would involve an implicit if not fully articulated acknowledgement of their partial whiteness by the Howard Beach residents—hence the teenagers' need to violently eject the men so as to secure the men's blackness in distinction from their own whiteness. Conversely, those people who protested the beating became black in a significant sense, regardless of the "objective" color of their skin. This is illustrated by a Howard Beach resident's description of an interracial crowd of protesters as "blacks and white-blacks."[8] Regardless of one's physiological features, to march in protest of the beatings was to be an outsider black presence infiltrating and challenging Howard Beach's white space. In this way, the racialization of Howard Beach's space effected the racialization of the various bodies in that space. Those bodies who "belonged" in Howard Beach were "pure" white, and those who did not were partially black. And not just the marchers who lived elsewhere than Howard Beach, but also the Howard Beach residents who participated in the march were marked as outsiders in this way. By marching, those who lived in Howard Beach designated themselves as part of the out-group of "black infiltrators" rather than the in-group of "white residents," even though they lived inside the city's boundaries and had pale skin and other physical characteristics that usually mark one as white.

In both the Howard Beach and the Benetton incidents, bodies produced raced spaces through their inhabiting of them. The Benetton clerk's white body and Williams's black body raced the spaces of inside and outside the store, respectively, as did the Howard Beach and Jamaica residents' bodies race the space of their towns. At the same time, those spaces raced the bodies existing in them. The whiteness of the inside of Benetton marked those who were admitted into the store as white and those who were denied admittance as black. The whiteness of the space of Howard Beach marked the bodies who were residents of the town as white, while the blackness of the space of Jamaica marked its residents' bodies as black. In that way, there exists a co-constitutive relationship between the racing of bodies by means of space and the racing of spaces by means of bodies. Each reinforces and makes possible the other such that the causal relationship between them is circular, not linear.

The unconscious racing of bodies and space is unique neither to the United States nor to contemporary times. Especially in its binary division of a civilized "us" from a wild "them," the phenomenon has a long history that stretches across Europe and, through European imperialism and colonialism, across the globe. The story that Europe told itself and others as it colonized huge parts of the world was that it had discovered wild spaces that needed taming. And not just spaces, but people also, lacked civilization since the space one inhabited helped determine what sort of person one was. The psychological-racial categories of wilderness and civilization operate precisely by "*spacing* the individual, that is, representing it as imprinted with the characteristics of a certain kind of space."[9] European spaces were civilized spaces, which made Europeans civilized people. Conversely, if one was not from Europe, then one was by definition savage. This reciprocal definition of wild and savage spaces was then used to justify the horrific treatment of those such as Native Americans and Africans who were deemed uncivilized.

I focus here on the division between civilized and wild found in settled versus nomadic habits of lived spatiality. This manifestation of the division is especially visible in the case of the Roma, commonly called Gypsies in English and Cikani (tsigani) in many European countries.[10] It is no coincidence that "bohemian," which describes an exotic, unconventional lifestyle, is a synonym for "Gypsy."[11] Like blackness—and, indeed, often taken as an instance of it—"Gypsiness" combines the exotic and sensual with a tinge of unruly danger. It often is packaged as a commodity to be bought by "civilized" people whose lives otherwise would lack spice. But outside of its sanitized commodification, the alleged wildness of actual Gypsies often is considered a menacing threat that must be eliminated. This perceived threat is due to Roma nomadism. While somewhat similar to Native American nomadism, Roma nomadism differs in that it concerns relationships to space and place broadly considered, rather than specifically to earth and land. Kinship with the land was the "problem" with Native American life; in contrast, an alleged deficiency of connections with the world around them is the "problem" with the Roma. While the division of wild and civilized spaces has been used to oppress and terrorize many non-white peoples, what is distinctive about the racial discrimination against the "wild" Roma is its explicit and primary focus on their "lack" of rootedness in place.

The Roma migrated to Europe from Northern India around the tenth century and have a long history of oppression and discrimination in Europe, which I will not recount in full detail here.[12] In general, European policy toward the Roma began as one of exclusion, that is, of driving the Roma out of countries in which they were not wanted.[13] But banishing the Roma was impractical since if neighboring countries were doing the same, then the banished from another country merely entered one's own. Banishing was also not economical; it consumed a great deal of time, money, and effort.[14] For these reasons, in the nineteenth century, strategies of exclusion were replaced with those of containment, which dominated until around 1950.[15] Containment took the form of segregated physical confinement and surveillance. The Roma often were forcibly separated from the rest of the population so that their activities could be watched and controlled. While exclusion increased the nomadism of the Roma, containment attempted to extinguish it by forcing the Roma to settle down in a designated Roma neighborhood with a wage labor job. From the failure of containment, but also from some of its tactics, came the strategy of inclusion. In the second half of the twentieth century, many European governments attempt to include the Roma by assimilating them through sedentarization, wage labor, and formal schooling.[16] This strategy also failed because the Roma continued to resist pressures to give up their distinctive way of life.

Today, the Roma commonly are denied job opportunities because they are Roma; Roma children are segregated from *gaje,* or non-Roma, children, often by placing them in schools for the mentally handicapped regardless of their mental capacities; arson is used to drive Roma families out of their homes and neighborhoods; and Roma women are sterilized without their consent, and sometimes without their knowledge.[17] Attacks on Central and East European Roma escalated particularly after the revolutions of 1989, when the forced integration of Roma into *gaje* communities carried out by Communist governments backfired and frustration over the painful transition to democracy was vented on the Roma.[18] Along with the Jews, the Roma have been used as scapegoats for radical political parties, a practice that is spreading to more mainstream groups, as the 2000 presidential elections in Romania demonstrated.[19]

Attempts to eliminate the Roma's way of life by means of exclusion, containment, and assimilation occur because their habits of lived spatiality are seen as threatening to *gaje* ways of life. The Roma are nomadic rather than settled, as *gaje* generally are. On one level, this means that Roma tend to physically move from location to location rather than settle permanently in one town or country. But just as important as geographical nomadism—and perhaps even more significant—is psychological nomadism. One way for a settled person to grasp this point is to try to imagine being nomadic and then to remind oneself that "the effort required for nomads to adjust to sedentarism is just as great as the effort it would take for a settled person to adjust to nomadism."[20] The psychological and geographical intertwine in habits of lived spatiality in such a way that the psychological takes on a weight equal to the geographical. A *gaje* can literally travel a great deal and still have a settled perspective, just as the Roma can literally stay in one location and have nomadic habits.[21]

While the distinction between settled and nomadic habits lies on a continuum that admits of gradation and mixture, significant differences between the two types of lived spatiality exist. A nomadic way of transacting with the world is characterized by its love for movement, fluidity, unboundedness, and uncertainty. As one Roma explained, "I am a man of the wilds, of the open air, of the fields and the woods, and I could not be this if a lived in a house. . . . I even like the constant change from extreme comfort to extreme discomfort [that occurs when living outdoors] that is an essential part of living a good healthy life, and I like the feeling of uncertainty, of never knowing quite what lies around the corner though I might know the area well."[22] A *gaje* traveling with Roma in the United States describes the mood of his companions the first day on the road after being in one location over the winter: "The joy of being on the road again was so intense and so overpowering, the first day was spent driving on while singing and laughing."[23] When the *gaje* asked the Roma why they came to the United States from Russia, he was laughed at in a good-natured way for asking such a foolish question.[24] It was as if he had asked the Roma why they breathe air or eat food: it was a ridiculous question because it presumed that not traveling was the norm for living and that travel needed a reason or explanation.

While ridiculous from a Roma's perspective, the question about the reason for traveling makes sense from and is a good example of a settled attitude. With settled habits, travel tends to be teleological. It is not for the sheer joy of movement but to get from one location to another. For the settled person, travel is not consummatory but only a means to an end. Or, put another way, in contrast to nomadism, settled habits are characterized by the quest for certainty, in which the unchanging and fixed have the highest value. As John Dewey explains, "the quest for certainty is a quest for a peace which is assured, an object which is unqualified by risk."[25] A settled way of transacting with the world seeks to eliminate the uncertainty of change and finds comfort in the lack of movement, understood both psychologically and geographically.

The nomadic attitude means that even when Roma live in permanent accommodations, their habits of living are not ones of permanence. The Roma tend not to be proprietary or territorial with regard to space: "the Gypsy's Territory lies within himself, and its frontiers are psychological, flexible but fragile, adaptable but absorbent."[26] Here one can begin to see how much nomadic and settled habits conflict, as well as why the Roma are discriminated against for being psychological and geographical travelers. Just as geographical space often is constituted by white privilege, so are habits of lived spatiality. Most accounts of space and place assume or argue that rootedness in place is fundamental to what it is to be human, and a proper relationship to place is one in which permanence is prioritized. For example, David Harvey describes " 'the process of place formation' as one of 'carving out permanences from the flow of process creating space.' "[27] And several of the contributors to *Philosophies of Place* contend that "a sense of rootedness in a place is an important part of what it means to be human."[28] From the perspective of settled habits, nomadism appears as an inhuman lack: nomadic habits are devoid of roots and groundedness and manifest an improper, even monstrous, relationship to space. The Roma's "inhuman" nomadism prevents them from being in place. Their lack of rootedness is perceived as a lack of industriousness, which means that they only waste space. Hence the derogatory descriptions of Roma in which nomadism is taken as proof of moral degeneration: in the 1950s, Czechoslovak law claims that " 'a nomadic life is led by someone who, whether in a group or individually, wanders from place to place and avoids honest work or makes his living in a disreputable way.' "[29] Likewise in Bulgaria in 1959, "unemployment, mendicity [*sic*], and wandering" were yoked together as descriptions of the Roma.[30] Today as in the 1950s, nomadism tends to be evaluated and understood from the perspective of sedentarism and is seen as nothing more than aimless vagrancy.[31]

But understood from the values embodied in nomadic habits, the Roma's relationship to space is not one of a lack. Nomadic life is not characterized by an absence of place or roots. The Roma's relationship to space is not marked by nostalgia, and, indeed, "his identity is not bound up in possessions or place."[32] The Roma experience what the sedentary attitude calls rootedness as stuckness, that is, as an impingement upon their independence and freedom to pick up and move whenever they desire. For the Roma, stopping points "are not bonds, but mere stages, and breaking off relations established in a given place is easy."[33] As a result, "*every* country is a 'foreign' country, a 'country of residence'; there is no homeland to go back to, or even to turn to in a symbolic capacity."[34] While from the perspective of a sedentary life, the connotations of this statement likely include nostalgia, regret, and sadness, from the perspective of a nomadic life, its connotations are that of joy, lightness, and freedom.

Another way of understanding the deprecation of Roma habits of lived spatiality is to view the Roma as punished for their ontological expansiveness. The Roma refuse to constrain or restrict the ways that they live space, as non-white people are supposed to do. They presume to embody space as white people do: as freely open for their easy movement in and out of it as they wish. Like the black men in Howard Beach who were beaten for attempting to live space as white people do, the Roma are persecuted because they challenge the rules of the racial contract that say that only white people have the right to freely roam. The right to roam complements, rather than conflicts with, *gaje* sedentary habits of lived spatiality. In this view, only if one has a proper, rooted relationship to space that makes it a place can one legitimately travel to other countries, lands, and spaces. The tourist, for example, travels properly precisely because she has a permanent home and is not nomadic. She is civilized and may enter other people's spaces if she pleases. The Roma, in contrast, are seen as inhuman because of their nomadism, and for that reason cannot be allowed to expand into *gaje* space. Ironically, only if and when they develop "civilized," settled habits of living space can the Roma be permitted to freely move about.

Although the comparison of sedentarism with a quest for certainty might suggest it, my point in contesting the hegemony of settled habits is not to claim that nomadic habits necessarily are superior to settled ways of life. The romanticization of border crossings, nomadism, and other types of unbounded movement problematically overlooks the fact that some people are forced to travel out of economic, political, and other necessities. Abstract celebrations of nomadism tend to appropriate the concrete situation of actual nomads for the needs and pleasure of settled people, flattening out the unequal political terrain that penalizes nomadic habits. My point instead is to illuminate the difference between nomadic and settled habits and to fully appreciate this difference as central to divergent ways of life. It also is to criticize the way in which settled habits often are taken to represent the normal, proper relationship to space. The rhetoric of place often combines with settled habits of space to simultaneously encourage the ontological expansiveness of white people and constrain the lived spatiality of non-white people.

The division of wild and civilized spaces combines with the hegemony of sedentary habits of lived spatiality to constitute the Roma as a dangerous wilderness that contrasts with *gaje* civilization. One way the wilding of the Roma operates is through "the microspace of the body."[35] Similar to the way that racism functions in the United States and many other parts of the world, in the case of the Roma skin color in particular is taken as a sign of whether someone is civilized or wild, and the white body serves as the somatic norm. For example, a *gaje* woman in the Czech Republic explains her objection to having Roma neighbors in this way: "Normal white people used to live in this building. The plumbing worked, electricity worked, everything was in order. But then they had to move out because of the Gypsies. They destroy everything. They don't know how to live like us."[36] Some Czech Republic restaurants display signs that say "Whites only" in order to keep Roma out.[37] And an employee of an employment office in Slovakia reports that Roma frequently are turned away by potential employers because "they're as black as coal . . . too black and nobody wants to hire [them]. . . . This way of thinking has always existed in the minds of people—that which is Gypsy is evil."[38] In all these examples, white bodies are associated with civilization, goodness, and desirability. The blackness of Roma bodies is taken as a sign of their destructiveness, evil, and uncivilized behavior. The Roma's body itself is seen as an uncivilized space, a "bubble of wilderness" that the Roma take wherever they go, transforming the space they enter into a black, wild zone because of their presence in it.[39]

The division of "wild" Roma and "civilized" *gaje* spaces also can be seen in something as simple and everyday as the use of the customary term for the Roma: "Gypsy." In Slovak, *ciganit* means to lie, and to say that someone is gypsying another person is to say that he or she is lying to another.[40] In both Czech and Slovak, the word *cikan* is an insult: to be like a Gypsy, is to be dirty, to steal, and to lie. Likewise, in English, to "gyp" someone is to take unfair financial advantage of someone, to rip someone off. "Gypsy" also connotes someone flashy, ostentatious, flamboyant, and saucy. The Roma are seen as dirty, dishonest, and colorfully gaudy, in contrast with the clean, honest, and tastefully modest *gaje*.

One example of this can be found in Germany, where the term for the Roma is *Zigeuner*. Potato chips called "Zigeuner Chips" are advertised as "crispier" and "spicier" than other brands of chips.[41] The "spiciness" of Zigeuner Chips demonstrates how Gypsiness often is commodified and then sold by and to *gaje* who perceive their life as bland. The allegedly dirty, dishonest dangerousness of the Roma can be intriguingly exotic, rather than terrifyingly harmful, as long as it is a temporary indulgence that does not permanently disrupt the life of the civilized *gaje*. The desirability of the Roma "wilderness" can be seen in the Roma bars that often serve as a refuge for former Yugoslavian Serbs. The bars are associated by *gaje* "with the inner human instincts, with wildness, with the lack of control that lurks in every body."[42] While the former Yugoslavian Serbs avoid interaction with the Roma in their everyday lives, they frequent their bars when they "wish to escape from the claustrophobic clutches of their regulated lives, a haven where people can quench their thirst for the wilder pleasures of life."[43] Because the wild aspects of human existence are not permissible, or at least must be heavily controlled in the "civilized" world, Roma bars are valued as one of the few spaces in which they can find expression. The Roma's wild danger is exotic and alluring, providing the "spice of life" that cannot be sampled otherwise.

Yet the popularity of Roma bars with *gaje,* as well as the occasional romanticization of Roma music, dancing, and general culture, also explains the opposite phenomenon, which is *gaje* aversion to the Roma. This recently has become an especially touchy situation for many countries in Central Europe. For them to break away from communism and the Soviet Union and establish themselves as "democratic" nations belonging to the Western world, Central European countries understand that Western Europe and the United States require them to establish themselves as "civilized" people in the eyes of the West. As one Serbian recently explained when discussing participation in the Eurovision Song Festival, "Yugoslavia, which is frightened of appearing underdeveloped, will never send someone like Lepa Brena [a popular singer of Balkan folk music]. . . . In the West they regard that music as exotic, and of course that cannot have any connection with us."[44]

Membership in the Western world hinges on a country's degree of alleged development. But "development" has become a stealthy way of enacting racist and colonialist practices that supposedly have nothing to do with racism or colonialism and instead promote "modernization."[45] The rhetoric of development and modernization used by Western Europe and the United States is similar to that of civilization: both operate in service of the division of a civilized, developed "us" (the West) from an undeveloped, wild "other" (the East, the mystical, and the "Oriental"). Caught in the border between East and West and seeking to prove that it is more West than East, Central Europe understands that it must satisfy Western demands that it disassociate itself from everything wild, or non-Western. As one of the prominent wild spaces in Central Europe, the Roma are seen as something to be tamed and settled, or else forcibly, if covertly, expelled to another part of the world (but not Western Europe), if Central Europe is to qualify for membership in the West. The expulsion must be covert because human rights are one of the criteria for admission into the European Union, and the West increasingly is scrutinizing Central and Eastern European countries' treatment of the Roma in this context. Ironically, discrimination and violence against the Roma in Europe can be seen as increasing precisely because of the "civilizing" influence of the Western world upon Central Europe.

The Roma's alleged wildness is necessary to *gaje* life because *gaje* life is defined in opposition to it. In areas of the world populated by Roma, part of how one knows one is a civilized person is to know that one is not a wild Gypsy. The Roma are also necessary as a repository for all the wild pleasures and thrills that are desired by *gaje* but cannot be permanently admitted into civilized life. But even though *gaje* require the existence of "Gypsies" in these ways, the Roma simultaneously are seen as in need of elimination—be that by reeducating, banishing, or killing them—precisely because of their lack of civilization. The Roma are "a threatening counteridentity" to the *gaje* that delimits what the *gaje* are by establishing what they are not, but whose necessary difference also is seen as threatening to the identity of the *gaje* because it is perceived as strange and foreign.[46]

The Benetton, Howard Beach, and Roma examples illustrate Michel Foucault's insight that "space is fundamental in any exercise of power."[47] Both within the United States and without, the racialization of space and habits of lived spatiality often enforces racism and white privilege. Yet the connection between race and space often is not seen because space is thought of as racially neutral. The domination of white habits of space is all the more effective because it presents itself as "color-free" standard. This tends to create the tunnel vision of white solipsism, an allegedly contextless perspective that sees race as insignificant in matters of existence or experience. The tight connection between white solipsism and racial neutrality means that the notion of space as an empty, neutral void must be rejected. The conception of space and habits of lived spatiality as race-free constitutes a false neutrality that makes invisible the inequalities of raced space, rendering one powerless in the face of, and often complicit with, racism. We can more fully combat racial oppression when we are better aware of how racialized space and habits of lived spatiality impact human existence. As long as racial inequalities exist, striving to make the racialization of space visible will be crucial to the fight against racism.

This "we" needs immediately qualification, for it is not everyone who tends to be oblivious to the connections between race and space.[48] Those who are stopped from entering a store, chased or burnt out of town, or involuntarily sterilized because they are not white tend to see all too well that spaces are not racially neutral arenas in which all may freely enter and move. It is white people who are particularly prone to complicity with racism because they tend not to acknowledge the asymmetrical racial constitution of space and place. Because in a white racist world, white people's race makes it easier for them to experience space as lacking magnetization, it is white people in particular who must work to become aware of the many different ways in which space is raced.

Because many habits of lived spatiality are unconscious, this awareness will be difficult for white people to achieve. Both psychically and somatically, white people's privilege is in part derived from the ways that they live their spatiality. That privilege is not merely lying at the fringes of awareness, waiting for the spotlight of consciousness to bring it to reflective attention. Often it instead hides, for example, in habits of controlling space, including the way that other people live space. These habits can seem unrelated to race; they often operate through the language of development, modernization, and progress. As such, they often are able to thwart conscious attempts to see them, operating invisibly to perpetuate the spatial aspects of white privilege.

And yet, white people cannot give up striving to become aware of the racialization of space and place. This is a crucial first step toward taking responsibility and being accountable for the ways in which they live space as the raced bodies that they are. Once they have achieved some measure of awareness of the racial magnetization of space—limited though it likely will be—they must work to devise ways of transacting with regard to space such that they fight against rather than help support white privilege. But what might this concretely mean?

To begin, challenging white privilege does not mean trying not to be a white person, as if a white person could shed her whiteness to either become raceless or adopt a new—for example, black—race. It also does not mean, for example, that she necessarily should try to transform her settled habits of lived spatiality into those of a nomad. As Lisa Heldke has argued in her account of what it is to be a responsible traitor to one's racial and other privileges, "[t]raitorness requires me to insist on my whiteness—to insist that I and others recognize my whiteness as always relevant, always a factor in the way that I conceive the world and others; and to detect that factor in the places where it is presently most undetectable to me."[49] For a white person to become or think of herself as raceless is for her to actively cultivate a harmful ignorance of the many ways in which race is relevant to her life. It does not make her privileges disappear, for in a white racist society, she will continue to be identified and treated, at least to some extent, as white. She will receive the social privileges of being white whether she wants them or not. A person's relationship to her race is not merely a matter of how she projects herself into the world, and merely having good intentions in terms of attempting to disidentify as white does not erase her whiteness. A person's race is the product of transaction with her world due to her social "location" in it, which means that other people help constitute the racialization of her experience through their perceptions of and reactions toward her.

Attempting to take on another race is just as problematic as attempting to shed one's whiteness, albeit in different ways. Attempting to take on another race, including the habits of lived spatiality characteristic of that race, might seem like an expression of a white person's respect for people of color and non-white lived experience. But it often is merely another example of white people's assumption that any and all spaces, whether geographical/physical or rhetorical/cultural, are open for white people to legitimately move about in. To see black and other non-white spaces as places for white people to decide they may properly inhabit is to appropriate those places in a gesture that is much closer to colonialism than one of respect.

So then, what are white people to do with respect to space if they wish to be "race traitors" but cannot and should not attempt to shed their whiteness?[50] How might white people live their spatiality such that they challenge rather than support racism? The distinction between being white and being whitely can help address these questions.[51] "Being white" refers to physical traits such as pale skin color, while "being whitely" refers to "a deeply ingrained way of being in the world" that includes behaviors, habits, and dispositions.[52] The connection between being white and being whitely is contingent, rather than necessary, which means that people who are white need not also be whitely. The fact that a person has physical features, such as pale skin, that tend to locate her as white does not necessarily mean that she has to think or behave as if white people are racially superior to non-white people. While biology contributes to a person's cultural, social, and political habits, it does not determine them.

The relationship between being white and being whitely is transactional, which means that their relationship is never as simple as one of cultural whiteliness overlaying biological whiteness. Biological whiteness—the fact that particular skin, hair, facial, and other physical features are identified as racially white—is not prior to, but is a product of whiteliness itself.[53] But the white-whitely distinction still can be used in meaningful ways; it can be invoked without resorting to a biologism of race. One can and should acknowledge that whiteness is not a "natural," physical substratum that is overlaid by cultural forms of whiteliness. One can and should understand whiteness as transactional and acknowledge that spatiality helps constitute who counts as white. One also can and should recognize that often troubling political motivations for appealing to the existence of white and black races are informed by the racism of whiteliness. One can and should do all of this at the same time that one retains the use of the category of whiteness. This is because even though being categorized as white may be a product of whiteliness, being white is no less real for being such. Even though it is psychically, socially, and materially constituted rather than biologically determined, whiteness will continue to be a necessary and useful category for philosophical analyses as long as white racist societies continue to discriminate invidiously against people based on their physical characteristics.

There are additional reasons to be cautious when using a white-

whitely distinction. To the extent that it implies that whiteness is fairly difficult (if not impossible) to change but that whiteliness is relatively simple to transform, the distinction is problematic. It is not the case that deeply ingrained ways of being in the world—habits, in other words—are easy to modify merely because they are not physical features. (And even this way of phrasing the concern is odd since many habits manifest themselves in one's physical features.) Especially when they are unconscious, habits of whiteliness can be extremely difficult to detect, let alone change. While acquired rather than innate, unconscious habits of white privilege can develop a relative fixity that makes them just as difficult to modify as one's physical features, if not more so.

Carefully qualified in these ways, the distinction between being white and whitely allows both the insistence that white people cannot and should not attempt to think of themselves as ceasing to be white and the realization that this insistence does not have to mean that acknowledging oneself as white dooms one to total complicity with racism. White people cannot willfully change the physical features that tend to result in their classification as white—at least, not many of them and only to a limited degree—but they can and should attempt to unlearn their whiteliness— even if here too those attempts must be partial and limited. White people can and need to find ways of transacting with the world as white that undermine white racism.

Doing so means that white people must find ways to use their racial privilege against racism. It also means that when fighting racism, white people do not become marginal in white racist societies in the same ways that non-white people are. Unlearning whiteliness does not mean pretending to have no racial privileges or thinking of oneself as having renounced all racial privileges. Instead, renouncing one's whiteliness often means acknowledging and using one's privilege as a white person to combat racism. This claim may seem paradoxical since one feature of whiteliness is the exercise of white privilege. To use one's privilege as a white person, even in the service of antiracist projects, may appear to only strengthen, rather than dismantle, that privilege. And, indeed, this is a danger that can never be completely eliminated. But if a person cannot step out of her skin and cease being white and if at least some privileges will continue to be awarded to white people in a racist society whether they want them or not, white people will continue to be privileged. Like it or not, a white person's "unjust privilege and power will not [completely] 'go away', no matter how hard one works to become a traitor."[54] The question for white race traitors is not will they continue to have some racial privileges, but what will they do with those privileges? The answer to

[161]

that question and a key to being a white race traitor at this point in history is finding ways to use white racial privilege against itself. "Privilege, in the hands of a traitor, [can] becom[e] a tool for democracy," rather than a tool for the increase of unjust privileges for white people.[55] White people need to be accountable for how and to what ends they use the tools of their privilege.

While unlearning whiteliness and becoming a race traitor mean giving up many privileges, they do not entail becoming marginal in the same ways that non-white people often are. The problem with describing white race traitors as marginal is that it "encourages a blurring or conflating of the location of the outsiders within [for example, black people working within white institutions] and the location of traitors [for example, white people working against racism within white institutions]. The description makes it sound as if traitors have a foot in each world and are caught equally between them, and this picture does not foreground white privilege."[56]

While white race traitors are often ostracized from white communities, they are not placed in the same social location as black people because, unlike black people, they have had access to the privileges of whiteness and continue to retain some of those privileges. Rather than seeing race traitors as marginalized, a cartography of race would better describe a white race traitor as "off center," that is, as destabilizing the center while still remaining in it. If the language of margin and center is to be retained when charting different ways of transacting with the world, one needs ways of acknowledging the subversive acts of race traitors that do not conflate traitors with outsiders, either those within or without the center.[57]

With regard to the racialization of space and place, the task of white people becomes how to traitorously inhabit space such that they use their white privilege to work against racism. Again, this task is fraught with danger because it provides a prime opportunity for unconscious habits of white privilege, especially those of ontological expansiveness, to perpetuate themselves in the name of their elimination. And yet, if white privilege cannot magically be made to disappear, it can be transformed into a tool for its dismantling. While there are many important ways by which to approach this issue, my analysis of the racialization of space clearly points to at least three things that white people should not do with regard to space. To begin, they should not accept the Western Protestant/capitalist ethic of settlement that requires rootedness in a space to consider it and its inhabitants meaningful or valuable. Because the opposition of meaningful place versus empty space covertly operates with this ethic, the rhetoric of place tends to implicitly divide different forms of lived spatiality into those that are "truly" human and others that are perceived as monstrously inhuman. This division paves the way for the "civilized" to invade or otherwise attempt to destroy "wild" spaces and their inhabitants, all in the name of "improving" them. The ethic of settlement and rhetoric of place make it all too easy to see the "wild" as not knowing their "proper" place. They are seen as refusing to stay in it, inappropriately roaming into civilized spaces where they are not wanted.

White people can challenge spatial forms of white privilege by contesting the ethic of settlement and rhetoric of place. This is not because all settled people are white, or vice versa, but because settled habits of lived spatiality are complicit with white habits of ontological expansiveness. This complicity suggests a second, related challenge to spatial forms of white privilege, which is for white people to attempt to combat that aspect of their whiteliness that leads them to think that all spaces are freely available for their legitimate and comfortable inhabitation. White people must curb the expansive, ubiquitous way in which they often transact, including the way that they transact as if no one else of significance does or should inhabit the world.

Phenomenological philosophy needs modification on this point. Maurice Merleau-Ponty, for example, describes lived existence in terms of projective intentionality, in which one projects meaning onto the world rather than receives it as a ready-made given.[58] But contra the conclusions of his analyses of "abnormal" patients who exhibit a failure of intentionality because of physical injury, projective intentionality should not be considered normal, that is, the appropriate ontological standard to be upheld for lived existence. This is not because the world is static or meaning is always already congealed. Merleau-Ponty rightly objects to this philosophical position. It is because projective intentionality tends to suggest that it is desirable that all people live in as ontologically an expansive manner as possible. This suggestion is problematic from an antiracist and feminist perspective because it licenses white people to live their space in racist ways. It implicitly encourages them not to concern themselves with other people's lived existence, including the ways in which other people's existence is inhibited by white people and institutions. In this way, the nontransactional, unidirectionality of projective intentionality lends itself toward ethical solipsism. Unlike metaphysical solipsism, which holds literally that only one subject exists, ethical solipsism holds that the interests, projects, desires, and values of the one subject are the main ones or the only ones of any significance. The promotion of a more expansive (though not ethically solipsistic) existence is needed for those, such as black people, who have not been allowed to transact freely. But just the opposite is needed in the case of those, such as white people, who often transact too expansively, aggressively, and solipsistically, living as if they are the only ones who should be allowed to do so.[59]

One can see white people's problematic appropriation of space in the example Williams gives of an all-white crowd, except for herself, taking a walking tour of Harlem. The tour took place on Easter Sunday, and the guide asked the group if they wanted to go inside some churches since " 'Easter Sunday in Harlem is quite a show.' "[60] Aside from discussing how much extra time this additional stop would take, there was no discussion of whether white people's gawking at black people in a church was ethically or politically problematic, nor did anyone ask whether the churches wanted to be observed by white people. Williams notes that the group was polite and well-intentioned but also that this well-intentioned attitude was precisely the problem: "no one [and, one might add, no space] existed for them who could not be governed by their intentions."[61] Here are unconscious habits of white privilege at work. Camouflaged behind the good intentions of the white people was their ethical solipsism. They viewed themselves as the only beings who possessed needs and desires worthy of consideration. While white tourists could legitimately roam into a black church, it is hardly imaginable that a group of underdressed, camera-toting black strangers would be allowed to observe the worshiping practices of a white congregation in, for example, white and wealthy Howard Beach. The white tour group's projection of its intentions into the world, which made the space of a black church into a kind of wild zoo for white people to wander through and observe its "exotic" inhabitants, is an instance of the lived relationship to spatiality supported by an ethic of settlement that white people must combat in their fight against whiteliness.

Complementing the realization that there are some spaces that white people should not enter and do not have legitimate authority to enter, fighting whiteliness vis-à-vis space also means that white people must recognize that it is not inappropriate or unjust for them to feel uncomfortable when they do enter spaces that are predominantly non-white. With this third guideline for living space in antiracist ways, I have in mind the example of a white relative who felt discriminated against when he and I went into a grocery store in a largely Latino/a section of south Dallas. He felt that he was—and indeed, he and I probably were—the target of hostile looks and other body language by the Latino/a inhabitants of the store. The space of the grocery store, in which he and I were the only white people, was a slightly forbidding space (to us), and after leaving the store, he somewhat angrily complained that he was the victim of "reverse discrimination," in which he was being treated inappropriately "just because" he was white.

The feeling of being unjustly discriminated against when entering a non-white (in this case, Latino/a) space is an example of the whiteliness that needs to be fought by white people. If white people transform their habit of claiming a "right" to project themselves into any and all spaces, then along with the transformation of that habit should come an acknowledgement of the fittingness of their lack of psychological comfort in some spaces. The lack of comfort and feeling of illegitimacy are entirely appropriate responses to the recognition that space is not racially neutral or empty and that white people do not have a legitimate claim to all space. Given a white racist society, white people should accept that when they enter Latino/a or other non-white spaces, it is entirely just that they receive hostile treatment "just because" they are white. I am not necessarily legitimizing all forms of hostile treatment of white people. Certainly some kinds, such as physical violence in particular, are not easily warranted even if a white person has entered a Latino/a grocery store or black church in a whitely way. But white people who are attempting to transform their habits of white privilege should accept as fitting, and not as "reverse discrimination," the angry reactions and stares that they might receive when they have entered into non-white spaces. The psychological privileges of whiteliness need to be relinquished just as much as economic and other ones do.

How might white privilege be not just something to combat, but a positive instrument to use in the fight itself? How might white people use the ontological expansiveness provided to them by their racial privilege to undercut the racist ways in which space is inhabited? An example involving the housing market can help answer these questions. In 1954, a white couple named Anne and Carl Braden purchased a house in a middle-class white neighborhood in Louisville, Kentucky, for the purpose of deeding it to a black couple, Charlotte and Andrew Wade. The reason for this arrangement was that the Wades were not able to purchase the house themselves due to residential segregation and the tacit agreement between white people that they sell their homes only to other white people. The Wades were barred from transacting expansively with respect to their housing; they were prevented from deciding for themselves which neighborhood space they would inhabit.[62]

Because they opposed segregation, the Bradens acted so as to make it possible for the Wades to buy the home they wanted. The Bradens' act was one of using their privilege as white people to fight against the racist practices of segregation. Unlike the white people who would only sell their homes to other white people, the Bradens used their whitely ability to transact expansively so as to make room for, rather than close out, the Wades' inhabiting of space. In doing so, the Bradens did not stop being white, nor did they lose all their whitely privileges as white people by subverting the whitely practice of residential segregation. The Bradens were ostracized by white communities by means of threatening phone calls and bomb threats. In that respect, Anne Braden's claim that "[t]o an extent, at least, we were thrown into the world of abuse where Negroes always live" is accurate.[63] But this extent is limited since the Bradens continued to be thought of as white by those who did not know about their traitorous act, and they retained their whitely privileges accorded to them through others' perception and treatment of them. A more accurate description of the Bradens' act than that provided by Anne Braden is that the Bradens used, rather than gave up, their privilege of being allowed to enter the space of the neighborhood in question to help dismantle the racist magnetization of that space. In that way, their whitely privilege became a tool of democracy, meaning in this case, a tool for the dismantling of spatial privilege awarded to white people, rather than one of mere oppression.

Not only do human beings "have" space because they "have" bodies, but in the United States, Europe, and elsewhere, human beings embody particular kinds of spaces because of the racing of bodies. The examples from Williams's work and the situation of the Roma show how space is raced by means of bodily existence and how bodies come to be raced through the spaces they are allowed to inhabit. They also open up questions about how white people might become race traitors with regard to their bodily inhabiting of space. I have suggested a few ways in which white people might do so, but they should not be taken as exhaustive. In particular, further thinking is needed about how white spatial privilege might be used as a positive tool against racism, as well as about the dangers of unconsciously perpetuating white privilege by using it in that way. Because space is not an empty, neutral arena, white people need to be held and hold themselves accountable for the ways that they live the racial magnetization of space, even though many of them operate unconsciously.

SEVEN

In Defense of Separatism

The main purpose of this book might present its biggest danger: a sustained focus on white privilege. Because white people are the primary benefactors and producers of white privilege, focusing on white privilege risks putting white people on center stage even as it tries to undermine their hegemony. In particular, examining the question of how white people can combat racism through the use of their racial privilege creates the danger that the story of race will become just another account of the importance of white people. There is no way to completely avoid this danger. Just as men's possible roles in feminist theory and practice must be explored if women's oppression is to be effectively countered, white people's possible roles in critical race theory and antiracist practice must be addressed if racism is to be successfully fought. The danger of supporting the primacy of white people's interests and needs by means of this focus nonetheless is very real. Unconscious habits of white privilege are too powerful to dismiss. It is all too easy for white people's good intentions to address racism in responsible, antiracist ways to reenact the very white privilege that they wish to undermine.

The work of pragmatist feminist Jane Addams provides an example of one such well-intentioned attempt to fight racism. Addams's case is fascinating because she was ahead of her time in arguing for the importance of reciprocity between white and non-white people. Her simultaneously theoretical and practical development of the notion of reciprocity recognized the diverse and marginalized perspectives of her immigrant neighbors in Chicago and demonstrated a profound awareness of how power and privilege affect relationships between different ethnic, racial, and class groups. Yet this very notion of reciprocity also furthered white privilege because it unintentionally allowed and even encouraged white people's ontological expansiveness. Addams's example points to the need for a kind of separatism. If white people want to counter their ontological expansiveness, they must attempt to determine when engagement with non-white people is and is not appropriate. It is not the case that eliminating white privilege, including the racist segregation that so often has accompanied white domination, necessarily or always requires the integration of white and non-white people. On the other hand, racial segregation can be a symptom of a white aversion to all things non-white, so the solution to white people's ontological expansiveness is not for them to retract into an all-white life. The story is more complex than either of these two extreme options allows. Different contexts will call for different types of behavior on the part of white people, and part of their learning to see their privilege involves developing habits that are attuned to the different ways that race and racism operate in specific situations.

It rightly has been claimed that "Addams's most original theoretical contributions concer[n] reciprocity among unequally positioned subjects," such as members of different races.[1] Addams makes clear throughout her writings that the idea of reciprocity is central to her understanding of the purpose of Hull-House. In an early piece published only four years after Hull-House began, Addams explains that it "was opened on the theory that the dependence of classes on each other is reciprocal."[2] If Hull-House was concerned to "add the social function to democracy," and " 'the social relation is essentially a reciprocal relation,' " then the goal of Hull-House was to increase reciprocity between new immigrants and Chicago's white middle class, as well as between the different immigrant groups themselves.[3]

In a reciprocal relationship, each side takes something and benefits from the other. It is necessary that the relationship not be unidirectional. This meant, in Addams's view, that members of the white middle class had something valuable to gain from the new immigrants just as the immigrants had something valuable to gain from them. Addams explicitly con-

firms this meaning when she writes that the people "of ability and refinement, of social power and university cultivation . . . who lose the most are
those who thus stay away" from the immigrant masses.⁴ But the self-
isolation of white middle-class people was not Addams's only concern. An
equally problematic obstacle to reciprocity, in her view, was the social and
geographical self-segregation of new immigrants. This is why Addams
claims that a white, middle-class house "situated in the midst of the large
foreign colonies which so easily isolate themselves in American cities,
would be in itself a serviceable thing for Chicago."⁵ Hull-House worked to
create reciprocity from both directions. It chipped away at the pattern of
white middle-class avoidance of immigrant culture, as well as exposed the
new immigrants to white middle-class America, reducing their isolation.

Addam's emphasis on reciprocity is especially striking given the common assumption of her day that non-white people had nothing of value to
offer white people. Three years after the 1889 establishment of Hull-
House, for example, Congress removed about nine million acres of North
Dakota land from the Chippewa Indians because of the alleged harm that
their segregation from white people was inflicting upon them. The con-
gressional committee wrote, "In the reservation the Indian children see
only a dull sameness in the culture of their surroundings. No man has
a better home than the other. . . . [T]he rearing of beautiful homes,
with their carpeted rooms, their cosy [sic] furniture, their pictures, and
the many articles of art and refinement, not forgetting cleanly and well-
dressed families, will have a greater civilizing effect . . . than anything that
has ever been attempted with the Indians."⁶ The Chippewa Indians were
seen as desperately needing the influence of white civilization, but the land
that was taken was not considered to be a reciprocal "gift" to white people.
The land was taken because the Chippewa lifestyle (allegedly) contained
nothing of value, and the Chippewa nation was seen as incapable of using
their resources to develop wealth and refinement. The situation of Native
Americans at the turn of the twentieth century was not identical to that of
newly arrived immigrants to the United States. One crucial difference was
that immigrants had a link to the "Old World" of Europe, against which
Euro-America was always measuring itself (even as it proclaimed its superiority) and which Native Americans lacked. But both Native Americans
and new immigrants were seen by most of Euro-America as uncivilized
and in need of assimilation because they "failed" to live up to white
middle-class standards. In that context, Addams's insistence that "uncivilized" people had something to contribute to white America was radically progressive.

I will return shortly to the question of what in particular Addams thought that new immigrants and white middle-class Americans had to gain from each other, and a bit later to the issue of immigrant isolation. Before doing so, let me address a strong challenge made to Addams's ideas that targets her attitude toward non-white groups. Historian Rivka Shpak Lissak argues that Addams ultimately was no different than other Euro-Americans in that her goal for new immigrants was assimilation, not reciprocity.[7] According to Lissak, rather than aiming to establish mutually respectful and influential relationships between native-born Americans and new European immigrants, Addams sought to eliminate immigrants' ethnic cultures by absorbing them into white middle-class American life.

Lissak claims that Addams envisioned the assimilation of immigrants as a two-step process.[8] Unlike most proponents of assimilation, who thought of it as a one-step transition in which racial-ethnic differences were quickly abandoned for the culture and ideals of white middle-class America, Addams allegedly insisted that the deliberate (but temporary) preservation of new immigrant cultures should precede their disintegration. This intermediate step was crucial for making the transition to white middle-class culture more gradual and less traumatic for the new immigrants and was, Lissak implies, a sign of Addams's genuine concern about the well-being of newcomers to the United States.[9] Nonetheless, according to Lissak, the end of Addams and other assimilationists was the same; they differed only on the means by which to reach it. Addams allegedly "thought that acculturation was bad insofar as it was undemocratically imposed," by which she supposedly meant that assimilation should occur "in an atmosphere of mutual respect, tolerance, and understanding," but the goal was still the ultimate elimination of non-white cultures.[10]

Addams clearly takes positions that do not fit within an assimilationist model.[11] She explicitly founded Hull-House on the theory that all classes were reciprocally dependent upon each other. She also claims that "[o]ne thing seemed clear in regard to entertaining immigrants [at Hull-House]; to preserve and keep whatever of value their past life contained," and she often speaks of the importance of cultivating immigrant children's respect for the "old ways" of their racial-ethnic cultures.[12] And Addams explicitly criticizes assimilation to whiteness when she charges that "in our overwhelming ambition to remain Anglo-Saxon, we have fallen into the Anglo-Saxon temptation of governing all peoples by one standard."[13] In these and other places, Addams indicates that immigrants have something distinctive to contribute to a reciprocal relationship with white middle-class America and that their assimilation into Anglo-Saxondom should be resisted.

Lissak is not able to satisfactorily handle Addams's anti-assimilationist claims because she misunderstands the concept of transaction. In the context of racial relationships, transaction means thinking of the relationship among different races along the metaphorical lines of neither the melting pot nor the tossed salad. It means instead understanding how different racial groups can and do constitutively, reciprocally, and dynamically influence one another, like a stew whose ingredients neither melt into one another nor remain totally separate.[14]

Lissak posits—helpfully, I think—that "the key to understanding Addams's views . . . is to examine her attitude toward ethnic-cultural persistence."[15] But she continues by claiming that

> Addams, like John Dewey and others, actually expressed two seemingly contradictory views simultaneously: she spoke of mutual esteem and respect of variety *and* in favor of cross-fertilization. Did this mean the perpetuation of ethnic-cultural uniqueness and the cultivation of distinct immigrant cultures through cultural institutions, or the gradual elimination of ethnic-cultural segregation after the absorption of immigrants and their contributions into a common fund through cross-fertilization? . . . The unresolved tension between unity and diversity in Addams's writings raises the question whether her pluralism was real or a matter of expediency and mere rhetoric.[16]

Lissak reveals that she (mis)understands cross-fertilization as assimilation, rather than as transaction. Working with a very atomistic understanding of racial groups, Lissak suggests that respect of variety and the constitutive influence of different groups on each other are mutually exclusive. For Lissak, pluralism can operate only atomistically, like vegetables thrown together in a salad bowl, side by side in hermetic juxtaposition with boundaries that are never porous or fluid. From this perspective, Addams's call for transactional cross-fertilization cannot but sound like a demand for assimilation, but Lissak's is a specific and contestable ontological position that Addams rejected. The two-stage process of assimilation Lissak attributes to Addams is founded on this mistaken assumption of atomism. Understood transactionally, Addams's pluralist desire for cross-fertilization allows her both to respect the distinctiveness of different racial groups and to attempt to develop continuities across them. Her pluralism is both non-atomistic and real.[17]

Yet Lissak is not completely wrong that there is something problematic about the way that Addams occasionally talks about the transactions between white middle-class and non-white immigrant groups. Let me return to the issue of what exactly each group contributes to the other in a reciprocal relationship. Addams is right that reciprocity is very important and sometimes even necessary to the establishment of respectful and non-racist relationships. But it is not sufficient. What each side is seen as having to contribute to and gain from the other in a reciprocal relationship also is crucial. Positing a reciprocal relationship between different races and classes does not, by itself, eliminate a white privileged understanding of the groups involved.

Addams asserted early on in her Hull-House career that what the white middle class brings to new immigrants is "as much as possible of social energy and the accumulations of civilization to those portions of the [human] race which have little."[18] In turn, the new immigrants allegedly provide the white middle class with an injection of the vitality and liveliness that it otherwise would lack. Similarly, writing in 1893 and 1910 to white middle-class Americans about their unrealized need for social settlements, Addams claims:

> We all bear traces of the starvation struggle which for so long made up the life of the [human] race. Our very organism holds memories and glimpses of that long life of our ancestors which still goes on among so many of our contemporaries. Nothing so deadens the sympathies and shrivels the power of enjoyment as the persistent keeping away from the great opportunities for helpfulness and a continual ignorance of the starvation struggle which makes up the life of at least half the [human] race. To shut one's self away from that half of the race life is to shut one's self away from the most vital part of it.[19]

Again in 1906, Addams said, "All the members of the community are equally stupid in throwing away the immigrant revelation of social customs and inherited energy."[20] And in 1930, toward the end of her life and career, Addams declared, "I believe that we may get, and should get, something of that revivifying and upspringing of culture from our contact with groups who come to us from foreign countries, and that we can get it in no other way."[21]

These depictions of a civilized-but-deadened white middle class and a primitive-but-lively non-white lower class both reflect and support a hierarchy in which white people are seen as fully human and non-white people as less than so. As in the case of Native Americans, this hierarchy operates by fusing images of wilderness and race. At the time that Addams lived in Hull-House, new immigrants were implicitly posited as being part of the untamed, energetic wilderness from which civilized, white Americans had distanced themselves. In the beginning of United States history, this distancing was seen as beneficial, as a way of securing both one's moral character and one's relationship to God. But as the wilderness was con-

quered, a romantic nostalgia for it arose in the second half of the nineteenth century. It then was transformed into something positive that civilization, now seen as sterile and lifeless, lacked. A racist appreciation of
non-white "primitives" for their perceived possession of life-energy began
at the turn of the twentieth century, the current manifestation of which
can be seen in the exoticization and gentrification of inner-city black
ghettos.[22]

That the civilized lack something that the primitive can provide does
not change the fact that the civilized are upheld as the epistemological,
moral, and social ideal to which the non-civilized should aspire. Reciprocity between the perceived lifeless and the alleged life-full can exist side by
side with an insidiously hierarchical relationship between them in which
one is seen as culturally and racially superior to the other. When Addams
explains what white middle-class Chicagoans and non-white immigrants
have to give to one another in terms of civilization and revivifying energy,
respectively, she implicitly endorses a problematic hierarchical reciprocity
between the two groups of people.

The term "hierarchical reciprocity" means something different than
asymmetrical reciprocity, which acknowledges that one side has more
power than the other.[23] Addams was far ahead of her time in recognizing
that reciprocity between white Chicagoans and non-white immigrants
was not symmetrical, and her work is full of rich examples in which
Addams "emphasize[s] the way power distorts relationships and show[s]
how to recognize and undo the harmful effects of privilege and disem-
powerment."[24] She explicitly insisted that the more powerful must do
things with the less powerful, not to them, consulting with them instead of
unilaterally deciding what is best for them.[25] But one can simultaneously
recognize and attempt to offset unequal power between parties by creating
a situation in which both fully participate and leave in place racist assump-
tions or stereotypes about the parties involved. Countering asymmetries
of top-down power with horizontal processes of negotiation and deliberation does not necessarily eliminate all forms of insidious hierarchy.[26]

In the case of the white middle-class Americans and the new immigrants described by Addams, each side has something of value to give
to the other, but they do not have equal ontological weight as human
beings.[27] The civilized culture of the one group makes them full persons,
and the primitive culture of the other makes them subpersons.[28] Addams
suggests as much when she implicitly describes new immigrants as living
in a sort of state of nature, "many of them without fellowship, without
local tradition or public spirit, without social organization of any kind."
As Addams depicts them, new immigrants, like Native Americans, are

destined to remain in this primitive, socially deficient state until they are brought into contact with the white middle class, who have "the social tact and training, the large houses, and the traditions and customs of hospitality" that are needed to transform the new immigrants into fully social human beings.[29] This hierarchical social ontology, which underlies Addams's account of reciprocity, partially undercuts the democratic thrust of her work. Alongside Addams's well-intentioned attempt to value immigrant life, unconscious habits of white privilege continue to operate. Indeed, those habits are all the more effective because they are camouflaged behind the purportedly antiracist notion of reciprocity.

A tension exists in Addams's work in which an implicitly racist view of new immigrants exists side by side with a genuine attempt to combat white Chicagoans' racist dismissal of them. An apparent second problem also exists, which concerns—to return to Lissak's guiding question—Addams's attitude toward the persistence of non-white racial cultures. Lissak's two-stage model of assimilation is a misguided means by which to understand Addams's goal for new immigrants. But Addams does make conflicting statements about the role or value of racial differences in the process of Americanization. Over the course of her life, she moves from a relative disregard to a high level of appreciation for racial differences, wanting to preserve rather than transcend them.[30] While Addams's appreciation for racial differences would seem to be a positive development in her later work, it raises serious questions about the concept of transaction. Lissak charges that transaction is a distinctly American (read: white middle-class) ideal that does not have the effect of equally drawing from and maintaining the distinctiveness of all those who are part of a transactional continuity, and she suggests that the transactional preservation of racial differences helps maintain the hegemony of white people by eroding the particular cultures of non-white people.

Taking the example of the ethnically mixed clubs that met at Hull-House, Lissak argues that they "were meeting places for otherwise segregated children and inculcated tolerance and respect for differences as a product of coexistence. They taught that the preconditions for democracy were the breaking down of national and cultural differences and the unification of American society on the basis of common interests, ideas, and feelings, and norms of behavior, as opposed to segregation and preservation of ethnic identity."[31] To pragmatist, feminist, and critical race theorist ears, inculcating respect for differences probably sounds like an ideal goal, but Lissak's very different claim is that doing so works against new immigrants' ability to maintain themselves as a distinct group. Key here is the link Lissak makes between self-segregation and the preservation of ethnic identity. In her view, in the United States, the self-segregation of non-white groups from white people is necessary to maintain those groups' racial cultures. To bring groups into intimate contact with one another, even for the well-intentioned purpose of increasing respect between them, is to contribute to the conditions that undermine their distinct identities.

The connection Lissak makes between self-segregation and the preservation of ethnic identity complements the disassociation she elsewhere effects between pluralism and cosmopolitanism. In her view, "Hull House was not an immigrant institution in the sense that it represented a pluralist cultural view of society. It was, rather, an American institute that sought to integrate individual newcomers of different backgrounds into a cosmopolitan, America-oriented society."[32] According to Lissak, a cosmopolitanism that cross-fertilizes different groups results not in pluralism, but in an erosion of non-white groups' identity and the inevitable assimilation into white culture. As she sees it, limiting the amount of significant interaction between different ethnic groups is the only way to bring about genuine pluralism.

The support Lissak offers for both her linkage of self-segregation and preservation of difference and her disassociation of pluralism and cross-fertilizing cosmopolitanism bears an uncanny affinity with one of John Dewey's criticisms of the separation of art from lived experience.[33] Just as Dewey was concerned about art products such as paintings being stuck in a museum, Lissak is worried about the lived traditions of immigrants' cultures being turned into dead objects for passive and distanced spectators. She argues that "[i]n the absence of ethnic sociocultural segregation, immigrants' 'folklore' and 'primitive art' would become museum exhibits within one or two generations."[34] As mere museum exhibits, immigrant traditions would no longer be live practices for the children and grandchildren of those who first came to the United States. Without those lived practices, the distinctive cultures of ethnic immigrants could not survive. For this reason, Lissak argues, self-segregation is needed to provide a space in which ethnic practices can continue as something other than dead museum pieces. Only in that way can the distinctive identity and culture of ethnic groups persist.

Lissak's opposition of cross-fertilization and pluralism demonstrates her assumption of an atomistic ontology, which is problematic in ways that I have already discussed. But I find her concern about the "museumification" of ethnic cultures and traditions to be compelling. It complements the concern I have about the exoticization of non-white cultures for the purposes of white middle-class consumption, pleasure, and profit.

Given the all too frequent tendency for a transactional relationship with dominant white culture to result in the reduction of non-white cultures to dead museum pieces and/or exotic consumables for white outsiders, history seems to point to the need for some sort of self-segregation from white culture to preserve non-white cultures as living traditions for their own members. Intertwined with Lissak's problematic atomism is a valid and important question: what role can and/or should self-segregation play in pluralist, cross-fertilizing relationships? Another way of phrasing this question is: can the concept of transaction allow or make room for that of separatism? If this question can be answered only negatively, then even if a hierarchical social ontology is removed from the notion of reciprocity, reciprocity could continue to operate as an implicit tool of white privilege.

At first glance, the question is a difficult one to address because segregation and separatism often are assumed to be atomistic by definition. On that definition, one group cuts itself off or is cut off rather sharply from other groups—or at least, this is the goal, even if it is never achieved wholly in fact. Whether the segregation occurs through choice or force, the boundaries between groups segregated from one another are not supposed to be porous or fluid. They are supposed to be rigid borders that seal off one group from another.

Because of this view of segregation and separatism, it can be easy to overlook the important role that self-segregation could play in a transactional world.[35] For all of Lissak's misunderstandings of pragmatist philosophy,[36] her work on Addams is potentially valuable because it encourages the hard work of rethinking separatism, contra Lissak, in non-atomistic ways. To begin this work, it is helpful to distinguish between two different senses of transaction. On a general level, transaction is always in play because in a world in which environments help constitute organisms, there is no such thing as a live organism completely isolated from its surroundings and, for that reason, there is no such thing as a live organism completely isolated from all other organisms. As Addams says, "we are bound to move forward or retrograde together . . . [because] . . . our feet are mired in the same soil, and our lungs breathe the same air."[37] But turning to a more local level, one can coherently speak of the relative presence or absence of transaction. In some situations, times, and places—such as early-twentieth-century Chicago—certain groups can be relatively isolated and have legitimate reasons to desire their isolation. In those cases, it might be beneficial not to try to end their self-enforced segregation, as Addams tried to do with immigrant groups. Or put another way, it can be important for those groups themselves to decide to what degree and when they wish to be brought into a more transactional relationship with other groups.[38] In these cases, one should be careful to ensure that the concept of transaction does not turn into a reason for one group to intrude upon another. This is especially true for those, such as white people, who belong to dominant social groups, who often are ontologically expansive, tending to see all spaces—physical, cultural, and otherwise—as available for their legitimate inhabitation.

The lack of transaction on the second, more local level can itself be described as the result of transaction on the first, more general level. Self-segregation can be seen as a transactional response to an oppressive environment that a person or group wishes to avoid. In that case, there is no thing such as "pure" segregation or separatism in which one has completely removed oneself or been removed from the transactional spiral that is life. All this is true, but its broad truth does not erase the need to recognize local restrictions of transaction. This is the grain of truth in Lissak's criticism of Addams's theory and practice of cross-fertilization. To fail to recognize the need for limitations on specific forms of transaction can undercut the conditions necessary for the survival and flourishing of minority groups.

A transactional transformation of self-segregation and separatism would understand these practices neither as attempts to completely isolate one's group from others, nor as efforts to create a space in which one's traditions and cultural activities remain unchanged. Understood transactionally, self-segregation and separatism instead would be practices that attempt to make greater room for the voices of dominated and oppressed groups in their transaction with dominant culture. The point of a transactional separatism would be not to completely eliminate transaction with others, but rather to make a change in how transactions with others take place. More specifically, this change in particular transactions would attempt to eliminate a situation in which the dominant group's desires are always or primarily that to which an oppressed group has to respond. If a dominant group will not voluntarily make room for oppressed groups' needs and desires—and dominant groups rarely do—then oppressed groups might need to create a separate space in which they can develop, nurture, and satisfy them. Without such a space, those needs and desires are in danger of being snuffed out in their transaction with more powerful, dominant groups.[39]

The racial integration of high schools that occurred in my hometown in West Texas in the early 1980s offers an example of this point. The two largest and wealthiest high schools were virtually all white, and the third, poorer and smaller, high school was predominantly black and Latino/a. To integrate the three schools, the black/Latino high school was abolished, and its student body was split up and bussed to the other two schools. Racial integration was achieved by making the black and Latino/a students, who had been in the majority at their original school, small minorities of non-white students at their new schools.

Here is a case that calls for transactional separatism, which would value the separate space of the third high school even though it was the product of racist housing patterns and the unfair school funding practices based on them. My point is not to praise the inequalities of the three schools but to highlight how one of the (unintended) results of segregating black and Latino/a students in their own high school was the creation of a safe space in which white domination could be challenged, or at least avoided for a while. Even though tensions and divisions between black and Latino students existed, the third high school enabled each group to form a place of belonging and togetherness that was destroyed when they were dispersed to other schools.[40] The black and Latino/a students and their families rightly were upset about the forced move to white schools. They were given little, if any, say in how integration of the schools was to take place. The needs and desires of white lawyers and administrators who had decided that integration should take place in the town dominated the situation, disregarding what the black and Latino/a families wanted, which was to leave their high school intact. (It probably goes without saying that the reason desegregation was delayed in my hometown until the early 1980s had nothing to do with black and Latino families' desires to preserve the non-white space of the third high school.)

Many white students and their families were also displeased with the decision to integrate, and they too did not have much say in how it would occur. But a significant difference between their situation and that of black and Latino/a families was that even when integrated, the two white high schools remained predominantly white. (Another important difference is that the group of city officials and school board administrators who decided how integration should occur was predominantly white.) White space was not destroyed by integration in the way that non-white space was. While I do not know the conscious intentions of the city leaders, the effect of their decision was to dismantle a concentrated space of non-whiteness and disempower the non-white people who occupied it. Sprinkling black and Latino/a students into white schools diluted them into innocuous bits of diversity that could be held up as "proof" that the town was non-racist and progressive. Enacted in this way, the integration of the town's schools harmed black and Latino/a students by using them for the sake of white interests—and all of this in the name of antiracist progress.

In contrast, a separatism that made room for black and Latino/a interests and voices would have done far more to combat white privilege and domination.

Separatism does not solve all problems; it presents dangers that could work against its ability to nurture marginalized and oppressed groups. Take, for example, the dangers of identity politics that separatism can involve: how are black or Latino/a people to separate from white people when racial categories are porous and fluid? Who has to—or gets to—do the work of policing identities that separatism seems to require? Another possible danger is that separatism could have the effect of only increasing mainstream culture's perception of oppressed groups as exotic others.[41] These problems are very real and cannot be completely eliminated. But they can be addressed. Each situation has its specific context and history that must be attended to when determining inclusion in and exclusion from any particular group, and the answer to the question of who is included and excluded should be considered fallible and in need of per-petual revision. Likewise, the effects of particular instances of separatism on the exoticization of minority groups must also be examined and re-examined to determine if separatist practices have undercut the flourish-ing of oppressed groups. These brief responses to questions about separa-tism do not fully address them; more could be and needs to be said. But objections to separatism do not necessarily or completely invalidate it as a possibly fruitful strategy for oppressed groups. Questions about when, where, and why limitations on transaction might be valuable are impor-tant to ask. Taking separatist practices seriously helps bring those ques-tions to the fore.

W. E. B. Du Bois perhaps saw this more clearly than anyone. In the latter half of his life, he argued for the need for black Americans' self-segregation to establish black churches, banks, schools, stores, and other institutions. A separate black community was required, in Du Bois's view, to build up black America's economic independence, which in turn was necessary in order to survive the long period of time that a psychological shift in white America's unconscious racist attitudes toward black people would take. Du Bois thought that without such self-segregation, black Americans would have difficulty surviving. While Lissak emphasizes cul-tural rather than economic independence for new immigrant groups, her point is similar: immigrant cultures often need a separate space of their own to ensure their ongoing existence. I agree with Du Bois and Lissak against Addams on this issue. White middle-class attempts to show re-spect for non-white people by means of reciprocal relationships with them can have the opposite effect of eroding non-white culture and identity.[42] Sometimes, in other words, the most respectful thing for white people to do is to leave non-white people alone.

The key to this claim is "sometimes." At other times, white people's distancing themselves from the interests and lives of non-white people can function as a racist dismissiveness of them. Instead of dismantling white privilege, a distancing way of living one's spatiality can serve to shore it up. But how can a white person tell the difference between those different times? How can she be sure that the distance established between her and another person is not "the distance of unconcern"?[43]

Part of the answer to these questions is that she cannot, at least not with any certainty or assurance of guarantee. As Lisa Heldke argues with respect to a bisexual person's disclosure of her sexuality, being honest and well-intentioned does not necessarily solve all political problems. In some contexts, to "pass" as a lesbian is more disruptive than to clarify that one is bisexual because in some heterosexist situations, to insist that one is bisexual rather than lesbian is to insist that one is "only half bad." In other contexts, in which a simplistic and rigid opposition between homosexuality and heterosexuality has been established, the strategy that tends to best disrupt the oppressiveness of monosexuality is for a bisexual to expose that her desire runs in more than one direction. For these reasons, the answer to the question of whether sexual honesty is important in relationships is both yes and no. Or, rather, the question cannot be answered in an abstract, universal way. The particular context of the question and the likely effects of one's answer in that situation must always be attended to.[44]

Likewise, the answer to the question of whether white people should engage more intimately and fully with the worlds of non-white people is both yes and no. It depends on the specific situation, and for white people to be well-intentioned in their engagement does not guarantee that their presence in non-white worlds will serve antiracist ends.[45] Anglo women who desire to work in respectful, reciprocal relationships with Latina women on feminist projects, for example, have to learn how to enter Latino/a space in nonintrusive ways.[46] Merely being earnest about "wanting to make things better" is not enough, for behind this wish can lurk an unconscious desire for self-aggrandizement. An Anglo woman can enter the world of a Latina woman in order to use the information she gains to profit herself, including the psychological profit that comes from feeling that one is a good person engaged in projects of self-growth. While self-growth, particularly on issues of racism, is a laudatory goal in some respects, in the context of entering Latino/a space solely for that end, that goal becomes a self-centered way to use Latino/a worlds for white pleasure and gain without any regard for the effects of one's intrusion on those worlds. In cases such as these, white women probably should stay in their own world because that is the way for them to do the least damage to women of color. Only if white women are willing to experience the psychological difficulty of being decentered in and criticized by the new world in which they enter—something very different from a feel-good project of self-growth—should they consider engaging in world-traveling. Their relocation to other worlds will always entail the need to be accountable for that movement.[47]

In addition to the difficulties that await white people who engage the worlds of non-white people in non-racist ways lie the problems that emerge from the exercise of white people's authority and power when deciding when and how to so. Take the example of an all-white group of women who met to try to honestly learn about race and confront their racism.[48] One manifestation of their white privilege was precisely their ability to decide when they wish to interact with non-white people. The women in this case decided to convene an all-white group so that they would not burden non-white women with the task of teaching them about race. The group recognized that it needed some "remedial" classes on race and that they should take responsibility for coming up to speed on racism. They were astonished, therefore, when a black woman was angry with them about their meetings. They could only see that they were earnestly trying to deal with problems with racism and failed to see that their decision to compose an all-white group was part of the very problem that they should be addressing. The precise problem, to be clear, was not that the group was entirely white. The black woman was angry because the white women were oblivious to the way that their white privilege continued to operate through the agency and power of their choices. For a group of white women to decide to convene a mixed race session on race would be to enact the very same problem, that problem being white people's taking it upon themselves to decide when they want to engage with non-white people and when they do not.

Another instance of the problem of white authority and control over world-traveling can be found in the issue of transracial adoption.[49] Most transracial adoptions in the United States take the form of white people adopting non-white babies, not the other way around. On one level, these adoptions do not appear problematic: a white person or couple wants to have a child and is able to give a home to a non-white baby whose biological mother cannot care for it. But on another level, such adoptions are problematic because they tend to contribute to a centuries-old pattern in the United States of white people moving into non-white worlds to take from them what they want. A racist culture creates conditions in which black and other women of color sometimes cannot care for their own children, which makes possible a transfer of those children to the most privileged sectors of American society that generally does nothing to change the conditions that enabled it.

The issue here is not whether white parents do a good job of raising non-white children. Important questions can and should be raised about whether white parents can teach non-white children the skills they need to survive in a racist world, but for the sake of the argument here, I accept the results of research on transracial adoption of black children that show that it is not harmful to black children.[50] Nor is the issue one of white parents' conscious intentions when adopting. I trust that few, if any, see their acts of adoption as ones of white control of non-white space through ontological expansion. I also am not categorically opposed to transracial adoption. There are cases in which transracial adoption is better than the alternative, for example, of a child's constant movement from one foster home to another until adulthood is reached. But none of these factors eliminates the broader problem that in transracial adoption, white needs and desires tend to unilaterally regulate a one-directional flow of valuable "goods" from non-white to white worlds. Transracial adoption often is part of a racist pattern of satisfying the demands and pleasures of white people at the expense of those of people of color. The facts that white people tend to experience this "forbidden" pleasure unconsciously and that it usually is accompanied by the consciously experienced, "permitted" pleasures of new parenthood do not mean that the unconscious pleasures are unreal.[51]

Some of the unconscious white pleasures found in having a non-white baby were exposed in a recent episode of the hilarious British sitcom *Absolutely Fabulous*. The television show revolves around two wealthy, middle-aged white women friends, Edina and Patsy, who are incredibly superficial, self-indulgent, pretentious, and nasty to other people. Edina, a public relations agent for the rich and famous, has a grown white daughter, Saffron, who lives with Edina and is pregnant by a man that Edina has never met. Edina and Patsy have been ridiculing Saffron throughout her pregnancy, mocking her figure and pleading for her to abort because they find babies to be disgusting and annoying. When one of Edina's visiting clients asks if Saffron is "pregnant by that big black guy" sitting with Saffron in the kitchen, Edina snaps to attention, ecstatically happy. Patsy pleads, "No Eddie . . ." and Edina whoops, "Black, he's black—Ah! Ah! I'm gonna have a mixed race baby, I'm gonna have a mixed race baby, darling!" With disgust dripping from her voice, Patsy sneers, "It doesn't make any

difference, it's still a *baby*." Edina then gushes, "Oh, oh, it *makes* a difference darling, a mixed raced baby is the finest accessory that anyone in my
position could ever have, sweetheart! Oh my God, it's the must-have of the
season, it's the Chanel of babies!" As Patsy groans, "Eddie, Eddie . . . ,"
Edina drifts into a reverie in which, dread-locked and outfitted in colorful
"street" clothes, she walks around London with a mixed-raced baby in her
arms, looking hip and cool as she greets friends. Snapping out of the
daydream, she dashes downstairs to the kitchen, babbling to Saffron as she
hugs her, "I want the baby! Love baby, love baby, love baby. . . ."

Edina makes conscious and explicit what often operates unconsciously
and is not supposed to exist: the fact that in a liberal society that embraces
multiculturalism and diversity, white people can receive a great deal of
cultural capital from having a mixed race or non-white baby. This is not to
say that white people do not genuinely love their non-white children. It is to
acknowledge the unspoken, hidden pleasures of white people that can
operate in transracial adoption, even (perhaps especially) alongside genuine, consciously felt love. White adoption of non-white babies is not a
simple matter of caring for "unwanted" children. It also is an instance of
white control over when and in what ways white people will engage with
people of color that maintains the primacy of white people's desires, values,
and goals. (It is interesting in this context to note that the cost of adopting a
white baby in the United States is double that of a non-white baby: $20,000
to $10,000, at least in Pennsylvania. While some white families desire or at
least will accept a non-white baby at a heavily discounted rate, adoption
agencies' pricing scales reflect white America's general opinion that white
people are worth more than people of color.)

The control of space by white people also was at issue in my hometown's integration of its high schools. Because integration did not take
place by having white students enter the space of the non-white high
school, it might appear that white ontological expansiveness was not involved in the situation and that non-white space was being respected in it.
But in the decision to abolish the non-white high school instead of one of
the white high schools, white people determined what spaces would be
allowed to exist. The space in which white students felt at home was
protected while the space that was home for non-white students was
destroyed. This protection of white space is the flip side of white ontological expansiveness; they are both part of the same coin of white spatial
control. Whether manifest through travel into non-white space or remaining at "home" in white space, white privilege operates through the man-
agement and control of white and non-white spaces alike.

A better alternative to integration might have been to maintain the segregation of the three high schools and refocus the agenda of the two white high schools so that it explicitly confronted white racism as a problem for people of all races.[52] Segregation need not support white racism, and racial diversity is not a panacea for the United States' racial problems. Segregation in the high schools should not have been maintained against the wishes of students and parents of color. But when segregation cannot be avoided without causing harm to people of color, there exist more options than merely bemoaning the "evils" of segregation. Like other forms of white privilege, segregation can be used to fight the very racism that initially produced it. White high schools—as well as other schools, such as colleges and universities—that honestly confronted the existence of white privilege and domination would do a great deal more to challenge white racism than ones that stubbornly held to the popular view that white privilege and domination can be eliminated by the sheer presence of a few non-white students sprinkled in the midst of white people.

White privilege has a way of reasserting itself in attempts to eliminate it, which means that there are no guarantees that an antiracist version of segregation would not backfire. The relentless operations of white privilege can create a frustrating situation for white people who want to challenge white domination. One white feminist asks, "Does being white make it impossible . . . to be a good person?"[53] The answer to this question is that, while understandable, it is the wrong one to ask. This is because it is a loaded question: it contains a psychological privilege that white people need to give up, which is the privilege of always feeling that they are in the right. White people should not wallow in guilt about their whiteness. Such wallowing tends to be self-indulgent and counterproductive to antiracist projects. But the purpose of critical race theory and other antiracist work is not to protect their fragile psyches, and so white people should not expect such protection if they are to participate in that work. It is difficult for most white people to see themselves as instruments of terror—perhaps especially after September 11, when the word "terrorist" has come to have the limited and racist connotation of "extremist Arab"—and yet that is what the work from Du Bois to bell hooks tells them that they, qua white, are. It probably is not possible for a white person to be wholly good, completely safe from painful accusations of racism, but it is possible for her to confront the reality of her white privilege and try—in attempts that inevitably will be "impure"—to use it for antiracist purposes.

Addams's work has the valuable but unintended effect of demonstrating how the terror of white domination can continue even in the midst of earnest gestures of reciprocity. It manifests the disadvantage of ethics and politics, which occurs when the pursuit of ethical or political improvement is itself a source of great harm.[54] In the case of white privilege, this disadvantage often and perhaps inevitably occurs because of the power of unconscious habit. Recognition of this disadvantage ideally should produce not paralysis and inactivity, but a "hyper- and pessimistic activism" or a "tragic meliorism" that attempts to change the world, knowing that many of those efforts will fail and that new dangers will be created in the place of the old.[55] A devastating feature of many of the efforts to improve the world by eliminating racism is that those efforts can only make it worse. The disadvantages and dangers presented by unconscious habits of white privilege are very powerful and real. Yet struggle against them must continue.

Conclusion

To understand white privilege as unconscious habit is to understand it as the product of a transactional relationship between psyche, body, and world that presents itself as nonexistent. In ongoing dynamic relationship, the psychosomatic organism and environing world help constitute each other. The world provides the psychical and physical food taken in by an organism. Transformed through digestion, that food nourishes (or poisons) both body and psyche and emerges, continuous with but distinct from its initial state, to fertilize (or pollute) the world in turn. In this transactional relationship, the concept of habit captures the process of digestion: what are the particular digestive predispositions of a particular organism? What is the particular style by which a particular organism takes from and contributes back to the world in its psychosomatic engagement with it?

While all habits tend to go unnoticed—at least when they are functioning smoothly—"forbidden" habits, such as those of white privilege, tend to be not just nonconscious, but unconscious. Increasingly socially and politically unacceptable in countries that have outlawed racial discrimination, habits of white privilege often block attempts to recognize them. They function as if nonexistent and actively thwart conscious attempts to pinpoint their presence. This unconscious, invisible mode of operation is what enables white privileged habits to be increasingly effective and pervasive. White privilege functions best when it appears not to be functioning at all, and it likes it that way, so to speak. The flashy obviousness of white supremacy will be its downfall in a "civilized" world that prides itself on its democratic tolerance and inclusiveness. White domination has learned that its future lies in the unobtrusiveness of white privilege, and so it perpetuates itself as inconspicuous and innocuous, a timid yet powerful wallflower that is happy to fade into the backdrop.

When I speak of racism's and white privilege's preferences, I am not so much personifying them as I am denying that intentionality occurs only at the level of individual consciousness. A person can have purposes that she seeks to fulfill but that she is not consciously aware of and even strives to remain unaware of. The same can be true on a larger, trans-individual scale. Entire societies or cultures can have goals that cannot be located in any specific individual or group of individuals. Often these are goals of which a society is consciously aware, but they also can be goals that a society pursues without realizing that it is doing so and without wanting to know exactly what it is pursuing. A white collective unconscious tends to pursue white privileged goals and perpetuate white privileged values, impacting an individual's unconscious habits but not reducible to them.

A white privileged world tends to produce white privileged processes of digestion for all the human organisms that inhabit it. This does not mean that all human have identical habits. Not only are white privileged habits differentially formed in co-constitutive relationships with a complex variety of other habits, but each human being also has a particular life experience and history that feeds her habits in distinctive ways. Society-wide patterns of transaction exist, however, forming around certain experiences and histories that are socially and politically meaningful and sometimes becoming transcultural and/or international when similar experiences and histories are found across nations and even the entire globe. White privilege is one of these global habits, ubiquitous in the northern and western parts of the world and, in part because of hegemony of the north and west, present in the east and south as well.

Personal habits cannot be understood apart from the global, institutional, and other nonpersonal habits with which they are transactionally formed. Yet one can make a functional (versus substantive) distinction between them, selectively attending to one or the other to gain a better understanding of it. A focus on personal habits can help reveal how white privilege gains a grip in individual lives. White privilege does not just exist in the dry realm of economic figures, educational statistics, and medical averages. It also exists in passionate and emotional commitments to it. Put another way, while international, economic, educational, health care, and other inequalities based on race exist, they maintain their existence in large part because of investments in the privileges and pleasures that they afford white people. It is this deeply personal, often unconscious attachment to white privilege that I find particularly fascinating. How does the racism produced by global, economic, educational, and other disparities rely upon and conspire with deeply rooted habits of white privilege that must somehow be targeted if attempts to eliminate institutional racism are to have any long-term success?

It does so by constituting human beings as the very selves that they are. Race and white privilege are ontological. Given that human beings are composed of habits formed in transaction with a white privileged world, their very being has been shaped—albeit always in constitutive relationship with other salient aspects of experience—by race and racism. This is true, although usually in different ways, for non-white as well as white people. In both cases, race and racist habits are not some sort of outer envelope that encloses a racially and racist-ly neutral core. On a transactional understanding, models of essential core versus incidental periphery ultimately break down. White privilege cannot be effectively countered by relegating it to an allegedly inessential part of the self. Its full ontological weight must be reckoned with.

This is also to say that its complicated history must be dealt with, for on a transactional understanding, ontology is always historical, contextual, and (trans-)cultural. This fact is what gives white privilege enduring stamina and malleable plasticity simultaneously. It is what makes white privilege both incredibly difficult to eliminate and potentially capable of elimination. It also is what makes white privilege more or less relevant depending on the particular historical situation and context, but never a mere façade hiding a racially neutral interior.

The ontological roots that white privilege puts down are bodily as well as psychical, or rather, engage a person's physicality and mentality in their co-constitution. White privilege is not just "in the head." It also is "in" the nose that smells, the back, neck, and other muscles that imperceptibly tighten with anxiety, and the eyes that see some but not all physical differences as significant. A person's psychological disposition toward the world can be found throughout her body, in her physical comportment, sensations, reactions, pleasures, and pains, just as her bodily (dis)functionings help constitute her mental tendencies and proclivities. And all of this, including the "properly" bodily aspects of white privilege, can function unconsciously. The body, in fact, often serves as a prime site of nonreflective resistance to the transformation of habits of white privilege. It can actively thwart conscious attempts to dismantle a psychosomatic sense of white superiority.

One of the implications of my claim that white privilege operates as unconscious habit is that white privilege is part of many people's experience and yet they are unaware of and struggle not to know this fact. In that sense, white privilege can be understood as an unconscious experience. This claim might strike readers as either unremarkable or preposterous, or perhaps both at once. On the one hand, it might appear to be the mundane claim that habits of white privilege exist and that many (especially white) people do not know this. And indeed, this is one of the main assertions of this book. But given the current popularity of strategies of colorblindness for countering racism, I do not find it trivial. Ignorance of race is not a viable solution to problems of racism and white privilege, at least not in this day and age. At best, colorblindness tends to be ineffective; at worst, it compounds the problem by allowing white privilege to continue to operate beneath conscious radar. Given white privilege's ability to grow and expand in an atmosphere of ignorance of race, countering that ignorance is important.

Doing so is much more difficult than one might think because of the unconscious operations of white privilege. In many cases, ignorance of white domination is not just an empty gap in knowledge nor the product of a mere epistemological oversight. Ignorance of it often is actively, dynamically, and even deliberately produced—albeit not consciously so—and it stubbornly maintains its existence as an allegedly mere lack through that uncanny type of production. Here the seemingly trivial claim about the existence of white privilege becomes much more momentous. As unconscious habit, white privilege exists as nonexistent, and the lack of knowledge about it helps structure all knowledge about one's self and the world. Human beings' experiences of white privilege profoundly shape who they are, what they do, and what kind of world they live in, and those experiences often do this without one's awareness of them.

It is at this point that my claims about the existence of white privilege might begin to sound preposterous. In addition to the paradox of unknown knowledge, this book testifies to the apparent oxymoron of unconscious experience. How can a person be unaware of her experience if she is the one experiencing it? On customary accounts of experience, unconscious experience seems as contradictory as an unfelt feeling. But just as the concept of unknown knowledge is paradoxical only if one limits knowledge to the realm of conscious reflection, the concept of unconscious experience is oxymoronic only if one limits experience to the realm of subjective, felt awareness. This limitation is refused by pragmatist philosophy, which radically rethinks experience, like habit, as transactional. This rethinking transforms experience from a single-barreled concept that concerns only the "subjective" feelings, ideas, or other "internal" states of organic life to a double-barreled concept that also includes the so-called external world that is the object of those states. As double-barreled, experience includes much more than conscious, felt awareness. Consciousness has fringes that both distinguish it from and connect it to something different from itself, and that "something different" is as much a part of lived experience as is conscious reflection.

A person's conscious, felt awareness of white privilege (or lack thereof) is not the totality of her experience of it, and the "something different" from conscious experience is not necessarily nonconscious. Often experience actively thwarts attempts to bring it to conscious awareness, which is why it is properly called unconscious. Much of contemporary experience of white privilege is unconscious in this sense. It is not the case that a person's white privilege just happens to go unnoticed but could easily become the object of conscious attention if only her focus was redirected. Formidable obstacles often exist to recognizing the existence of white privilege, and these obstacles, as well as the "nonexistence" of white privilege, are part of the experience of it.

In the United States and other countries that have outlawed racial discrimination, the obstacles to recognizing the sheer existence of white domination are increasing. The end of de jure racism did not mean the end of racism as such. White domination morphed into de facto racism against non-white people, and this transformation corresponded with a shift from relatively conscious to relatively unconscious forms of racial oppression, which I have distinguished respectively as white supremacy and white privilege. This is not to deny that a great deal of racism continues to operate on a conscious level. The ongoing activities of race-based hate groups, whose numbers in the United States increased markedly after the September 11 attacks, make it impossible to think that all racism is unconscious.[1] Nor it is to claim that unconscious racism did not exist in the days of slavery and Jim Crow. But the mixture of white supremacy and white privilege existing in the United States is more heavily weighted with unconscious racism today than it was two hundred, one hundred, or even forty years ago, and this overall trend of increasing white privilege and decreasing white supremacy is likely to continue.

This shift helps explain the current popularity of strategies of color-blindness for fighting racism. Even though colorblindness usually is intended as a strategy for the elimination of racism and white domination, it actually tends to fuel and be fueled by white privileged habits. Colorblindness attempts to erase all race and make it invisible: "I don't see race, I just see people." Habits of white privilege support these attempts by making the invisibility of race seem like the goal that all people should aim for. Whiteness and its concomitant privileges tend to operate as invisible, and since whiteness is the standard to which all should aspire, then people of color too should aspire to give up their race and become race-free (= white). The colorblindness that results in turn fuels habits of white privilege by creating a social, political, and psychological atmosphere of racial invisibility in which white privilege can thrive. It is as if, with their style of hidden invisibility, habits of white privilege provide ready-made grooves for colorblindness to slide into, and those grooves in turn are deepened as colorblindness grows.

Colorblindness also fuels white privilege by strengthening its obsessional desire to be rid of everything that would contaminate white purity. As an alleged contaminant, non-white people are a threat to whiteness that should be eliminated, and colorblindness provides a socially acceptable method of doing so. As an antiracist strategy, colorblindness does not eliminate non-white people in the sense of literally attempting to kill them. But in its claim to not see race, colorblindness metaphorically kills non-white people because its refusal to recognize them as black, Latino/a, Asian, or other people of color is a refusal to recognize them as the specific people they are. The non-white person must become a mere person, while the white person's ontology—and all the privileges it confers—goes unchallenged because whiteness is not considered a visible race in the first place. The freedom from race offered by colorblindness is a freedom to be secure in a space of pure whiteness. And it is a freedom that can be gained without even mentioning the word "race" at all.

Colorblindness can appeal to white middle-class women in particular by allowing them to simultaneously (appear to) fight white domination and avoid confrontation with others. The desire to please others, keep the peace, and avoid conflict tends to be particularly well engrained in the habits of white, middle-class women. While feminists have noted how these habits affect the way white women take up (or avoid) the struggle against sexist oppression, less attention has been paid to how they affect white women's relationship to racism. Habits of avoiding conflict can lead them to wish to completely avoid topics of race and racism. When those topics are engaged, colorblindness presents itself as the perfect antiracist strategy for feminine keep-the-peace habits. With colorblindness, white middle-class women can have their cake and eat it too: they can struggle against racism without openly struggling with anyone because the contentious topic of race is erased from all possible discussion. Any attempt to (re)introduce it can be parried with the claim that one does not see race at all. Confrontation, anger, disagreement around issues of race—all can be avoided at the same time that one is on record as opposing racism.[2]

The concepts of multiculturalism and diversity can appear to be improvements over that of colorblindness. At least with multiculturalism and diversity, cultural and ethnic differences between people are explicitly acknowledged. But too often the notion of multiculturalism functions as an acknowledgment of some differences that simultaneously conceals others. It tends to be used to recognize only the relatively easy differences of style of dress, cultural customs, and types of food, remaining silent about the difficult differences of access to power, economic opportunities, and ontological status. In many settings such as mainstream colleges and universities, words such as "racism," "oppression," and "inequality" rarely are used in discussions of multiculturalism, which often take on an apolitical tone of celebration that assumes all ethnic or cultural groups are situated on a level playing field. Multicultural events held on college campuses or hosted by city councils tend to rotate from one ethnic group to another, focusing on their distinctive foods, rituals, and traditions but in such a way that they seem strangely interchangeable. A Native American pow-wow one week, Cinco de Mayo the next, followed by an Indian curry feast or German Oktoberfest—over the course of a semester or year, a (sometimes literal) smorgasbord of different cultures might be presented for college students and local citizens to sample. Each ethnic or cultural tradition can be consumed without confronting the painful, non-celebratory subject of the past and present oppressive relationships between different groups and, above all, between white and non-white people.[3]

The elimination through the apolitical aestheticization of issues of racial justice even has occurred in Supreme Court cases that have upheld affirmative action, a program that was designed to address racial (and other) inequalities. In the 2003 Michigan affirmative action case, *Grutter v. Bollinger,* the majority argued in support of the use of affirmative action in law schools not because doing so would help further racial justice, but because of the educational benefits of diversity to law school students, a population that is overwhelmingly white. Somewhat ironically, it was Justice Clarence Thomas, arguing for the minority, who pointed out that the majority's position merely appealed to the "faddish slogan of the cognoscenti." Thomas argued that law schools were using racial discrimination to achieve a certain "diverse" look that currently is fashionable, rather than to help the truly underprivileged, whatever their race, who are too

CONCLUSION

poor or uneducated to participate in elite institutions of higher education. While Thomas drew from these arguments an unfortunate conclusion about the uselessness of affirmative action, he is right that the majority's reduction of issues of justice to ones of aesthetic interest is extremely problematic. In the name of eliminating white privilege through the continuation of affirmative action, the majority's reasons for its decision further entrenched that privilege by reducing race to a cosmetic enhancement of the lives of white people. Even though the Court upheld the use of affirmative action, the case arguably did more harm than good to struggles for racial justice.[4]

The Michigan affirmative action case helps solve the puzzle of how the rhetoric of multiculturalism and diversity manages to complement that of colorblindness. On one level, the two strategies for ending racism are entirely incompatible. Multiculturalism and diversity explicitly recognize differences between people, while colorblindness explicitly prides itself on not seeing difference all. Given this clash, how can multiculturalism, diversity, and colorblindness operate together as the predominant modes of (supposed) antiracist activity in contemporary U.S. society? How do they so happily coexist? One answer is found in the recognition of a kind of racial fetishism at work in their coexistence. If the logic of fetishism involves simultaneously seeing and not seeing something, then contemporary proponents of multiculturalism, diversity, and colorblindness can be said to fetishize race, seeing it when they desire to celebrate it and not seeing it when the political stakes are much higher than those involved in mere celebration.[5] Yet one still needs to ask how the logic of fetishism gains a foothold in the specific terrain of race. The more complete answer is that multiculturalism, diversity, and colorblindness are not as different as they initially seem. Both multiculturalism and diversity, on the one hand, and colorblindness, on the other, tend to be blind to issues of racial justice. The rhetoric of multiculturalism and diversity generally acknowledges only apolitical, non-contentious differences between people, avoiding the more emotionally charged term "race" and using the more placid "ethnicity" instead. Like colorblindness, the rhetoric and strategy of multicultural diversity eschews difficult discussions of institutional racism, of economic, material, and educational inequalities across racial divides, of restitution and reparation for past injustices committed against people of color, and so on. Multicultural diversity and colorblindness work hand in hand to both see and not see racial differences, a contradictory vision that has the ultimate effect of blinding people to issues of racial (in)justice.

Diversity is not a cure-all for white privilege, and celebrations of multiculturalism do not necessarily eliminate racism.[6] They can enable the ontological expansiveness of white people into non-white worlds—and all in the name of antiracist intentions and practices, which makes them potentially powerful cover-ups for white domination. This does not mean that programs such as the Multicultural Resource Center, located at my university, do not perform valuable work as they "promote and reflect the ethnic richness and diversity of its students within the University community and . . . advocate for their needs." Programs at predominantly white universities that offer counseling and other educational support services to non-white students are greatly needed. Yet I am concerned in this case that the terms "multiculturalism" and "diversity" continue the white privileged practice of assuming that only non-white people have a race, ethnicity, or culture. The center's services are not designed for the "ethnic richness and diversity" of all the university's students. They explicitly target "African/Black American, Latino/Hispanic American, Asian & Pacific American, and American Indian/Alaskan Native undergraduate students."[7] My claim is not that the center should focus instead on the needs of white students—there are plenty of other organizations that implicitly and even explicitly do that—but that using "multiculturalism" and "diversity" as code words for non-white people continues the racist practice of assuming that white people are the neutral, homogeneous standard against which all other, "diverse," peoples should be measured.

My initial reaction was that the center should be named something like "The Center for Helping Students of Color Deal with Racism," ungainly though the name is. But I cannot imagine that such a bald admission of problems of racism at my university would be allowed by its administration. As is the case at many mainstream (read: white-dominated) colleges and universities, people at my university struggling against racism in higher education generally have had to fight tooth and nail for every hire made, every new program established, and every other success achieved. While my concerns about the rhetoric of multicultural diversity remain, given the resistant atmosphere to antiracist change, I acknowledge that the choice of the name "Multicultural Resource Center" could be a wise strategy rather than a wimpy sellout. At the same time that it covers over the fact that the center's purpose is to help non-white students deal with racism as they navigate a white-centered university, it does achieve that purpose. Better put: precisely because it covers over its purpose, it is better able to achieve it. The reality of the current environment at my university is that a proposal for "The Center for Helping Students of Color Deal with Racism" probably would be rejected because it too directly forces white people to confront problems of racism. It would be seen as too confrontational, not sufficiently tactful. It would, in other words, too greatly clash with middle-class white habits of white privilege. In contrast, the name "Multicultural Resource Center" plays into those habits, using the more acceptable terms of "multiculturalism" and "diversity" to avoid too much overt disruption of them. By doing so, it is able covertly to use those habits against themselves. While the concept embodied in the center's name is flawed, it allows the center to exist and thereby accomplish its antiracist work. This is nothing to belittle as complicit or half-baked. Uses of the concept of multicultural diversity that only or primarily further white privilege must be protested, but uses of it that chip away at white privilege, even if imperfectly, can and often should be endorsed. "Impure" victories over habits of white domination always are preferable to "pure" positions that are easily defeated.

For similar reasons, one might be tempted to view the Michigan affirmative action case as a partial rather than a pyrrhic victory. Huge losses for the side of racial justice were sustained in the defeat of opponents of affirmative action, but the majority's decision does allow law schools to continue to use race as a factor in their admissions processes, enabling them to counter somewhat the systematic privileging of white people in the United States. Yet I am concerned that, on balance, the Supreme Court's decision does more to further white privilege than to challenge it. Especially when the majority concluded its opinion with the invitation for future litigation against affirmative action, remarking that in twenty-five years the use of racial preferences likely will no longer be needed because the current interest in them will have evaporated, one can see how thoroughly the case supports white interests as the governing factor in racial matters.[8] I am not attempting to take a position of purity with regard to the Court's decision, but I am pointing out that not all "impure" victories over white privilege are equal. Some do more than others to use white privilege against itself, and I am not sure that the Michigan case does enough.

In part, this is because the case involves white people using the language and interests of diversity (albeit not necessarily consciously) to further white privilege, rather than to counter it. The majority's decision can be seen, in other words, as an instance of white ontological expansiveness. The white judges moved into the terrain of affirmative action and racial justice for the purpose of furthering white privileged interests. In contrast, the Multicultural Resource Center can be considered an example of a transactional separatism in which non-white people used white privilege against itself. The Center created a predominantly non-white space in which students of color can nurture and develop their needs and desires rather than be forced to respond to those of a white-dominated university.

[195]

(I say "predominantly" since several of the counselors that work for the center are white.) By temporarily limiting students' transactions with a white privileged world, the center can serve as an obstacle to white ontological expansiveness.

White people also need to find ways to use white privilege against itself. In a white-dominated university, for example, white students, faculty, and administrators need to abandon strategies of colorblindness and openly acknowledge the roles that race, racism, and white interests play in the structure and functioning of the school. This is not necessarily equivalent to affirming the exclusionary character of whiteness. I disagree with scholars who argue that whiteness must be abolished if white domination is to end.[9] The origins of whiteness are rooted in oppression, colonialism, and slavery, but this is not all that whiteness might mean in the future. To eliminate whiteness at this historical moment would be to eliminate the possibility for material, psychological, and ontological reparations to be made to people of color by white people *as white people* making amends for the past to help build a different future. While there are no guarantees, whiteness could be transformed, even "rehabilitated" by this process, a process that is too important to undercut with the elimination of racial categories.[10]

I say all this as a white person who is constituted by white privilege. What does that mean for the normative status of the claims in this book? My account of white privilege, including the judgment that it needs to be challenged and transformed, is neither timeless nor ahistorical. It admittedly and perhaps inevitably (because of my race) is grounded in white privileged values themselves: in the desire to see myself as good and to eradicate any guilt that I feel as a racially privileged person. But it also is grounded experientially in the felt need to eliminate demoralizing pain and suffering that, while not essential or timeless, stretches across different historical moments, geographical locals, and racial groups. Whiteness and white privilege are not monolithic, which means that most white people also have had experiences of hardship and pain. And this is true for virtually all people: we are composed of habits born out of experiences that are a mix of joy and suffering, privilege and disadvantage, ecstasy and agony. Not all people's hardships are equivalent, and some surely suffer more than others. But experience, broadly and pragmatically conceived in all its complexity, can provide a naturalistic grounding for ethical and political judgments against racism and white privilege.

It also can provide a grounding for the development of habits of resistance—for effective resistance is habitual. Antiracist activism is as much ontological as is white privilege, and effective resistance against white privilege means a transformation of the self via one's modes of activity. Yet the ultimate goal of this book is not to leave people with a specific number of activities they can or should do to transform their habits from ones of white privilege to ones of resistance. Most white people, and especially the likely readers of this book, already know or can easily imagine what to do to encourage such transformation. They can, for example, include people of color in their syllabi in substantial ways; give money to groups that support people of color, such as the United Negro College Fund; speak out against incidents of racism when they witness them, in person or via letters to the local newspaper editor; support political candidates who work against white privilege; and so on. Instead of providing a detailed recipe for the "what" of activism—an approach that inevitably would fail because it cannot address the specific situation of every reader—this book addresses the "how" of engaging in practices of resistance. Attempts to transactionally (re)make both the self and world less white-privileged can easily have the effect of only shoring up that privilege. All people, and white people in particular, need to be aware that white privilege often subtly operates in allegedly nonracist or even antiracist practices. Rather than rest assured that she is effectively fighting white privilege, when engaging in resistance a person needs to continually be questioning the effects of her activism on both self and world.

Like all habits, both habits of white privilege and habits of resistance to it are as much about the "external" world as they are about the individual organism. In fact, habit perhaps is best described as existing between or across organism and world, rather than "inside" an individual. Yet in some situations, it can make sense to speak of certain habits as belonging to a particular individual. Thinking of habits of white privilege and resistance as "owned" by a particular person rather than as existing between her and a racist world, for example, uses the appropriative patterns of white privilege to make it more likely that a person will take responsibility for her habits. While a person's habits are not her own in the sense of being totally manufactured "inside" her, independent of "external" input, they are hers in that they make up who she is and in that she can exercise some influence over their constitution and deployment. I hope this book has encouraged such ownership. While unconscious habits of white privilege will continue to thwart attempts to expose and change them, change can occur and habits of resistance can be developed, but only if a person takes responsibility for her unconscious life.

NOTES

INTRODUCTION

1. I will not take up here the question of exactly when the modern concept of race was invented. For a persuasive argument that Kant introduced it, see Robert Bernasconi, "Who Invented the Concept of Race? Kant's Role in the Enlightenment Construction of Race," in *Race* (Malden, Mass.: Blackwell, 2001). Given that Enlightenment conceptions of race explained it as a result of climate and other environmental factors, the origin of the modern concept of race might be dated instead around 1830, when scientific notions of race as inherent in one's nature began to challenge environmentalism (George M. Fredrickson, *The Black Image in the White Mind: The Debate on Afro-American Character and Destiny, 1817–1914* [Hanover, N.H.: Wesleyan University Press, 1971], 1–2).

2. The term "non-white" is problematic, but I do not see a way to avoid the problems it involves, given the need for a term that broadly describes people who are disadvantaged by white privilege. The drawback to "non-white" is that it centers on whiteness and can seem to posit white people as the standard against which all others should be measured. But the most satisfactory alternative, "people of color," implies that white people do not have a race. And so I use "non-white" somewhat unhappily, recognizing that the language I utilize to combat racial privilege is complicit with it.

3. The classic example of this argument is found in the journal *Race Traitor*.

4. Thanks to Vincent Colapietro (personal conversation) for this observation.

5. For more on these issues, see Richard Dyer, *White* (New York: Routledge, 1997), especially pp. 12, 19–20, and 52–53; and Noel Ignatiev, *How the Irish Became White* (New York: Routledge, 1995).

6. For more on "bodying," see Shannon Sullivan, *Living Across and Through Skins: Transactional Bodies, Pragmatism, and Feminism* (Bloomington: Indiana University Press, 2001), especially p. 30.

7. James Allen, ed., *Without Sanctuary: Lynching Photography in America* (Santa Fe, N.M.: Twin Palms Publishers, 2000).

8. Charles Mills describes this phenomenon in terms of an "epistemology of ignorance" in which white people cannot understand the racist world that they live in, benefit from, and helped create. See Mills, *The Racial Contract* (Ithaca, N.Y.: Cornell University Press, 1997), 18, 93.

9. Perhaps other forms of racism, such as black-Asian, black-Latino, and Latino–Native American racism, also are increasingly operating unconsciously,

but my focus in this book is on the specific form of racism that is white domination of non-white people.

10. Patricia Williams, *Seeing a Color-Blind Future: The Paradox of Race* (New York: Farrar, Straus and Giroux, 1997), 61.

11. The following three paragraphs are adapted from pages 195–97 of Shannon Sullivan, "The Unconscious Life of Race: Freudian Resources for Critical Race Theory," in *Rereading Freud: Psychoanalysis through Philosophy,* ed. Jon Mills (Albany: SUNY Press, 2004).

12. Sullivan, *Living Across and Through Skins,* 124–28.

13. I refer here to Maurice Merleau-Ponty's claim that consciousness, which is always bodily on his account, is a matter of "I can" (Merleau-Ponty, *Phenomenology of Perception,* trans. Colin Smith [New York: Routledge, 1962], 137).

14. I take the term "white solipsism" from Adrienne Rich, *On Lies, Secrets, and Silence: Selected Prose, 1966–1978* (New York: Norton, 1979), 306.

15. As Carol Kennedy has pointed out (private correspondence), Asians are conspicuously absent from this book. In part, this is because I often ground discussion of race in my life experiences, which tend to involve black people, Latinos/as, Native Americans, and (to a lesser degree) the Roma. But I suspect that the absence of Asians and Asian Americans from my perceived experience is itself a sign of unconscious habits of white privilege, and as such it deserves much more attention than I give it here.

1. IGNORANCE AND HABIT

1. Joseph L. Graves, Jr., *The Emperor's New Clothes: Biological Theories of Race at the Millennium* (New Brunswick, N.J.: Rutgers University Press, 2001). See also Anthony Kwame Appiah, "The Conservation of 'Race,' " *Black American Literature Forum* 23(1) (1989): 37–60; Naomi Zack, *Race and Mixed Race* (Philadelphia: Temple University Press, 1993) and *Philosophy of Science and Race* (New York: Routledge, 2002).

2. What is also misleading is the claim that the concept of race has been completely scientifically discredited. The concept of race was not necessarily eliminated when it was replaced by that of population in biomedical research, and debate continues over whether there is scientific validity in racial and ethnic self-characterizations. For a sample of these debates, see Lisa Gannett, "Racism and Human Genome Diversity Research: The Ethical Limits of 'Population Thinking,' " *Philosophy of Science* 68 (2001): S479–S492; Sandra Soo-Jin Lee, Joanna Mountain, and Barbara A. Koenig, "The Meanings of 'Race' in the New Genomics: Implications for Health Disparities Research," *Yale Journal of Health Policy, Law, and Ethics* 1(1) (2001): 33–75; and Neil Risch, Esteban Burchard, Elad Ziv, and Hua Tang, "Categorization of Humans in Biomedical Research: Genes, Race, and Disease," *Genome Biology* 3(7) (2002): 1–12. Thanks to Malia Fullerton for her seminar on "The Dilemma of Difference: 'Race' as a Research Variable in Biomedical Research," which provided these references. See also Stephanie Malia

Fullerton, "On the Absence of Biology in Philosophical Considerations of Race," in *Race and Epistemologies of Ignorance,* ed. Shannon Sullivan and Nancy Tuana (Albany: SUNY Press, forthcoming).

3. The following six paragraphs are adapted from pages 206–13 of Shannon Sullivan, "Remembering the Gift: Du Bois on the Unconscious and Economic Operations of Racism," *Transactions of the C. S. Peirce Society* 39(2) (Spring 2003): 205–25.

4. W. E. B. Du Bois, *Dusk of Dawn: An Essay toward an Autobiography of a Race Concept* (New York: Schocken Books, 1984), 64.

5. Bobby M. Wilson, "Critically Understanding Race-Connected Practices: A Reading of W. E. B. Du Bois and Richard Wright," *Professional Geographer* 54(1) (2002): 32.

6. W. E. B. Du Bois, *Darkwater: Voices from Within the Veil* (New York: Harcourt, Brace, and Company, 1999), 17.

7. Du Bois, *Darkwater,* 47.

8. Marilyn Frye, *The Politics of Reality: Essays in Feminist Theory* (Freedom, Calif.: Crossing Press, 1983), 118–19.

9. Du Bois, *Dusk of Dawn,* 283. The change in Du Bois's opinion about white people also helps explain his departure from the NAACP in the late 1930s.

10. Bernard Boxill has claimed that Du Bois was "imbued with the scientific spirit" such that he underplayed "the irrational element in race prejudice" (Boxill, "Du Bois and Fanon on Culture," *Philosophical Forum* 9[1] [1978]: 326, 335). But Boxill misses the shift in Du Bois's work and so misunderstands Du Bois's early approach to racial prejudice as the only one of his career.

11. W. E. B. Du Bois, *The Autobiography of W. E. B. Du Bois: A Solioquy on Viewing My Life from the Last Decade of Its First Century* (New York: International Publishers, 1968), 228.

12. Du Bois, *Dusk of Dawn,* 296.

13. William James, *The Principles of Psychology,* 2 vols. (New York: Dover Publications, 1955).

14. I wonder if James's conservative portrayal of habit might explain why Du Bois initially omitted it in his work, but there is nothing in Du Bois's corpus that sheds light on this speculation.

15. Du Bois, *Darkwater,* 41.

16. Du Bois, *Darkwater,* 41. The tension between these optimistic statements and the more pessimistic ones about white people above—all from *Darkwater*—is a result of Du Bois's gradual shift from a naive liberal to a Freudian position on racism, which in 1920 had begun but was not yet fully made.

17. For more on the connections between Du Bois and James, see James Campbell, "Du Bois and James," *Transactions of the C. S. Peirce Society* 28(3) (1992): 569–81.

18. Du Bois, *Dusk of Dawn,* 194.

19. Du Bois, *Dusk of Dawn,* 171.

20. John Dewey, *Human Nature and Conduct,* vol. 14 of *The Middle Works, 1899–1924,* ed. Jo Ann Boydston (Carbondale: Southern Illinois University Press, 1988), 21.

21. John Dewey, *Experience and Nature,* vol. 1 of *The Later Works: 1925–1953,* ed. Jo Ann Boydston (Carbondale: Southern Illinois University Press, 1988), 64–65.

22. For more on habit, especially gendered bodily habits, see Shannon Sullivan, *Living Across and Through Skins* (Bloomington: Indiana University Press, 2001).

23. The following four paragraphs are adapted from pages 113–15 of Shannon Sullivan, "(Re)construction Zone: Beware of Falling Statues," in *In Dewey's Wake: Unfinished Work of Pragmatic Reconstruction,* ed. William Gavin (Albany: SUNY Press, 2003), 109–27.

24. Alexis de Tocqueville, *Democracy in America,* vol. 1 (New York: Vintage Books, 1990) 379.

25. Tocqueville, *Democracy in America,* 394.

26. bell hooks also comments on the importance to black safety during slavery of "cultivating the habit of casting the gaze downward to as not to appear uppity" (hooks, "Representations of Whiteness in the Black Imagination," in *Black on White: Black Writers on What It Means to Be White,* ed. David R. Roediger [New York: Schocken Books, 1998], 168).

27. Tocqueville, *Democracy in America,* 394.

28. Tocqueville, *Democracy in America,* 375.

29. Tocqueville, *Democracy in America,* 360.

30. Tocqueville, *Democracy in America,* 360.

31. Tocqueville, *Democracy in America,* 375.

32. Tocqueville, *Democracy in America,* 367. Tocqueville makes the more limited observation about the transfer of slaves from North to South when the North abolished slavery.

33. The following five paragraphs are adapted from pages 121–23 of Sullivan, "(Re)construction Zone.

34. Meyer Weinberg, *A Chance to Learn: The History of Race and Education in the United States* (New York: Cambridge University Press, 1977), 149.

35. The following example of turn-taking comes from chapter two of Thomas Kochman, *Black and White Styles in Conflict* (Chicago: University of Chicago Press, 1981). In chapter 10 of her *Black Feminist Thought: Knowledge, Consciousness, and the Politics of Empowerment* (Boston: Unwin Hyman, 1990), Patricia Hill Collins also uses Kochman's work on black styles of dialogue to build an "afrocentric feminist epistemology." On a similar point, see also Amanda E. Lewis, *Race in the Schoolyard: Negotiating the Color Line in Classrooms and Communities* (New Brunswick, N.J.: Rutgers University Press, 2003) 69; and bell hooks, *Teaching to Transgress: Education as the Practice of Freedom* (New York: Routledge, 1994), 187. Thanks to Lisa Heldke for reminding me about the relevance of hooks's work to these issues.

36. Patricia Williams discusses additional examples of the subtle but harmful

ways that law school can be a racist, as well as a sexist, space in chapter five of *The Alchemy of Race and Rights: Diary of a Law Professor* (Cambridge, Mass.: Harvard University Press, 1991).

37. hooks, *Teaching to Transgress*, 187.

38. For more on racism in contemporary education, see Jonathan Kozol, *Savage Inequalities: Children in America's Schools* (New York: Crown Publishers, 1991).

39. Jason D. Hill, *Becoming a Cosmopolitan: What It Means to Be a Human Being in the New Millennium* (Lanham, Md.: Rowman and Littlefield, 2000), 14–15. For additional work on pragmatism and race, see Bill E. Lawson and Donald F. Koch, eds., *Pragmatism and the Problem of Race* (Bloomington: Indiana University Press, 2004).

40. Hill, *Becoming a Cosmopolitan*, 14.

41. Hill, *Becoming a Cosmopolitan*, 14–15.

42. Hill, *Becoming a Cosmopolitan*, 15.

43. Hill, *Becoming a Cosmopolitan*, 45.

44. Hill, *Becoming a Cosmopolitan*, 4.

45. Hill, *Becoming a Cosmopolitan*, 16–17.

46. Hill, *Becoming a Cosmopolitan*, 17.

47. Hill, *Becoming a Cosmopolitan*, 2.

48. Hill, *Becoming a Cosmopolitan*, 3.

49. Dewey, *Experience and Nature*, 214.

50. Hill, *Becoming a Cosmopolitan*, 21.

51. This paragraph is adapted from page 89 of Shannon Sullivan, "The Racialization of Space: Toward a Phenomenological Account of Raced and Anti-Racist Spatiality," in *The Problems of Resistance: Studies in Alternate Political Cultures,* ed. Steve Martinot (Atlantic Highlands, N.J.: Prometheus/Humanity Books, 2001).

52. Linda Martín Alcoff, "Towards a Phenomenology of Racial Embodiment," *Radical Philosophy* 95 (May/June 1999): 19, emphasis in original.

53. This experience can happen to white people too. See Robert Bernasconi, "Waking Up White and in Memphis," in *White on White/Black on Black,* ed. George Yancy (Lanham, Md.: Rowman and Littlefield, 2005).

54. I am influenced by Lucius Outlaw's argument that the baby of race need not and should not be thrown out with the bathwater of racism; see Outlaw, *On Race and Philosophy* (New York: Routledge, 1996). Additionally, racial categories have sometimes been created and used by non-white people, such as Native Americans, as terms of pride. In instances such as this, the elimination of the category of race might do more harm than good. See Nancy Shoemaker, "How Indians Got to Be Red," *American Historical Review* 102 (1997): 625–44.

55. Dewey, *Human Nature and Conduct*, 29.

56. John Dewey, "Racial Prejudice and Friction," in vol. 13 of *The Middle Works, 1899–1924,* ed. Jo Ann Boydston (Carbondale: Southern Illinois University Press, 1988), 242–54.

57. The following six paragraphs are adapted from pages 139–42 of Shannon Sullivan, "Racialized Habits: Dewey on Race and the Roma," in *Pragmatism and Values: The Central European Pragmatist Forum, Volume One*, ed. John Ryder and Emil Višòovský (Amsterdam: Rodopi Press, 2004).

58. Dewey, "Racial Prejudice and Friction," 243.

59. Dewey, "Racial Prejudice and Friction," 243.

60. Dewey, "Racial Prejudice and Friction," 243.

61. Dewey, "Racial Prejudice and Friction," 244.

62. Gregory Pappas, "Dewey's Philosophical Approach to Racial Prejudice," *Social Theory and Practice* 22(1) (1996): 53.

63. Dewey, "Racial Prejudice and Friction," 246.

64. Dewey, "Racial Prejudice and Friction," 245.

65. Dewey, "Racial Prejudice and Friction," 253.

66. Dewey, "Racial Prejudice and Friction," 253.

67. Dewey, "Racial Prejudice and Friction," 253.

68. My reading of Dewey's "Racial Prejudice and Friction" contrasts with that of Pappas in his "Dewey's Philosophical Approach to Racial Prejudice," which credits Dewey with successfully resisting a reductivist account of racial prejudice.

69. John Dewey, "Address to the National Association for the Advancement of Colored People," in vol. 6 of *The Later Works: 1925–1953*, ed. Jo Ann Boydston (Carbondale: Southern Illinois University Press, 1989), 229.

70. Dewey, "Address," 226.

71. Dewey, "Address," 225.

72. Dewey, "Address," 226.

73. Dewey, "Racial Prejudice and Friction," 251.

74. James, *Principles of Psychology*, vol. 1, 121.

75. See James, *Principles of Psychology*, vol. 1, 121–22. Perhaps this helps explain why the early Du Bois overlooked or ignored James's concept of habit.

76. Dewey, *Experience and Nature*, 64–65.

77. Dewey, *Experience and Nature*, 214.

78. Vincent Colapietro, "Further Consequences of a Singular Capacity," in *Peirce, Semiotics, and Psychoanalysis*, ed. John Muller and Joseph Brent (Baltimore, Md.: John Hopkins University Press, 2000), 139.

79. Luce Irigaray, *This Sex Which Is Not One*, trans. Catherine Porter with Carolyn Burke (Ithaca, N.Y.: Cornell University Press, 1985), 75.

80. Another meaningful inconsistency in Dewey's remarks on racial prejudice is his very intellectualist-sounding claim that "mental preparation" must be secured before increased interaction between different racial groups can be a source of improvement of racial friction. Until that preparation is secured, immigration into the United States must be restricted ("Racial Prejudice and Friction," 252). These comments are odd given the analysis Dewey elsewhere provides of the need for increased friction to produce social change by breaking up sedimented habits (see Dewey, *Human Nature and Conduct*, 90).

81. Dewey, "Racial Prejudice and Friction," 243.

82. Luce Irigaray, *An Ethics of Sexual Difference,* trans. Carolyn Burke and Gillian C. Gill (Ithaca, N.Y.: Cornell University Press, 1993), 73–81.

83. Dewey, "Racial Prejudice and Friction," 246.

84. For an account of the ways that Dewey recognizes wonder in other areas of his work, see Beatrice H. Zedler, "Wonder in John Dewey," *Modern Schoolman* 54(1) (1976): 1–14.

85. Native traditions of hospitality toward strangers would also seem to reveal other options. Interestingly, Dewey specifically dismisses them, claiming that their rites of hospitality spring from dread of, not regard for, the other (Dewey, "Racial Prejudice and Friction," 244).

86. Thanks to Phillip McReynolds for bringing up this point.

87. I take the concept of world-traveling from María C. Lugones, "Playfulness, 'World'-Traveling, and Loving Perception," *Hypatia* 2(2) (1987): 3–19.

88. hooks, "Representations of Whiteness," 50. See also George Yancy's account of "white terrorism" in his introduction to *White on White/Black on Black,* ed. George Yancy (Lanham, Md.: Rowman and Littlefield, 2005). As Yancy explains, "[t]he experience of terrorism is not new to Black people living in racist white America" (3).

89. Du Bois, *Darkwater,* 17.

90. Dewey, "Racial Prejudice and Friction," 246.

91. Another notable problem with Dewey's "solution" to racial friction, associated with his perception of racial difference as threatening, involves increasing standards of living in particular foreign countries so that the lowering of their birth rates will reduce "the menace of [their] numbers" ("Racial Prejudice and Friction," 251).

92. Vincent Colapietro and Teresa de Lauretis underscore this point in their fruitful exchange on Peircean habit. See Colapietro, "Further Consequences of a Singular Capacity," and Teresa de Lauretis, "Gender, Body, and Habit Change," in *Peirce, Semiotics, and Psychoanalysis,* ed. John Muller and Joseph Brent (Baltimore, Md.: John Hopkins University Press, 2000). Dewey frequently discusses imagination but neglects its unconscious dimensions: "the conscious adjustment of the new and the old *is* imagination" (Dewey, *Art as Experience,* vol. 10 of *The Later Works: 1925–1953,* ed. Jo Ann Boydston [Carbondale: Southern Illinois University Press, 1989], 276; emphasis in original).

93. Charlene Haddock Seigfried, "John Dewey's Pragmatist Feminism," in *Feminist Interpretations of John Dewey,* ed. Charlene Haddock Seigfried (University Park: Pennsylvania State University Press, 2002), 55–56.

94. Elisabeth Young-Bruehl, *The Anatomies of Prejudice* (Cambridge, Mass.: Harvard University Press, 1996), 167, 185, 562 n. 17.

95. Young-Bruehl, *Anatomies of Prejudice,* 77.

96. Young-Bruehl, *Anatomies of Prejudice,* 96.

97. Cynthia Willett, *The Soul of Justice: Social Bonds and Racial Hubris* (Ithaca, N.Y.: Cornell University Press, 2001), 20.

98. Willett, *Soul of Justice,* 20.

NOTES TO PAGES 43–46

99. Gregory Pappas (private conversation) has helped me see the insights into whiteness provided by "Racial Prejudice and Friction" if it is understood as a descriptive account of racism. I disagree with Pappas, however, that the essay can be read in this way.

100. Colapietro, "Further Consequences," 144; de Lauretis, "Gender," 172.

101. Colapietro, "Further Consequences," 146.

102. Cf. Morton Levitt, *Freud and Dewey on the Nature of Man* (Westport, Conn.: Greenwood Press, 1960), 165. Levitt characterizes Dewey in this way in comparison with Freud.

103. Cornel West, *Keeping Faith: Philosophy and Race in America* (New York: Routledge, 1993): "Dewey failed . . . [to define] the relation of democratic ways of thought and life to a profound sense of evil" (108). This also is true of Richard Rorty's appropriation of the Freudian unconscious as "the sensitive, whacky [*sic*], backstage [conversational] partner who feeds us our best lines" (Rorty, "Freud and Moral Reflection" in *Pragmatism's Freud: The Moral Disposition of Psychoanalysis,* ed. Joseph H. Smith and William Kerrigan [Baltimore, Md.: Johns Hopkins University Press, 1986], 7, 9). As Richard H. King points out, "Rorty takes the bite out of Freud's description of the self . . . , trivializ[ing] the unconscious and minimize[ing] intrapsychic conflict" (King, "Self-realization and Solidarity: Rorty and the Judging Self" in *Pragmatism's Freud,* ed. Smith and Kerrigan, 41).

104. Dewey, "Racial Prejudice and Friction," 244.

105. Dewey, *Human Nature and Conduct,* 29.

2. ENGAGING THE ISOLATED UNCONSCIOUS

1. Freud quoted in Max Eastman, *Heroes I Have Known: Twelve Who Lived Great Lives* (New York: Simon and Schuster, 1942), 267. I was alerted to this quote by Morton Levitt's *Freud and Dewey on the Nature of Man* (Westport, Conn.: Greenwood Press, 1960), 167.

2. I recognize that not all psychoanalytic theory is atomistic and that some psychoanalytic philosophy avoids this problematic aspect of Freud's legacy. For important work that extends psychoanalysis to social and political issues, see, for example, Kelly Oliver and Steve Edwin, eds., *Between the Psyche and the Social: Psychoanalytic Social Theory* (Lanham, Md.: Rowman and Littlefield, 2002); and Kelly Oliver, *The Colonization of Psychic Space: A Psychoanalytic Social Theory of Oppression* (Minneapolis: University of Minnesota Press, 2004).

3. Even though William James is the better-known psychologist, I appeal to Dewey here because of his stronger stance against individualism, especially in the case of habit.

4. John Dewey, *Human Nature and Conduct,* vol. 14 of *The Middle Works, 1899–1924,* ed. Jo Ann Boydston (Carbondale: Southern Illinois University Press, 1988), 61.

5. Dewey, *Human Nature and Conduct,* 61–62.

6. Dewey, *Human Nature and Conduct,* 93, 114.

7. Dewey, *Human Nature and Conduct,* 93, 27.

8. For accounts that risk this conclusion, see Jon Mills and Janusz A. Pola-
nowski, *The Ontology of Prejudice* (Amsterdam: Rodopi Press, 1997) and Elisabeth
Young-Bruehl, *The Anatomies of Prejudice* (Cambridge, Mass.: Harvard University
Press, 1996). In contrast, some scholars read Freud's claims as historical and
contextual; see, for example, Juliet Mitchell, *Psychoanalysis and Feminism* (New
York: Pantheon Books, 1974); and Michael S. Roth, *Psycho-Analysis as History:
Negation and Freedom in Freud* (Ithaca, N.Y.: Cornell University Press, 1987),
especially pp. 89–90. While I acknowledge that not all scholars read Freud's work
as making universal or timeless claims, I continue to find that his theory is insuffi-
ciently transactional.

9. This section is adapted from pages 205–11 of Shannon Sullivan, "The
Unconscious Life of Race: Freudian Resources for Critical Race Theory," in *Re-
reading Freud: Psychoanalysis through Philosophy,* ed. Jon Mills (Albany: SUNY
Press, 2004).

10. I will use "ego ideal" and "superego" interchangeably, as does Freud in
both his 1921 *Group Psychology and the Analysis of the Ego* (ed. and trans. James
Strachey [New York: W. W. Norton, 1959]) and 1923 *The Ego and the Id* (ed. and
trans. James Strachey [New York: W. W. Norton, 1960]). Freud later distinguishes
the ego ideal as a function of (and not strictly synonymous with) the superego by
which the ego measures itself in his 1932/33 *New Introductory Lectures on Psycho-
Analysis* (in volume 22 of *The Standard Edition of the Complete Psychological
Works of Sigmund Freud,* ed. and trans. James Strachey [London: Hogarth Press,
1964], 64–65).

11. See also Sigmund Freud, "On Narcissim: An Introduction," in vol. 4 of
Collected Papers, trans. Joan Riviere (London: Hogarth Press, 1950), 31.

12. Freud, *Group Psychology,* 41.

13. Freud, "Thoughts for the Times on War and Death," in vol. 4 of *Collected
Papers,* 295, 316.

14. Freud, *Group Psychology,* 42.

15. Freud, "Thoughts for the Times," 289–90.

16. Freud does not discuss conscious versus unconscious leading ideas in
Group Psychology, but in "The Unconscious" he does make clear that there are
conscious and unconscious ideas, which presumably could include leading ideas.
See Freud, "The Unconscious," in vol. 4 of *Collected Papers,* 109.

17. This is not to say that this is the only way race can be or is relevant to
them. It can be something positive to endorse, but not on a Freudian account.

18. Freud, "The Unconscious," 109–11.

19. Marilyn Frye, *The Politics of Reality: Essays in Feminist Theory* (Freedom,
Calif.: Crossing Press, 1983), 86–87.

20. This difference between white supremacists and white privilegists is reflected in James Weldon Johnson's depiction of Southerners and Northerners,
respectively, in Johnson, *The Autobiography of an Ex-Colored Man* (New York:
Dover Publications, 1995), 80.

21. Young-Bruehl, *The Anatomies of Prejudice,* 240.

22. Freud, *Group Psychology*, 57.

23. Freud, *Group Psychology*, 57.

24. Freud, *The Ego and the Id*, 26, 30, 48, 53, 56, 60. I use "his" advisedly here since in its primary form, the Oedipus complex detailed below involves a male child.

25. Freud, *The Ego and the Id*, 30.

26. Freud, *The Ego and the Id*, 31; see also page 49.

27. Freud, *The Ego and the Id*, 48; Freud, *Group Psychology*, 52–53.

28. Jean Laplanche, *Essays on Otherness* (New York: Routledge, 1999), 147, emphasis in original.

29. Jean Laplanche, *New Foundations for Psychoanalysis*, trans. David Macey (Cambridge, Mass.: Basil Blackwell, 1989), 124.

30. Freud, *The Ego and the Id*, 33.

31. Freud, *Group Psychology*, 3.

32. Freud, *Group Psychology*, 4–5.

33. Philip Rieff, *Freud: The Mind of a Moralist* (Chicago: University of Chicago Press, 1979), 33. Rieff's comment is made in the context of an explicit comparison of Freud and Dewey.

34. Freud, *Civilization and Its Discontents*, ed. and trans. James Strachey (New York: W. W. Norton, 1961), 92–93; and Freud, "Thoughts for the Times," 298. See also Freud, "Three Essays on Sexuality," in vol. 7 of *The Standard Edition of the Complete Psychological Works of Sigmund Freud*, ed. and trans. James Strachey (New York: W. W. Norton, 1960), 105.

35. Freud, "Three Essays on Sexuality," 43–44. One can see from this quote why Dewey found Freud's psychoanalysis so objectionable.

36. Franz Fanon, *Black Skin, White Masks*, trans. Charles Lam Markmann (New York: Grove Press, 1967), 85.

37. Fanon, *Black Skin, White Masks*, 100.

38. "In an individual neurosis we take as our starting point the contrast that distinguishes the patient from his environment, which is assumed to be 'normal' " (Freud, *Civilization and Its Discontents*, 110). As the quotes around the word "normal" suggest, Freud realized that standards for normalcy often vary from community to community and may be questionable, even neurotic or pathological. This does not alter my point that Freud's psychoanalysis (unlike that of Fanon, for example) too easily lends itself to changing the individual at the expense of transforming his or her environments.

39. Fanon, *Black Skin, White Masks*, 213.

40. Gilles Deleuze and Felix Guattari, *Anti-Oedipus: Capitalism and Schizophrenia*, trans. Robert Hurley, Mark Seem, and Helen R. Lane (Minneapolis: University of Minnesota Press, 1983), 278.

41. On the distinction between raciation and racism, see Lucius Outlaw, *On Race and Philosophy* (New York: Routledge, 1996), 8; and Lewis R. Gordon, *Bad Faith and Anti-Black Racism* (Atlantic Highlands, N.J.: Humanities Press, 1995), 92.

NOTES TO PAGES 62-69

42. Vincent Colapietro, "Notes for a Sketch of a Peircean Theory of the Unconscious," *Transactions of the Charles S. Peirce Society* 31(3) (1995): 499, emphasis in original.

3. SEDUCTIVE HABITS OF WHITE PRIVILEGE

1. Jean Laplanche, *New Foundations for Psychoanalysis*, trans. David Macey (Cambridge, Mass.: Basil Blackwell, 1989), 113.

2. Laplanche, *New Foundations for Psychoanalysis*, 89; John Fletcher and Martin Stanton, eds., *Jean Laplanche: Seduction, Translation and the Drives*, trans. Martin Stanton (London: Institute of Contemporary Arts, 1992), 55.

3. Jean Laplanche, *Essays on Otherness* (New York: Routledge, 1999), 73, 183, 108.

4. Fletcher and Stanton, eds., *Jean Laplanche*, 25.

5. *Le Robert de Poche* (Paris: Dictionnaires Le Robert, 1995). The use of "seduction" to mean leading someone aside or astray, used by Laplanche below, is more explicit in the English than the French definition of the word. See *Webster's Encyclopedic Unabridged Dictionary of the English Language* (New York: Portland House, 1989).

6. See also James Baldwin, *The Fire Next Time* (New York: Dell Publishing Co., 1963), 41, where Baldwin explains the importance of a parent's tone of voice to a young black child in conveying fear and transgression of boundaries established by white people.

7. Toni Morrison, *The Bluest Eye* (New York: Pocket Books, 1972), 15, 16.

8. Gilles Deleuze and Felix Guattari, *Anti-Oedipus: Capitalism and Schizophrenia*, trans. Robert Hurley, Mark Seem, and Helen R. Lane (Minneapolis: University of Minnesota Press, 1983); and *A Thousand Plateaus: Capitalism and Schizophrenia*, trans. Brian Massumi (Minneapolis: University of Minnesota Press, 1987).

9. Laplanche, *Essays on Otherness*, 136.

10. Laplanche, *New Foundations for Psychoanalysis*, 142, 137, emphasis in original.

11. Freud, *The Ego and the Id*, ed. and trans. James Strachey (New York: W. W. Norton, 1960), 20.

12. On the role of hearing in race, see Matthew Jordan, "Recorded Jazz and 'La Voix Negre': The Sound of Race in the Age of Mechanical Reproduction," *Nottingham French Studies* 43(1) (2004): 89–99. On the role of vision, see Linda Alcoff, "Towards a Phenomenology of Racial Embodiment," *Radical Philosophy* 95 (1999): 15–23.

13. Laplanche, *New Foundations*, 49.

14. Peter Osborne, *Philosophy in Cultural Theory* (New York: Routledge, 2000), 109, emphasis in original. Osborne adds that "[p]rimal communication is . . . always across *three*, not two, generations" (109).

15. Deleuze and Guattari, *A Thousand Plateaus*, 29.

16. Deleuze and Guattari, *Anti-Oedipus*, 38.

17. Deleuze and Guattari, *Anti-Oedipus*, 97.

18. Fletcher and Stanton, eds., *Jean Laplanche*, 188, emphasis in original.

19. Laplanche, *Essays on Otherness*, 171, 108.

20. Jean Laplanche, *New Foundations for Psychoanalysis*, 124, emphasis in original.

21. Laplanche, *Essays on Otherness*, 127–28.

22. It is important to note that even though it is Laplanche's favorite example of seduction, the breast is not necessarily a privileged site for that process. Laplanche's appeal to the breast is not a covert return to familialism. For Laplanche, "[t]he example of the breast is perhaps only a fable, particularly for the modern child who increasingly has infrequent contact with it. It [merely] has the advantage of making clear on what basis the constitution of the first *source-objects*, these interiorised or rather introjected objects, occurs" (Laplanche, *Essays on Otherness*, 128).

23. Laplanche, *New Foundations*, 91.

24. Osborne, *Philosophy in Cultural Theory*, 109.

25. Morrison, *The Bluest Eye*, 19, 20.

26. Morrison, *The Bluest Eye*, 21.

27. Morrison, *The Bluest Eye*, 62.

28. Morrison, *The Bluest Eye*, 22.

29. Robert Proctor, *Racial Hygiene: Medicine under the Nazis* (Cambridge, Mass.: Harvard University Press, 1988), 78. See also Dr. William Lee Howard's 1903 description alleging that black males have "'racial instincts that are about as amenable to ethical culture as is the inherent odor of the race'" (quoted in George M. Fredrickson, *The Black Image in the White Mind: The Debate on Afro-American Character and Destiny, 1817–1914* [Hanover, N.H.: Wesleyan University Press, 1971], 279).

30. Polish psychiatrist Antoni Kepínski, quoted in Robert Jay Lifton, *The Nazi Doctors: Medical Killing and the Psychology of Genocide* (New York: Basic Books, 1986), 147.

31. Julia Kristeva, *Powers of Horror: An Essay on Abjection*, trans. Leon S. Roudiez (New York: Columbia University Press, 1982), 69; Elizabeth Grosz, *Volatile Bodies: Toward a Corporeal Feminism* (Bloomington: Indiana University Press, 1994), 192.

32. Laplanche, *Essays on Otherness*, 160.

33. Fletcher and Stanton, eds., *Jean Laplanche*, 21.

34. See, for example, Jon Mills and Janusz A. Polanowski, *The Ontology of Prejudice* (Amsterdam: Rodopi Press, 1997): "Every person by nature is racist" (11), and "[t]he belief that humanity is capable of purging itself of prejudice is not only philosophically incredulous but also psychologically infantile" (1). See also Lawrence A. Hirschfeld, *Race in the Making: Cognition, Culture, and the Child's Construction of Human Kinds* (Cambridge: MIT Press, 1996), which claims that us-them distinctions are biologically given, which do not have to result in racism but are the ineradicable foundation for it. For criticism of a similar problem in

Elisabeth Young-Bruehl's *The Anatomy of Prejudice* (Cambridge, Mass.: Harvard University Press, 1996), see Shannon Sullivan, "Pragmatism, Psychoanalysis, and Prejudice: Elisabeth Young-Bruehl's *The Anatomy of Prejudice*," *Journal of Speculative Philosophy* 15(2) (2001): 162–69.

35. Fletcher and Stanton, eds., *Jean Laplanche*, 190.

36. Fletcher and Stanton, eds., *Jean Laplanche*, 190.

37. Laplanche, *New Foundations*, 93.

38. Fletcher and Stanton, eds., *Jean Laplanche*, 104.

39. Laplanche, *Essays on Otherness*, 126. See also *New Foundations*, 75.

40. Elizabeth Grosz uses the term "naturalism" this way in her rejection of it (*Volatile Bodies*, 14 and 212 n. 15). See also Donna Haraway's rejection of naturalism because of its (alleged) appeal to organic wholeness and Sonia Kruk's description of naturalism as necessity "given in nature" in her account of Simone de Beauvoir's alleged anti-naturalism (Haraway, *Simians, Cyborgs, and Women: The Reinvention of Nature* [New York: Routledge, 1991], 150; Kruks, *Retrieving Experience: Subjectivity and Recognition in Feminist Politics* [Ithaca, N.Y.: Cornell University Press, 2001], 39). While definitions of naturalism as essentialist and biologistic are common in feminist theory, other (and richer) understandings of naturalism exist, as work in pragmatism and feminist epistemology shows.

41. Fletcher and Stanton, eds., *Jean Laplanche*, 10.

42. Fletcher and Stanton, eds., *Jean Laplanche*, 10.

43. Fletcher and Stanton, eds., *Jean Laplanche*, 10.

44. Laplanche, *Essays on Otherness*, 195.

45. Fletcher and Stanton, eds., *Jean Laplanche*, 36.

46. Fletcher and Stanton, eds., *Jean Laplanche*, 36. Laplanche uses "implantation" rather than "introjection" because he claims that introjection also is ipsocentric. This is one reason why Laplanche would disagree with Kleinian theory, despite their shared emphases on the early months of infant psychical life and the infant's psychical taking in of (part of) the (m)other, especially the breast.

47. Fletcher and Stanton, eds., *Jean Laplanche*, 37.

48. Fletcher and Stanton, eds., *Jean Laplanche*, 57. This explains Laplanche's objection to phenomenology, which he views as attempting "to restore to the human being his quality of 'first person' subject" and "to find the intentionality of a subject at the heart of all psychical acts" (*Essays on Otherness*, 113). In this context, it is noteworthy that before training with Lacan, Laplanche studied at the Ecole Normale Superiéure with Merleau-Ponty (as well as Hippolyte), receiving highest accommodations on his *aggregation de philosophie* (Fletcher and Stanton, eds., *Jean Laplanche*, 225).

49. See, for example, Laplanche's call for a return to the Cartesians—Descartes, Spinoza, and Leibniz—to define passivity and activity (Laplanche, *New Foundations*, 123; Fletcher and Stanton, eds., *Jean Laplanche*, 80, 175). A return to Descartes would seem to be a return to an atomistic view of human beings as closed off from the world around them. Spinoza's relational ontology, on the other hand, would bring out the transactional aspects of Laplanche's account.

50. Patricia Williams, *Seeing a Color-Blind Future: The Paradox of Race* (New York: Farrar, Straus and Giroux, 1997), 3.

51. Williams, *Seeing a Color-Blind Future*, 8.

52. Williams, *Seeing a Color-Blind Future*, 8–9.

53. Laplanche, *Essays on Otherness*, 93. See also Laplanche, *New Foundations*, 103: "given that the child lives on in the adult, an adult faced with a child is particularly likely to be deviant and inclined to perform bungled or even symbolic actions because he is involved in a relationship with his other self, with the other he once was. The child in front of him brings out the child within him."

54. Laplanche, *Essays on Otherness*, 93 n. 24.

55. Laplanche, *Essays on Otherness*, 73.

56. Philippe Van Haute, "Fatal Attraction: Jean Laplanche on Sexuality, Subjectivity, and Singularity in the Work of Sigmund Freud," *Radical Philosophy* 73 (1995): 10.

57. Laplanche, *Essays on Otherness*, 65.

58. Laplanche, *Essays on Otherness*, 114, 62 n. 21.

59. Laplanche, *Essays on Otherness*, 65, 114.

60. Laplanche, *Essays on Otherness*, 44.

61. Richard Kearney, *Strangers, Gods and Monsters* (New York: Routledge, 2003). The following three paragraphs have been adapted from page 86 of my review of this book in *Teaching Philosophy* 27(1) (2004): 85–87.

62. Julia Kristeva, *Strangers to Ourselves* (New York: Columbia University Press, 1991), 1, 192.

63. Kearney, *Strangers, Gods and Monsters*, 77.

64. Kearney, *Strangers, Gods and Monsters*, 67.

65. Kearney, *Strangers, Gods and Monsters*, 100.

66. Laplanche, *Essays on Otherness*, 173.

67. Given Laplanche's explicit criticism of hermeneutic philosophy, it might seem odd to charge Laplanche with operating with a radical (or any other type of) hermeneutics. Laplanche's criticism is that hermeneutic interpretation claims to give meaning to a meaningless past, which denies the reality of the enigmatic message transmitted in seduction (see Laplanche, *Essays on Otherness*, 87, 165; "Psychoanalysis as Anti-Hermeneutics," *Radical Philosophy* 79 (1996): 7–12). Since Kearney uses the term to address the issue of communication between self and other, not only is Kearney's appeal to hermeneutics not invalidated by Laplanche's objection to it, but Kearney's particular use of hermeneutics also complements Laplanche's concern with the relationship between infant and adult other. Some of Laplanche's most recent work is more open to hermeneutics, as long as it is understood as "a *hermeneutics of the message*" (Laplanche, "Narrativity and Hermeneutics: Some Propositions," *New Formations* 48 (2002): 28, emphasis in original).

68. Laplanche, *New Foundations*, 93.

69. Laplanche, *New Foundations*, 93, emphasis in original.

70. Laplanche, *New Foundations*, 103.

71. Laplanche, *Essays on Otherness*, 237–38, 237 n. 9. Laplanche's discussion here is of four different levels of time—the time of the world, the time of the living being, the time of memory and the individual project, and the time of human history and society—not of self-preservation and seduction, per se. But self-preservation clearly is an instance of level II (the living being) while seduction is an instance of levels III and IV (the individual project and humanity as a whole). Levels III and IV are "clearly connected" with level II in that the former are built upon the latter (just as level II is built upon level I), but that connection does not minimize their "shar[p] distinct[ion]." As Laplanche claims, "only the relation between levels III and IV is more complex than the simple ideal of superimposition would suggest" (237 n. 9).

72. Laplanche, *New Foundations*, 103–104; see also 108.

73. Laplanche, *Essays on Otherness*, 97, 212; *New Foundations*, 103.

74. Osborne, *Philosophy in Cultural Theory*, 104. See also Jacqueline Lanouzière, "Breast-Feeding as Original Seduction and Primal Scene of Seduction," *New Formations* 48 (2002–03): 54.

75. Laplanche, *New Foundations*, 89–90, emphasis in original.

76. Laplanche, *New Foundations*, 41.

77. But twelve months apparently is not too young for babies to use sign language. According to Linda Acredolo and Susan Goodwyn, babies can begin to sign between nine and twelve months and to understand sign language as young as six to seven months, well before they are able to speak vocally (*Baby Signs: How to Talk with Your Baby before Your Baby Can Talk* [Chicago: Contemporary Books, 2002], 34–35).

78. Laplanche, *Essays on Otherness*, 73; emphasis in original. I omit the second reason because it is not relevant here. For the record, it is that "emphasizing 'language' effaces the alterity of the other in favour of trans-individual structures" (73), a point discussed above.

79. Of course, for many children, especially in the non-Western world, this would place their age well beyond twelve to twenty-four months. To the extent that Laplanche's account assumes that seduction ends at one to two years because breast-feeding is terminated then, it operates with a problematic Eurocentrism. Eliminating that Eurocentrism from his account would furnish further support for my claim that seduction can extend beyond early childhood.

80. Laplanche, *Essays on Otherness*, 154.

81. Laplanche, *Essays on Otherness*, 154.

82. Sigmund Freud, "'A Child Is Being Beaten': A Contribution to the Study of the Origin of Sexual Perversions," in vol. 17 of *The Standard Edition of the Complete Psychological Works of Sigmund Freud*, ed. and trans. James Strachey (London: Hogarth Press, 1955), 183.

83. Freud, "'A Child Is Being Beaten,'" 184.

84. Carol Gilligan's *In a Different Voice: Psychological Theory and Women's Development* (Cambridge, Mass.: Harvard University Press, 1993) offers one of the best-known criticisms of this developmental story. For criticisms that do not

support gender stereotyping as Gilligan's account tends to do, see Lorraine Code, "Naming, Naturalizing, Normalizing: 'The Child' as Fact and Artifact," in *Toward a Feminist Developmental Psychology,* ed. Patricia Miller and Ellin Scholnick (New York: Routledge, 2000); and Cynthia Willett, *The Soul of Justice: Social Bonds and Racial Hubris* (Ithaca, N.Y.: Cornell University Press, 2001).

85. Laplanche, *Essays on Otherness,* 126.

86. Laplanche, *Essays on Otherness,* 90.

87. On habit as a mode of mechanization, see Shannon Sullivan, *Living Across and Through Skins: Transactional Bodies, Pragmatism and Feminism* (Bloomington: Indiana University Press, 2001), 31–32.

88. Deleuze and Guattari, *Anti-Oedipus,* 109.

89. Deleuze and Guattari, *A Thousand Plateaus,* 51.

90. Deleuze and Guattari, *A Thousand Plateaus,* 257.

91. This approximates a concern that an audience member raised when I presented a portion of chapter 2 of this book at Seattle University's conference on "Race, Space, and Place," November 8–9, 2002.

92. Haraway, *Simans, Cyborgs, and Women,* 190.

93. Laplanche, *Essays on Otherness,* 165.

94. Ward Churchill, *Indians Are Us* (Monroe, Maine: Common Courage Press, 1994), 213.

95. Deleuze and Guattari, *A Thousand Plateaus,* 176

96. Deleuze and Guattari, *A Thousand Plateaus,* 190, 188.

97. Laplanche, *Essays on Otherness,* 129; see also Fletcher and Stanton, eds., *Jean Laplanche,* 191. For Laplanche, Freud was right about the id's inaccessibility even though he wrongly argued the point based on the id's supposed origin in inherited memory traces.

98. Laplanche, *Essays on Otherness,* 121.

99. Laplanche, *Essays on Otherness,* 111; Laplanche, *New Foundation,* 149–50.

100. Vincent Colapietro, "Notes for a Sketch of a Peircean Theory of the Unconscious," *Transactions of the Charles S. Peirce Society* 31(3) (1995): 489.

4. GLOBAL HABITS, COLLECTIVE HAUNTINGS

1. Franz Fanon, *Black Skin, White Mask,* trans. Charles Lam Markmann (New York: Grove Press, 1967), 63. The following section on Fanon is adapted from pages 10–17 and 20 of Shannon Sullivan, "Ethical Slippages, Shattered Horizons, and the Zebra Striping of the Unconscious: Fanon on Social, Bodily, and Psychical Space." *Philosophy and Geography* 7(1) (2004): 9–24.

2. María C. Lugones, "Playfulness, 'World'-Traveling, and Loving Perception," *Hypatia* 2(2) (1987): 3–19.

3. Franz Fanon, *Peau Noire, Masques Blancs* (Paris: Editions du Seuil, 1952), 175.

4. Fanon, *Black Skin, White Masks,* 192.

5. Fanon, *Black Skin, White Masks,* 192–93.

6. Fanon, *Black Skin, White Masks,* 144–45, 187–91.

7. Fanon, *Black Skin, White Masks,* 147.

8. Fanon, *Black Skin, White Masks,* 146.

9. Fanon, *Black Skin, White Masks,* 110.

10. Fanon, *Black Skin, White Masks,* 143–44.

11. David Macey, "The Recall of the Real," *Constellations* 6(1) (1999): 103.

12. Fanon, *Black Skin, White Masks,* 145.

13. Fanon, *Black Skin, White Masks,* 145.

14. Fanon, *Black Skin, White Masks,* 192.

15. Fanon, *Black Skin, White Masks,* 191.

16. Fanon, *Black Skin, White Masks,* 193.

17. Fanon, *Black Skin, White Masks,* 192, 193.

18. Franz Fanon, *The Wretched of the Earth,* trans. Constance Farrington (New York: Grove Press, 1963), 81.

19. Fanon, *Black Skin, White Masks,* 194.

20. Franz Fanon, *Toward the African Revolution,* trans. Haakon Chevalier (New York: Grove Press, 1967), 15.

21. Fanon, *Black Skin, White Masks,* 111, emphasis in original.

22. Fanon, *Black Skin, White Masks,* 111.

23. Maurice Merleau-Ponty, *Phenomenology of Perception,* trans. Colin Smith (New York: Routledge, 1962), 142.

24. Merleau-Ponty, *Phenomenology of Perception,* 252.

25. Fanon, *Black Skin, White Masks,* 111.

26. Fanon, *Black Skin, White Masks,* 112.

27. Fanon, *Black Skin, White Masks,* 112.

28. Fanon, *Black Skin, White Masks,* 112, 217. Fanon's analysis of the triple existence that a black person is forced to live reveals the misunderstanding behind Macey's criticism that Fanon focuses on the theme of being-for-others rather than on being-with-others (Macey, "Fanon, Phenomenology, Race," *Radical Philosophy* 95 [1999]: 10). Fanon's point is precisely that black people are not allowed to exist *with* other (white) people—a relationship that suggests their existential equality—but instead are forced by their racial-epidermal schema to exist *for* (white) others as thing-like subpersons.

29. Fanon, *Black Skin, White Masks,* 139. For an account of Fanon's three bodily schemas that aligns them with Sartre's understanding of alienation, see Jeremy Weate, "Fanon, Merleau-Ponty, and the Difference of Phenomenology," in *Race,* ed. Robert Bernasconi (Malden, Mass.: Blackwell Publishers, 2001), 173–75.

30. Fanon, *Black Skin, White Masks,* 216–17, emphasis added.

31. Cynthia Willett, *The Soul of Justice: Social Bonds and Racial Hubris* (Ithaca, N.Y.: Cornell University Press, 2001), 165. See also Kelly Oliver, *Witnessing: Beyond Recognition* (Minneapolis: University of Minnesota Press, 2001).

32. Willett, *The Soul of Justice,* 21.

33. Charles Mills, *The Racial Contract* (Ithaca, N.Y.: Cornell University Press, 1997), 89.

34. Willett, *The Soul of Justice,* 215.

35. Willett, *The Soul of Justice*, 215.

36. Fanon, *Black Skin, White Masks*, 11.

37. Fanon, *Black Skin, White Masks*, 97.

38. Merleau-Ponty, *Phenomenology of Perception*, 101.

39. See, for example, Simone de Beauvoir's *The Second Sex*, trans. H. M. Parshley (New York: Vintage Books, 1989) for a phenomenological examination of the shattering of women's bodily horizons that occurs because of sexist oppression.

40. Merleau-Ponty, *Phenomenology of Perception*, 143.

41. Franz Fanon, *A Dying Colonialism*, trans. Haakon Chevalier (New York: Grove Press, 1965), 59.

42. Fanon, *A Dying Colonialism*, 59.

43. Fanon, *Black Skin, White Masks*, 123.

44. Fanon, *Black Skin, White Masks*, 135. See also Irene L. Gendzier, *Franz Fanon: A Critical Study* (New York: Pantheon Books, 1973), 228. As Gendzier notes (38, 227), Fanon's ultimate position on Negritude is very close to Sartre's, which is somewhat ironic given Fanon's initial dismay at Sartre's dismissal of Negritude as a minor term in a dialectical movement toward universalism.

45. Fanon, *Wretched of the Earth*, 234, 247.

46. Thanks to Phillip McReynolds for discussing with me the effects of the different histories of French colonialism in the Caribbean and North Africa.

47. Fanon, *Black Skin, White Masks*, 11.

48. D. Caute quoted in Renée T. White, "Revolutionary Theory: Sociological Dimensions of Fanon's *Sociologie d'une revolution*," in *Fanon: A Critical Reader*, ed. Lewis R. Gordon, T. Denean Sharpley-Whiting, and Renée T. White (Maldon, Mass.: Blackwell Publishers, 1996), 101.

49. John Fletcher and Martin Stanton, eds., *Jean Laplanche: Seduction, Translation and the Drives*, trans. Martin Stanton (London: Institute of Contemporary Arts, 1992), 190.

50. Fanon, *Black Skin, White Mask*, 213.

51. Hussein Abdilahi Bulhan, *Franz Fanon and the Psychology of Oppression* (New York: Plenum Press, 1985), 195.

52. Maurice Merleau-Ponty, *The Structure of Behavior*, trans. Alden L. Fisher (Boston: Beacon Press, 1963), 179; and Merleau-Ponty, *The Phenomenology of Perception*, 380.

53. For discussions of Merleau-Ponty's relationship to psychoanalysis, including the question of how close he came to psychoanalysis in his later work, see Jacques Lacan, "Merleau-Ponty: In Memoriam," *Review of Existential Psychology and Psychiatry* 18(1–3) (1983): 73–81; Joseph Lyons, "The Lived Body in Phenomenology and Psychoanalysis," in *Phenomenology and Psychoanalysis: The Sixth Annual Symposium of the Simon Silverman Phenomenology Center* (Pittsburgh, Pa.: Simon Silverman Phenomenology Center, 1988), 1–30; Maurice Merleau-Ponty, "Phenomenology and Psychoanalysis: Preface to Hesard's *L'Oeuvre de Freud*,"

Review of Existential Psychology and Psychiatry 18(1–3) (1983): 67–72; Dorothea Olkowski, "Merleau-Ponty's Freudianism: From the Body of Consciousness to the Body of Flesh," *Review of Existential Psychology and Psychiatry* 18(1–3) (1983), 97–115; Dorothea Olkowski and James Morley, eds., *Merleau-Ponty, Interiority and Exteriority, Psychic Life and the World* (Albany: SUNY Press, 1999); James Phillips, "Lacan and Merleau-Ponty: The Confrontation of Psychoanalysis and Phenomenology," in *Disseminating Lacan,* ed. David Pettigrew and François Raffoul (Albany: SUNY Press, 1996); James Phillips, "Latency and the Unconscious in Merleau-Ponty," in *Phenomenology and Psychoanalysis: The Sixth Annual Symposium of the Simon Silverman Phenomenology Center* (Pittsburgh, Pa.: Simon Silverman Phenomenology Center, 1988), 31–63; and J. B. Pontalis, "The Problem of the Unconscious in Merleau-Ponty's Thought," *Review of Existential Psychology and Psychiatry* 18(1–3) (1983), 83–96.

54. Fanon, *Black Skin, White Masks,* 192–93.

55. Fanon, *Black Skin, White Masks,* 153.

56. Nicolas Abraham and Maria Torok, *The Shell and the Kernel: Renewals of Psychoanalysis,* ed. and trans. Nicholas T. Rand (Chicago: University of Chicago Press, 1994).

57. Nicholas Rand, introduction to Abraham and Torok, *The Shell and the Kernel,* 18.

58. Toni Morrison, *Beloved* (New York: Penguin Books, 1987), 200–201.

59. Morrison, *Beloved,* 62.

60. Morrison, *Beloved,* 203.

61. Rand, introduction to *The Shell and the Kernel,* 22

62. Morrison, *Beloved,* 29.

63. Morrison, *Beloved,* 274.

64. Sam Durrant, *Postcolonial Narrative and the Work of Mourning: J. M. Coetzee, Wilson Harris, and Toni Morrison* (Albany: SUNY Press, 2004), 99.

65. Morrison, *Beloved,* 36.

66. Morrison, *Beloved,* 36.

67. Durrant, *Postcolonial Narrative and the Work of Mourning,* 167.

68. Toni Morrison quoted in Danielle Taylor-Guthrie, ed., *Conversations with Toni Morrison* (Jackson: University Press of Mississippi, 1994), 247.

69. Abraham and Torok, *The Shell and the Kernel,* 167.

70. Morrison quoted in Taylor-Guthrie, *Conversations with Toni Morrison,* 249.

71. Thanks to Lisa Heldke for pointing this out in our discussion of the incident.

72. Brent Staples, "Just Walk on By: A Black Man Ponders His Power to Alter Public Space," *Ms.,* September 1986, 54.

73. Rand, introduction to *The Shell and the Kernel,* 22.

74. Morrison quoted in Taylor-Guthrie, *Conversations with Toni Morrison,* 247–48.

75. Morrison quoted in Taylor-Guthrie, *Conversations with Toni Morrison,* 247.

76. Paul Connerton, *How Societies Remember* (New York: Cambridge University Press, 1989).

5. APPROPRIATE HABITS OF WHITE PRIVILEGE

1. This paragraph and the subsequent section on Du Bois and the gifts of black folk are adapted from pages 208 and 213–18 of "Remembering the Gift: Du Bois on the Unconscious and Economic Operations of Racism," *Transactions of the C. S. Peirce Society* 39(2) (Spring 2003): 205–25.

2. W. E. B. Du Bois, *Darkwater: Voices from Within the Veil* (New York: Harcourt, Brace, 1999), 23.

3. Du Bois, *Darkwater,* 22, emphasis in original.

4. Du Bois, *Darkwater,* 18.

5. W. E. B. Du Bois, *The Gift of Black Folk: The Negroes in the Making of America* (New York: Washington Square Press, 1970).

6. For another example of Freud's implicit impact on Du Bois's work around the same time, see chapter 2 of Claudia Tate, *Psychoanalysis and Black Novels: Desire and the Protocols of Race* (New York: Oxford University Press, 1998), which provides a psychoanalytic reading of Du Bois's 1928 novel *Dark Princess: A Romance.*

7. Du Bois, "The Conservation of Races," in *W. E. B. Du Bois Speaks: Speeches and Addresses, 1980–1919,* ed. Philip S. Foner (New York: Pathfinder Press, 1970), 75–76.

8. Du Bois, "The Conservation of Races," 75–76.

9. Du Bois, *The Gift of Black Folk,* 1.

10. For a discussion of whiteness itself as a kind of property owned by white people, see Cheryl Harris, "Whiteness as Property," in *Black on White: Black Writers on What It Means to Be White,* ed. David R. Roediger (New York: Schocken Books, 1998), 103–18.

11. Gilles Deleuze and Felix Guattari, *Anti-Oedipus: Capitalism and Schizophrenia,* trans. Robert Hurley, Mark Seem, and Helen R. Lane (Minneapolis: University of Minnesota Press, 1983).

12. Joel Kovel, *White Racism: A Psychohistory* (New York: Pantheon Books, 1970), 218.

13. bell hooks and Cornel West cited in Stephen Nathan Haymes, *Race, Culture, and the City: A Pedagogy for Black Urban Struggle* (Albany: SUNY Press, 1995), 59.

14. Haymes, *Race, Culture, and the City,* 100.

15. John Shuford, "Four Du Boisian Contributions to Critical Race Theory," *Transactions of the Charles S. Peirce Society* 37(3) (2001): 318.

16. Arlene Dávila, *Latinos, Inc.: The Marketing and Making of a People* (Berkeley: University of California Press, 2001).

17. Haymes, *Race, Culture, and the City*, 23.

18. bell hooks, *Black Looks: Race and Representation* (Boston: South End Press, 1992), 31.

19. Kovel, *White Racism*, 187.

20. Du Bois, *Dusk of Dawn*, 170.

21. bell hooks, "Representations of Whiteness in the Black Imagination," in *Black on White: Black Writers on What It Means to Be White*, ed. David R. Roediger (New York: Schocken Books, 1998), 51.

22. Toni Morrison, *Playing in the Dark: Whiteness and the Literary Imagination* (Cambridge, Mass.: Harvard University Press, 1990), 9–10.

23. Patricia Williams, *Seeing a Color-Blind Future: The Paradox of Race* (New York: Farrar, Straus, and Giroux, 1997), 27.

24. Williams, *Seeing a Color-Blind Future*, 27.

25. Du Bois, *Dusk of Dawn*, 138.

26. Du Bois, *Dusk of Dawn*, 171–72.

27. Du Bois, *Dusk of Dawn*, 172.

28. Du Bois, *Dusk of Dawn*, 6.

29. Chief Seattle, *How Can One Sell the Air? The Manifesto of an Indian Chief* (Dorchester, England: Prism Press, 1984), no page numbers provided. I acknowledge that it is debatable whether Chief Seattle actually said this. This particular quotation is usually attributed to a letter to President Pierce rather than to Seattle's speech to Governor Stevens. However, both sources are questionable; see the U.S. National Archives and Records Administration's site, http://www.archives.gov/publications/prologue/print_friendly.html?page=spring_1985_chief_seattle_content.html&title=NARA%20%7C%20Prologue%20%7C%20Prologue%3A%20Selected%20Articles#F3. The earliest evidence found of this quotation is in an article written more than thirty years after the fact by a white man, who claimed that Seattle said it. Thanks to Carol Kennedy for providing this information.

30. Vine Deloria, *God Is Red: A Native View of Religion* (Golden, Colo.: Fulcrum Publishing, 1994), 172. I do not mean to romanticize Native relations with the land; Native American nations did fight each other over territory. But the general difference between Native and white attitudes toward land described here (and by Deloria) is one that makes a difference, to borrow from William James.

31. Anonymous, in "How Can One Sell the Air?" no page number.

32. To be more precise, the Euro-American attitude toward Indians that I describe is more accurate of the British than the Spanish colonists of the Americas. On this point, see David J. Weber, ed., *Foreigners in Their Native Land: Historical Roots of the Mexican Americans* (Albuquerque: University of New Mexico Press, 1973), especially p. 20.

33. J. E. Chamberlin, *The Harrowing of Eden: White Attitudes toward Native Americans* (New York: Seabury Press, 1975), 19.

34. Chamberlin, *The Harrowing of Eden*, 39.

35. Chamberlin, *The Harrowing of Eden*, 51.

36. Emily Greenwald, *Reconfiguring the Reservation: The Nez Perces, Jicarilla Apaches, and the Dawes Act* (Albuquerque: University of New Mexico Press, 2002), 19.

37. Greenwald, *Reconfiguring the Reservation,* 31.

38. Greenwald, *Reconfiguring the Reservation,* 32.

39. Greenwald, *Reconfiguring the Reservation,* 39–40.

40. Paula Mitchell Marks, *In a Barren Land: American Indian Dispossession and Survival* (New York: William Morrow, 1998), xxiii.

41. Marks, *In a Barren Land,* xxiii.

42. Roderick Nash, *Wilderness and the American Mind,* 3rd ed. (New Haven, Conn.: Yale University Press, 1982), 1, 7, 28.

43. Frederick Turner, *The Frontier in American History* (New York: Holt, Rinehart, and Winston, 1962), 3, 11, 24.

44. Grund quoted in Turner, *The Frontier in American History,* 7.

45. Nash, *Wilderness and the American Mind,* 67. 69.

46. Maureen Smith, "An Enduring American Indian Myth: The Exercise of Religious Freedom in America," *Maine Scholar: A Journal of Ideas and Public Affairs* 11 (1998): 191–208.

47. Robert Bly, quoted in Ward Churchill, *Indians Are Us* (Monroe, Maine: Common Courage Press, 1994), 209.

48. Phillip Deloria, *Playing Indian* (New Haven, Conn.: Yale University Press, 1998), 171.

49. Churchill, *Indians Are Us,* 228.

50. Phillip Deloria, *Playing Indian,* 176–77.

51. Franz Fanon, *The Wretched of the Earth,* trans. Constance Farrington (New York: Grove Press, 1963), 44.

52. See, for example, Fanon's claim that "muscular action must substitute itself for concepts" (Fanon, *The Wretched of the Earth,* 220).

53. Hussein Abdilahi Bulhan and Renée T. White draw attention to the relationship between land and psyche. See Bulhan, *Franz Fanon and the Psychology of Oppression* (New York: Plenum Press, 1985), 101; and White, "Revolutionary Theory: Sociological Dimensions of Fanon's *Sociologie d'une revolution,*" in *Fanon: A Critical Reader,* ed. Lewis R. Gordon, T. Denean Sharpley-Whiting, and Renée T. White (Maldon, Mass.: Blackwell Publishers, 1996), 102.

54. White, "Revolutionary Theory," 104.

55. Randall Robinson, *The Debt: What America Owes to Blacks* (New York: Plume, 2000).

56. Jamal E. Watson, "Lawyers Plan Suit for Slavery Reparations," *Boston Globe,* April 13, 2001.

57. Charles Mills, *Blackness Visible* (Ithaca, N.Y.: Cornell University Press, 1998).

58. Robinson, *The Debt,* 208, emphasis in original.

59. Du Bois, "The Class Struggle," in vol. 2 of *The Seventh Son: The Thought*

and Writings of W. E. B. Du Bois, ed. Julius Lester (New York: Random House, 1971), 266; Du Bois, "Karl Marx and the Negro," in vol. 2 of Lester, ed., *The Seventh Son,* 289; Du Bois, "Marxism and the Negro Problem," in vol. 2 of Lester, ed., *The Seventh Son,* 295. See also Bobby M. Wilson, "Critically Understanding Race-Connected Practices: A Reading of W. E. B. Du Bois and Richard Wright," *Professional Geographer* 54(1) (2002): 36.

60. Du Bois, "Marxism and the Negro Problem," 295.

61. Du Bois, "The Class Struggle," 266.

62. Du Bois, "The Class Struggle," 266.

63. Du Bois, "The Class Struggle," 266.

64. Du Bois, "The Class Struggle," 266.

65. Du Bois, "The Class Struggle," 267.

66. Du Bois, "The Class Struggle," 267.

67. Marks, *In a Barren Land,* 354.

68. Marks, *In a Barren Land,* 357.

69. For more on Indian tribes' adoption of modern corporate strategies to fight Euro-American capitalism's exploitation of them and their resources, see Donald L. Fixico, *The Invasion of Indian Country in the Twentieth Century: American Capitalism and Tribal Natural Resources* (Niwot: University Press of Colorado, 1998).

70. Anahad O'Connor, "Rise in Income Improves Children's Behavior," *New York Times on the Web,* October 21, 2003, www.nytimes.com.

71. Fanon, *The Wretched of the Earth,* 100.

72. Fanon, *The Wretched of the Earth,* 101.

73. Fanon, *The Wretched of the Earth,* 103.

74. Dávila, *Latinos, Inc.,* 4.

75. Dávila, *Latinos, Inc.,* 9.

76. Haymes, *Race, Culture, and the City,* 49.

77. Ward Churchill, *Struggle for the Land* (Monroe, Maine.: Common Courage Press, 1993), 424.

78. Churchill, *Struggle for the Land,* 424.

79. Churchill, *Struggle for the Land,* 432–33.

80. David Horowitz's criticisms of reparations for slavery made in an ad placed in several U.S. college newspapers caused an uproar on many campuses in the spring of 2001. For more on the issue, including the full text of Horowitz's ad, see Associated Press, "Ad in Brown University Newspaper Sparks Protests," *Centre Daily Times,* State College, Pa.: March 18, 2001, page 9A; and http://www.newsmax.com/archives/articles/2001/3/7/221937.shtml.

81. Loria quoted in Turner, *The Frontier in American History,* 11.

82. Cathy Caruth, "Unclaimed Experience: Trauma and the Possibility of History," in *Yale French Studies: Literature and the Ethical Question #79* (New Haven, Conn.: Yale University Press, 1991), 192.

83. Churchill, *Struggle for the Land,* 437.

6. RACE, SPACE, AND PLACE

1. This section is adapted from pages 90–95 of Shannon Sullivan, "The Racialization of Space: Toward a Phenomenological Account of Raced and Anti-Racist Spatiality," in *The Problems of Resistance: Studies in Alternate Political Cultures*, ed. Steve Martinot (Atlantic Highlands, N.J.: Prometheus/Humanity Books, 2001), 86–104.

2. Patricia J. Williams, *The Alchemy of Race and Rights: Diary of a Law Professor* (Cambridge: Harvard University Press, 1991).

3. Williams, *The Alchemy of Race and Rights*, 44–45.

4. Williams, *The Alchemy of Race and Rights*, 58.

5. Williams, *The Alchemy of Race and Rights*, 69.

6. Williams, *The Alchemy of Race and Rights*, 68.

7. Thanks to Terrance MacMullan for offering this observation during discussion of a version of this paper at the third meeting of the Radical Philosophy Association, November 1998, San Francisco, Calif.

8. Quoted in Williams, *The Alchemy of Race and Rights*, 70.

9. Charles Mills, *The Racial Contract* (Ithaca, N.Y.: Cornell University Press, 1997), 42.

10. See Philip Deloria, *Playing Indian* (New Haven, Conn.: Yale University Press, 1998) for an account of how Native Americans have served as objects of desire and repulsion for white Americans.

11. *Webster's Encyclopedic Unabridged Dictionary of the English Language* (New York: Portland House, 1989).

12. Helsinki Watch Report, *Struggling for Ethnic Identity: Czechoslovakia's Endangered Gypsies* (New York: Human Rights Watch, 1992), ix. The following eight paragraphs are adapted from pages 93–95 of Shannon Sullivan, "Racialized Habits: Dewey on Race and the Roma," in *Pragmatism and Values: The Central European Pragmatist Forum, Volume One*, ed. John Ryder and Emil Višòovský (Amsterdam: Rodopi Press, 2004), 139–48.

13. The following historical information comes from Jean-Pierre Liégeois, *Roma, Gypsies, Travellers* (Strasbourg: Council of Europe Press, 1994), 121–55.

14. Liégeois, *Roma, Gypsies, Travellers*, 136.

15. Liégeois, *Roma, Gypsies, Travellers*, 135.

16. Liégeois, *Roma, Gypsies, Travellers*, 148.

17. Helsinki Rights Watch, *Struggling for Ethnic Identity*.

18. Isabel Fonseca, *Bury Me Standing: The Gypsies and Their Journey* (New York: Alfred Knopf, 1995), 140, 143, 150.

19. Maria Bucur, *Eugenics and Modernization in Interwar Romania* (Pittsburgh, Pa.: University of Pittsburgh Press, 2002), 231.

20. Liégeois, *Roma, Gypsies, Travellers*, 185.

21. Liégeois, *Roma, Gypsies, Travellers*, 79.

22. Manfri Frederick Wood, *In the Life of a Romany Gypsy* (London: Routledge and Kegan Paul, 1973), 115–16.

23. Konrad Bercovici, *Gypsies: Their Life, Lore, and Legends* (New York: Greenwich House, 1983), 241.

24. Bercovici, *Gypsies*, 242.

25. John Dewey, *The Quest for Certainty*, vol. 4 of *The Later Works: 1925–1953*, ed. Jo Ann Boydston (Carbondale: Southern Illinois University Press, 1988), 7; see also page 18.

26. Liégeois, *Roma, Gypsies, Travellers*, 225.

27. Harvey quoted in Andrew Light and Jonathan M. Smith, eds. *Philosophies of Place* (Lanham, Md.: Rowman and Littlefield, 1998), 4.

28. Light and Smith, *Philosophies of Place*, 10.

29. Quoted in Fonseca, *Bury Me Standing*, 230.

30. Liégeois, *Roma, Gypsies, Travellers*, 235.

31. Liégeois, *Roma, Gypsies, Travellers*, 235.

32. Liégeois, *Roma, Gypsies, Travellers*, 111.

33. Liégeois, *Roma, Gypsies, Travellers*, 78.

34. Liégeois, *Roma, Gypsies, Travellers*, 225.

35. Mills, *The Racial Contract*, 51.

36. Helsinki Rights Watch, *Struggling for Ethnic Identity*, 69.

37. Helsinki Rights Watch, *Struggling for Ethnic Identity*, 122.

38. Helsinki Rights Watch, *Struggling for Ethnic Identity*, 84.

39. I take the phrase "bubble of wilderness" from Mills, *The Racial Contract*, 53. In this context, it is interesting to note the particular comparison made by the United Nations Human Development Office when critically documenting the marginalization of the Roma: Eastern Europe's "four to five million Roma endure conditions closer to those of sub-Saharan Africa than Europe" (Human Development Report Office, *Avoiding the Dependency Trap: The Roma Human Development Report* [New York: United Nations Development Programme, 2002], quoted in publicity available at http://hdr.undp.org/reports/detail'reports.cfm?view=708).

40. Helsinki Rights Watch, *Struggling for Ethnic Identity*, ix.

41. Fonseca, *Bury Me Standing*, 228.

42. Mattijs van de Port, *Gypsies, Wars, and Other Instances of the Wild: Civilisation and Its Discontents in a Serbian Town* (Amsterdam: Amsterdam University Press, 1998), 155.

43. Van de Port, *Gypsies, Wars, and Other Instances of the Wild*, 6–7.

44. Van de Port, *Gypsies, Wars, and Other Instances of the Wild*, 59.

45. Donna Haraway, *Simians, Cyborgs, and Women: The Reinvention of Nature* (New York: Routledge, 1991), 162.

46. Liégeois, *Roma, Gypsies, Travellers*, 199.

47. Michel Foucault, "Space, Knowledge, and Power" in *The Foucault Reader*, ed. Paul Rabinow (New York: Pantheon Books, 1984), 252.

48. The remainder of this chapter has been adapted from pages 96–102 of Sullivan, "The Racialization of Space," 86–104.

49. Lisa Heldke, "On Being a Responsible Traitor: A Primer," in *Daring to be*

Good: Essays in Feminist Ethico-Politics, ed. Bat-Ami Bar On and Ann Ferguson (New York: Routledge, 1998), 93.

50. I do not use the term "race traitor" in the same sense that the journal *Race Traitor* has been taken to mean. The journal's call for the abolishment of the white race sometimes has been interpreted as claiming that white people can and should attempt to refuse or to step outside their racial identity (see, for example, Joe Kincheloe, ed. *White Reign: Deploying Whiteness in America* [New York: St. Martin's Press, 1998]). Whether or not this interpretation of *Race Traitor* is accurate, I agree with Lisa Heldke when she says, "I am more inclined to see the process [of being a race traitor] as one of dismantling an identity I inhabit, in order to rebuild it, rather than attempting to step outside that identity, in order to rebuild it from without, as it were" (Heldke, "On Being a Responsible Traitor," 93).

51. Charles Mills makes a similar distinction between being white and being White in *The Racial Contract*, 106.

52. Marilyn Frye, "White Woman Feminist," in *Overcoming Racism and Sexism*, ed. Linda A. Bell and David Blumenfeld (Lanham, Md.: Rowman and Littlefield, 1995), 117.

53. Frye acknowledges this point as well. See Frye, "White Woman Feminist," 133 n. 9.

54. Heldke, "On Being a Responsible Traitor," 95.

55. Heldke, "On Being a Responsible Traitor," 95.

56. Alison Bailey, "Locating Traitorous Identities: Toward a View of Privilege-Cognizant White Character," *Hypatia* 13(3) (1998): 32.

57. Bailey, "Locating Traitorous Identities," 32–33.

58. Merleau-Ponty, Maurice, *Phenomenology of Perception*, trans. Colin Smith (New York: Routledge, 1962), 110–12.

59. For more on problems with Merleau-Ponty's concept of projective intentionality, see chapter 3 of Sullivan, *Living Across and Through Skins: Transactional Bodies, Pragmatism, and Feminism* (Bloomington: Indiana University Press, 2001).

60. Quoted in Williams, *The Alchemy of Race and Rights*, 71. I am reminded here of Ward Churchill's biting criticism (quoting Sherman Alexie) of the men's movement's appropriation of Native American spiritual practices that "the sweat lodge is a church" (Churchill, *Indians Are Us* [Monroe, Maine: Common Courage Press, 1994], 219).

61. Williams, *The Alchemy of Race and Rights*, 72.

62. Bailey summarizes the Bradens' story in "Locating Traitorous Identities," 31.

63. Quoted in Bailey, "Locating Traitorous Identities," 31.

7. IN DEFENSE OF SEPARATISM

1. Charlene Haddock Seigfried, "Introduction to the Illinois Edition," in Jane Addams, *Democracy and Social Ethics* (Chicago: University of Illinois Press, 2001), xxxv n. 8.

2. Jane Addams, "The Subjective Necessity for Social Settlements," in Jane

Addams, Robert A. Woods, J. O. S. Huntington, Franklin H. Giddings, and Bernard Bosanquet, *Philanthropy and Social Progress* (New York: Thomas Y. Crowell, 1893), 1. Portions of the essay were incorporated into chapter 6 of Addams, *Twenty Years at Hull-House with Autobiographical Notes* (New York: Macmillan Co., 1910).

3. Addams, "The Subjective Necessity," 1–2; see also 25. Addams does not indicate the source of the inner quote in the second phrase here.

4. Addams, "The Subjective Necessity," 5.

5. Addams, "The Subjective Necessity," 1.

6. J. E. Chamberlin, *The Harrowing of Eden: White Attitudes toward Native Americans* (New York: Seabury Press, 1975), 59–60.

7. Rivka Shpak Lissak, *Pluralism and Progressives: Hull-House and the New Immigrants, 1890–1919* (Chicago: University of Chicago Press, 1989).

8. Lissak, *Pluralism and Progressives*, 30, 40–41.

9. Sometimes, in contrast, Lissak makes it seem as if this alleged first stage was not evidence of real concern, but instead merely a trick played on new immigrants to lure them into assimilation. For example, Lissak claims that Liberal Progressive talk of the value of contributions of new immigrants was "mere rhetoric" that "served as a psychological device designed to make newcomers feel that their cultures were respected and found worthy of inclusion in the American common fund" (*Pluralism and Progressives*, 161).

10. Lissak, *Pluralism and Progressives*, 60, 61.

11. In all fairness, I should point out one place in which Addams *does* sound like a two-stage assimilationist. See page 213 of Addams, "Americanization," *American Sociological Society Proceedings* 14 (1919): 206–14, in which Addams argues for an "evolutionary conception" of nationalism by which to Americanize new immigrants, in which Americanization takes place "gradually" and through "free opportunity for modification" rather than suddenly and forcefully. Warren S. Thompson's "Discussion" of Addams's essay (on pages 214–15 of the same issue) elaborates this "evolutionary" approach.

12. Addams, *Twenty Years at Hull-House*, 231, 234, 244.

13. Jane Addams, *Newer Ideals of Peace* (New York: Macmillan Co., 1906), 47.

14. For more on the melting pot, tossed salad, and stew metaphors in the context of transaction, see Shannon Sullivan, *Living Across and Through Skins: Transactional Bodies, Pragmatism, and Feminism* (Bloomington: Indiana University Press, 2001), especially chapter 1.

15. Lissak, *Pluralism and Progressives*, 8.

16. Lissak, *Pluralism and Progressives*, 8–9, emphasis added.

17. The story here needs to be complicated slightly in that Addams sometimes makes remarks that endorse the transcendence of racial differences (see note 30 below). Given that these remarks can make Addams sound like an assimilationist, Lissak's atomism is not the only reason for her misreading of Addams's notion of cross-fertilization. But Addams ultimately comes out on the side of valuing racial differences, which is why I think both that her pluralism is real and that Lissak's analysis of it is misguided.

18. Addams, "The Subjective Necessity," 2.

19. Addams, "The Subjective Necessity," 10–11; reprinted in Addams, *Twenty Years at Hull-House,* 116–17.

20. Addams, *Newer Ideals of Peace,* 79.

21. Addams, *The Second Twenty Years at Hull-House* (New York: Macmillan Co., 1930), 410.

22. Lissak makes a similar argument in *Pluralism and Progressives,* 164. A recent example of the exoticization and commodification of black ghettos can be found in Chaka Ferguson, "Harlem Hopping Again," *Spokesman-Review,* October 7, 2001, pages H3 and H5.

23. My use of this term is similar to Iris Marion Young's development of it, although Young focuses more explicitly on the irreversibility of particular perspectives in a reciprocal relationship than I do here. See Young, "Asymmetrical Reciprocity: On Moral Respect, Wonder, and Enlarged Thought," in *Intersecting Voices: Dilemmas of Gender, Political Philosophy, and Policy* (Princeton, N.J.: Princeton University Press, 1997).

24. Seigfried, "Introduction to the Illinois Edition," xxi.

25. Addams, *Democracy and Social Ethics,* 70.

26. Cf. Seigfried's discussion of Addams on page 210 of Seigfried, "Socializing Democracy: Jane Addams and John Dewey," *Philosophy of the Social Sciences* 29(2) (1999): "The horizontal linkage of persons, no one of whom is granted antecedent advantage, that constitutes democratic forms of organization profoundly challenges the assertion of privilege that underlies hierarchical forms of government in which power flows from the top down." I am not so much disagreeing with Seigfried as I am drawing attention to the different types of antecedent advantages that can be at play in racial relationships, not all of which can be eliminated by changing the direction of power. Or put another way, I am arguing that Addams has not yet challenged a particular type of power found in the different social ontologies that people bring to the democratic table.

27. This pattern of hierarchical reciprocity has a long history, going back at least as far as Aristotle's *The Politics,* trans. H. Rackham (Cambridge, Mass.: Harvard University Press, 1944), which argues that slaves and masters, like husbands and wives, reciprocally need each other for self-preservation, each lacking something crucial that the other provides. Slaves and women furnish masters and husbands with the needs of their daily lives, and masters and husbands furnish slaves and women with rational direction of their activities. Thanks to Hasana Sharp for reminding me of this connection.

28. I take the term "subperson" from Charles Mills, *The Racial Contract* (Ithaca, N.Y.: Cornell University Press, 1997); and *Blackness Visible* (Ithaca, N.Y.: Cornell University Press, 1998).

29. Addams, "The Subjective Necessity," 4.

30. For a detailed account of this shift in Addams' thought, see pages 49–51 of Shannon Sullivan, "Reciprocal Relations between Races: Jane Addams's Ambiguous Legacy," *Transactions of the C. S. Peirce Society* 39(1) (Winter 2003).

31. Lissak, *Pluralism and Progressives*, 45.

32. Lissak, *Pluralism and Progressives*, 47.

33. See Dewey, *Art as Experience*, vol. 10 of *The Later Works, 1925–1953*, ed. Jo Ann Boydston (Carbondale: Southern Illinois University Press, 1989).

34. Lissak, *Pluralism and Progressives*, 166.

35. As I now think my own earlier work on transaction might do. See Sullivan, *Living Across and Through Skins*, especially pp. 151–52.

36. And her occasional problematic use of its texts. In at least two places, Lissak either quotes or paraphrases Addams and Dewey in misleading ways. Compare Lissak, *Pluralism and Progressives*, 156, with Dewey's "Nationalizing Education," in vol. 10 of *The Middle Works, 1899–1924*, ed. Jo Ann Boydston (Carbondale: Southern Illinois University Press, 1985); and Lissak, *Pluralism and Progressives*, 30, with Addam's "Americanization," especially p. 210.

37. Addams, *Democracy and Social Ethics*, 112.

38. In case it is necessary, let me make clear that I am not arguing for the imposition of segregation on those who do not wish to be geographically or otherwise isolated, which of course is one of the primary forms that white privilege has taken and continues to take in the United States.

39. This account bears an affinity to Sarah Lucia Hoagland's description of conceptual separatism, which is an activity of refusal, disruption, and disloyalty to dominant systems that is distinct from purism. See Hoagland, "Resisting Rationality," in *Engendering Rationalities*, ed. Nancy Tuana and Sandra Morgen (Albany: SUNY Press, 2001).

40. bell hooks describes the loss she felt when the schools in her Kentucky hometown were desegregated, in hooks, *Yearning: Race, Gender, and Cultural Politics* (Boston: South End Press, 1990), 34–35.

41. Thanks to Phillip McReynolds for bringing up these points.

42. Lissak, *Pluralism and Progressives*, 169.

43. Sonia Kruks, *Retrieving Experience: Subjectivity and Recognition in Feminist Politics* (Ithaca, N.Y.: Cornell University Press, 2001), 154–55.

44. Lisa Heldke, "In Praise of Unreliability," *Hypatia* 12(3) (1997): 174–82.

45. Linda Martín Alcoff makes a similar point about the context-sensitive practice of speaking for others in "The Problem of Speaking for Others," in *Overcoming Racism and Sexism*, ed. Linda A. Bell and David Blumenfeld (Lanham, Md.: Rowman and Littlefield, 1995).

46. María Lugones and Elizabeth Spelman, "Have We Got a Theory for You! Feminist Theory, Cultural Imperialism and the Demand for 'The Woman's Voice,'" *Hypatia* (WSIF) 1 (1983): 573–81.

47. Donna Haraway, *Simians, Cyborgs, and Women: The Reinvention of Nature* (New York: Routledge, 1991), 192.

48. Marilyn Frye, *The Politics of Reality: Essays in Feminist Theory* (Freedom, Calif.: Crossing Press, 1983), 111–12.

49. Twila L. Perry, "Transracial Adoption: Mothers, Hierarchy, Race, and

Feminist Legal Theory," in *Critical Race Feminism: A Reader,* 2nd ed., ed. Adrien Katherine Wing (New York: New York University Press, 2003), 176–85.

50. Perry, "Transracial Adoption," 180–81.

51. Cf. Susan Bordo's thoughtful reflections on adoption, including transracial adoption, in which Bordo claims that it is "academics—both black and white—[that] are much more likely to have problems with transracial adoption than [non-academics]" (Bordo, "Adoption," *Hypatia* 20[1] [2005]: 233).

52. I adapt this suggestion from Lisa Heldke, "A Du Boisian Proposal for Persistently White Colleges," *Journal of Speculative Philosophy* 18(3) (2004): 224–38.

53. Frye, *The Politics of Reality,* 113.

54. Charles Scott, *The Advantages and Disadvantages of Politics and Ethics* (Bloomington: Indiana University Press, 1997).

55. The first phrase is from Michel Foucault, "On the Genealogy of Ethics: An Overview of Work in Progress," in *The Foucault Reader,* ed. Paul Rabinow (New York: Pantheon Books, 1984), 343. The second was suggested to me by Jim Albrecht (personal conversation).

CONCLUSION

1. See "The Year in Hate," in the Southern Poverty Law Center's *Intelligence Report,* Issue 105 (Spring 2002), www.splcenter.org.

2. For more on the appeal of colorblindness to white women, see Ruth Frankenberg, *White Women, Race Matters: The Social Construction of Whiteness* (Minneapolis: University of Minnesota Press, 1993), especially pp. 142–57.

3. On the relationship of food and eating to racist and colonialist attitudes, see Lisa Heldke, *Exotic Appetites: Ruminations of a Food Adventurer* (New York: Routledge, 2003).

4. Eduardo Mendieta, "A Pyrrhic Victory: Racial Justice not Aesthetic Diversity," paper presented at Suffolk County Community College Spring Conference, April 24, 2004.

5. Kelly Oliver discusses colorblindness as a fetish in Oliver, *Witnessing: Beyond Recognition* (Minneapolis: University of Minnesota Press, 2001), 167.

6. For more on this point in the context of white universities, see Lisa Heldke, "A Du Boisian Proposal for Persistently White Colleges," *Journal of Speculative Philosophy* 18(3) (2004): 224–38.

7. www.equity.psu.edu/mrc/.

8. Mendieta, "A Pyrrhic Victory."

9. See, for example, Noel Ignatiev's abolitionist position in Ignatiev, "Abolitionism and the White Studies Racket," *Race Traitor* 10 (1999): 3–7.

10. Lucius Outlaw, "Rehabilitate Racial *Whiteness?*" in *What White Looks Like: African-American Philosophers on the Whiteness Question,* ed. George Yancy (New York: Routledge, 2004). While I am in basic agreement with Outlaw, I am less sanguine than he is about the success of this process because of the unconscious nature of white privilege.

BIBLIOGRAPHY

Abraham, Nicolas, and Maria Torok. 1994. *The Shell and the Kernel: Renewals of Psychoanalysis*. Ed. and trans. Nicholas T. Rand. Chicago: University of Chicago Press.

Acredolo, Linda, and Susan Goodwyn. 2002. *Baby Signs: How to Talk with Your Baby before Your Baby Can Talk*. Chicago: Contemporary Books.

Addams, Jane. 1893. "The Subjective Necessity for Social Settlements." In Jane Addams, Robert A. Woods, J. O. S. Huntington, Franklin H. Giddings, and Bernard Bosanquet, *Philanthropy and Social Progress*. New York: Thomas Y. Crowell.

——. 1906. *Newer Ideals of Peace*. New York: Macmillan Co.

——. 1910. *Twenty Years at Hull-House with Autobiographical Notes*. New York: Macmillan Co.

——. 1919. "Americanization." *American Sociological Society Proceedings* 14: 206–14.

——. 1930. *The Second Twenty Years at Hull-House*. New York: Macmillan Co.

——. 2001. *Democracy and Social Ethics*. Chicago: University of Illinois Press.

Alcoff, Linda Martín. 1995. "The Problem of Speaking for Others." In *Overcoming Racism and Sexism*. Ed. Linda A. Bell and David Blumenfeld. Lanham, Md.: Rowman and Littlefield.

——. 1999. "Towards a Phenomenology of Racial Embodiment." *Radical Philosophy* 95 (May/June): 15–23.

Allen, James, ed. 2000. *Without Sanctuary: Lynching Photography in America*. Santa Fe, N.M.: Twin Palms Publishers.

Appiah, Kwame Anthony. 1989. "The Conservation of 'Race.'" *Black American Literature Forum*, 23(1): 37–60.

Aristotle. 1944. *The Politics*. Trans. H. Rackham. Cambridge, Mass.: Harvard University Press.

Associated Press. 2001. "Ad in Brown University Newspaper Sparks Protests." *Centre Daily Times* (State College, Pa.), March 18, page 9A.

Bailey, Alison. 1998. "Locating Traitorous Identities: Toward a View of Privilege-Cognizant White Character." *Hypatia* 13(3): 27–42.

Baldwin, James. 1963. *The Fire Next Time*. New York: Dell Publishing Co.

Beauvoir, Simone de. 1989. *The Second Sex*. Trans. H. M. Parshley. New York: Vintage Books.

Bercovici, Konrad. 1983. *Gypsies: Their Life, Lore, and Legends*. New York: Greenwich House.

Bernasconi, Robert. 2001. "Who Invented the Concept of Race? Kant's Role in the Enlightenment Construction of Race." In *Race*. Ed. Robert Bernasconi. Malden, Mass.: Blackwell.

———. 2005. "Waking Up White and in Memphis." In *White on White/Black on Black*. Ed. George Yancy. Lanham, Md.: Rowman and Littlefield.

Bordo, Susan. 2005. "Adoption." *Hypatia* 20(1): 230–36.

Boxill, Bernard R. 1978. "Du Bois and Fanon on Culture." *Philosophical Forum* 9(1): 326–38.

Bucur, Maria. 2002. *Eugenics and Modernization in Interwar Romania*. Pittsburgh, Pa.: University of Pittsburgh Press.

Bulhan, Hussein Abdilahi. 1985. *Franz Fanon and the Psychology of Oppression*. New York: Plenum Press.

Campbell, James. 1992. "Du Bois and James." *Transactions of the Charles S. Peirce Society* 28(3): 569–81.

Caruth, Cathy. 1991. "Unclaimed Experience: Trauma and the Possibility of History." In *Yale French Studies: Literature and the Ethical Question #79*. New Haven, Conn.: Yale University Press.

Chamberlin, J. E. 1975. *The Harrowing of Eden: White Attitudes toward Native Americans*. New York: Seabury Press.

Churchill, Ward. 1993. *Struggle for the Land*. Monroe, Maine: Common Courage Press.

———. 1994. *Indians Are Us*. Monroe, Maine: Common Courage Press.

Code, Lorraine. 2000. "Naming, Naturalizing, Normalizing: 'The Child' as Fact and Artifact." In *Toward a Feminist Developmental Psychology*. Ed. Patricia Miller and Ellin Scholnick. New York: Routledge.

Colapietro, Vincent. 1995. "Notes for a Sketch of a Peircean Theory of the Unconscious." *Transactions of the Charles S. Peirce Society* 31(3): 482–506.

———. 2000. "Further Consequences of a Singular Capacity." In *Peirce, Semiotics, and Psychoanalysis*. Ed. John Muller and Joseph Brent. Baltimore, Md.: John Hopkins University Press.

Collins, Patricia Hill. 1990. *Black Feminist Thought: Knowledge, Consciousness, and the Politics of Empowerment*. Boston: Unwin Hyman.

Connerton, Paul. 1989. *How Societies Remember*. New York: Cambridge University Press.

Dávila, Arlene. 2001. *Latinos, Inc.: The Marketing and Making of a People*. Berkeley: University of California Press.

Deleuze, Gilles, and Felix Guattari. 1983. *Anti-Oedipus: Capitalism and Schizophrenia*. Trans. Robert Hurley, Mark Seem, and Helen R. Lane. Minneapolis: University of Minnesota Press.

———. 1987. *A Thousand Plateaus: Capitalism and Schizophrenia*. Trans. Brian Massumi. Minneapolis: University of Minnesota Press.

Deloria, Philip. 1998. *Playing Indian*. New Haven, Conn.: Yale University Press.

Deloria, Vine, Jr. 1994. *God Is Red: A Native View of Religion*. Golden, Colo.: Fulcrum Publishing.

Dewey, John. 1985. "Nationalizing Education." In vol. 10 of *The Middle Works, 1899–1924*. Ed. Jo Ann Boydston. Carbondale: Southern Illinois University Press.

———. 1988. *Experience and Nature*. Vol. 1 of *The Later Works: 1925–1953*. Ed. Jo Ann Boydston. Carbondale: Southern Illinois University Press.

———. 1988. *Human Nature and Conduct*. Vol. 14 of *The Middle Works: 1899–1924*. Ed. Jo Ann Boydston. Carbondale: Southern Illinois University Press.

———. 1988. *The Quest for Certainty*. Vol. 4 of *The Later Works: 1925–1953*. Ed. Jo Ann Boydston. Carbondale: Southern Illinois University Press.

———. 1988. "Racial Prejudice and Friction." In vol. 13 of *The Middle Works, 1899–1924*. Ed. Jo Ann Boydston. Carbondale: Southern Illinois University Press.

———. 1989. "Address to the National Association for the Advancement of Colored People." In vol. 6 of *The Later Works: 1925–1953*. Ed. Jo Ann Boydston. Carbondale: Southern Illinois University Press.

———. 1989. *Art as Experience*. Vol. 10 of *The Later Works: 1925–1953*. Ed. Jo Ann Boydston. Carbondale: Southern Illinois University Press.

Du Bois, W. E. B. 1968. *The Autobiography of W. E. B. Du Bois: A Solioquy on Viewing My Life from the Last Decade of Its First Century*. New York: International Publishers.

———. 1970. "The Conservation of Races." In *W. E. B. Du Bois Speaks: Speeches and Addresses, 1980–1919*. Ed. Philip S. Foner. New York: Pathfinder Press.

———. 1970. *The Gift of Black Folk: The Negroes in the Making of America*. New York: Washington Square Press.

———. 1971. "The Class Struggle." In vol. 2 of *The Seventh Son: The Thought and Writings of W. E. B. Du Bois*. Ed. Julius Lester. New York: Random House.

———. 1971. "Karl Marx and the Negro." In vol. 2 of *The Seventh Son: The Thought and Writings of W. E. B. Du Bois*. Ed. Julius Lester. New York: Random House.

———. 1971. "Marxism and the Negro Problem." In vol. 2 of *The Seventh Son: The Thought and Writings of W. E. B. Du Bois*. Ed. Julius Lester. New York: Random House.

———. 1984. *Dusk of Dawn: An Essay toward an Autobiography of a Race Concept*. New York: Schocken Books.

———. 1999. *Darkwater: Voices from Within the Veil*. New York: Harcourt, Brace.

Durrant, Sam. 2004. *Postcolonial Narrative and the Work of Mourning: J. M. Coetzee, Wilson Harris, and Toni Morrison*. Albany: SUNY Press.

Dyer, Richard. 1997. *White*. New York: Routledge.

Eastman, Max. 1942. *Heroes I Have Known: Twelve Who Lived Great Lives*. New York: Simon and Schuster.

Fanon, Franz. 1952. *Peau Noire, Masques Blancs*. Paris: Editions du Seuil.

———. 1963. *The Wretched of the Earth*. Trans. Constance Farrington. New York: Grove Press.

———. 1965. *A Dying Colonialism*. Trans. Haakon Chevalier. New York: Grove Press.

———. 1967. *Black Skin, White Masks.* Trans. Charles Lam Markmann. New York: Grove Press.

———. 1967. *Toward the African Revolution.* Trans. Haakon Chevalier. New York: Grove Press.

Ferguson, Chaka. 2001. "Harlem Hopping Again." Spokane, Wash., *Spokesman-Review,* October 7, pages H3 and H5.

Fixico, Donald L. 1998. *The Invasion of Indian Country in the Twentieth Century: American Capitalism and Tribal Natural Resources.* Niwot: University Press of Colorado.

Fletcher, John, and Martin Stanton, eds. 1992. *Jean Laplanche: Seduction, Translation, and the Drives.* Trans. Martin Stanton. London: Institute of Contemporary Arts.

Fonseca, Isabel. 1995. *Bury Me Standing: The Gypsies and Their Journey.* New York: Alfred A. Knopf.

Foucault, Michel. 1984a. "On the Genealogy of Ethics: An Overview of Work in Progress." In *The Foucault Reader.* Ed. Paul Rabinow. New York: Pantheon Books.

———. 1984b. "Space, Knowledge, and Power." In *The Foucault Reader.* Ed. Paul Rabinow. New York: Pantheon Books.

Frankenberg, Ruth. 1993. *White Women, Race Matters: The Social Construction of Whiteness.* Minneapolis: University of Minnesota Press.

Fredrickson, George M. 1971. *The Black Image in the White Mind: The Debate on Afro-American Character and Destiny, 1817–1914.* Hanover, N.H.: Wesleyan University Press.

Freud, Sigmund. 1950. "On Narcissim: An Introduction." In vol. 4 of *Collected Papers.* Trans. Joan Riviere. London: Hogarth Press.

———. 1950. "Thoughts for the Times on War and Death." In vol. 4 of *Collected Papers.* Trans. Joan Riviere. London: Hogarth Press.

———. 1950. "The Unconscious." In vol. 4 of *Collected Papers.* Trans. Joan Riviere. London: Hogarth Press.

———. 1955. "'A Child Is Being Beaten': A Contribution to the Study of the Origin of Sexual Perversions." In vol. 17 of *The Standard Edition of the Complete Psychological Works of Sigmund Freud.* 24 vols. Ed. and trans. James Strachey. London: Hogarth Press.

———. 1959. *Group Psychology and the Analysis of the Ego.* Ed. and trans. James Strachey. New York: W. W. Norton.

———. 1960. *The Ego and the Id.* Ed. and trans. James Strachey. New York: W. W. Norton.

———. 1960. "Three Essays on Sexuality." In vol. 7 of *The Standard Edition of the Complete Psychological Works of Sigmund Freud.* 24 vols. Ed. and trans. James Strachey. New York: W. W. Norton.

———. 1961. *Civilization and Its Discontents.* Ed. and trans. James Strachey. New York: W. W. Norton.

——. 1964. *New Introductory Lectures on Psycho-Analysis.* In vol. 22 of *The Stan-dard Edition of the Complete Psychological Works of Sigmund Freud.* 24 vols. Ed. and trans. James Strachey. London: Hogarth Press.

Frye, Marilyn. 1983. *The Politics of Reality: Essays in Feminist Theory.* Freedom, Calif.: Crossing Press.

——. 1995. "White Woman Feminist." In *Overcoming Racism and Sexism.* Ed. Linda A. Bell and David Blumenfeld. Lanham, Md.: Rowman and Littlefield.

Fullerton, Stephanie Malia. Forthcoming. "On the Absence of Biology in Philo-sophical Considerations of Race." In *Race and Epistemologies of Ignorance.* Ed. Shannon Sullivan and Nancy Tuana. SUNY Series on Philosophy and Race, ed. Robert Bernasconi and T. Denean Sharpley-Whiting (Albany: SUNY Press).

Gannett, Lisa. 2001. "Racism and Human Genome Diversity Research: The Ethical Limits of 'Population Thinking.'" *Philosophy of Science* 68: S479–S492.

Gendzier, Irene L. 1973. *Franz Fanon: A Critical Study.* New York: Pantheon Books.

Gilligan, Carol. 1993. *In a Different Voice: Psychological Theory and Women's De-velopment.* Cambridge, Mass.: Harvard University Press.

Gordon, Lewis R. 1995. *Bad Faith and Anti-Black Racism.* Atlantic Highlands, N.J.: Humanities Press.

Graves, Joseph L., Jr. 2001. *The Emperor's New Clothes: Biological Theories of Race at the Millennium.* New Brunswick, N.J.: Rutgers University Press.

Greenwald, Emily. 2002. *Reconfiguring the Reservation: The Nez Perces, Jicarilla Apaches, and the Dawes Act.* Albuquerque: University of New Mexico Press.

Grosz, Elizabeth. 1994. *Volatile Bodies: Toward a Corporeal Feminism.* Bloom-ington: Indiana University Press.

Haraway, Donna J. 1991. *Simians, Cyborgs, and Women: The Reinvention of Na-ture.* New York: Routledge.

Harris, Cheryl. 1998. "Whiteness as Property." In *Black on White: Black Writers on What It Means to Be White.* Ed. David R. Roediger. New York: Schocken Books.

Haymes, Stephen Nathan. 1995. *Race, Culture, and the City: A Pedagogy for Black Urban Struggle.* Albany: SUNY Press.

Heldke, Lisa. 1997. "In Praise of Unreliability." *Hypatia* 12(3): 174–82.

——. 1998. "On Being a Responsible Traitor: A Primer." In *Daring to Be Good: Essays in Feminist Ethico-Politics.* Ed. Bat-Ami Bar On and Ann Ferguson. New York: Routledge.

——. 2003. *Exotic Appetites: Ruminations of a Food Adventurer.* New York: Rout-ledge.

——. 2004. "A Du Boisian Proposal for Persistently White Colleges." *Journal of Speculative Philosophy* 18(3): 224–38.

Helskini Watch Report. 1992. *Struggling for Ethnic Identity: Czechoslovakia's En-dangered Gypsies.* New York: Human Rights Watch.

Hill, Jason D. 2000. *Becoming a Cosmopolitan: What It Means to Be a Human Being in the New Millennium.* Lanham, Md.: Rowman and Littlefield.

Hirschfeld, Lawrence A. 1996. *Race in the Making: Cognition, Culture, and the Child's Construction of Human Kinds.* Cambridge: MIT Press.

Hoagland, Sarah Lucia. 2001. "Resisting Rationality." In *Engendering Rationalities.* Ed. Nancy Tuana and Sandra Morgen. Albany: SUNY Press.

hooks, bell. 1990. *Yearning: Race, Gender, and Cultural Politics.* Boston: South End Press.

——. 1992. *Black Looks: Race and Representation.* Boston: South End Press.

——. 1994. *Teaching to Transgress: Education as the Practice of Freedom.* New York: Routledge.

——. 1998. "Representations of Whiteness in the Black Imagination." In *Black on White: Black Writers on What It Means to Be White.* Ed. David R. Roediger. New York: Schocken Books.

Human Development Report Office. 2002. *Avoiding the Dependency Trap: The Roma Human Development Report.* New York: United Nations Development Programme.

Ignatiev, Noel. 1995. *How the Irish Became White.* New York: Routledge.

——. 1999. "Abolitionism and the White Studies Racket." *Race Traitor* 10: 3–7.

Irigaray, Luce. 1985. *This Sex Which Is Not One.* Trans. Catherine Porter with Carolyn Burke. Ithaca, N.Y.: Cornell University Press.

——. 1993. *An Ethics of Sexual Difference.* Trans. Carolyn Burke and Gillian C. Gill. Ithaca, N.Y.: Cornell University Press.

James, William. 1955. *The Principles of Psychology.* 2 vols. New York: Dover Publications.

Johnson, James Weldon. 1995. *The Autobiography of an Ex-Colored Man.* New York: Dover Publications.

Jordan, Matthew. 2004. "Recorded Jazz and 'La Voix Negre': The Sound of Race in the Age of Mechanical Reproduction." *Nottingham French Studies* 43(1): 89–99.

Kearney, Richard. 2003. *Strangers, Gods and Monsters.* New York: Routledge.

Kincheloe, Joe, ed. 1998. *White Reign: Deploying Whiteness in America.* New York: St. Martin's Press.

King, Richard H. 1986. "Self-realization and Solidarity: Rorty and the Judging Self." In *Pragmatism's Freud: The Moral Disposition of Psychoanalysis.* Ed. Joseph H. Smith and William Kerrigan. Baltimore, Md.: Johns Hopkins University Press.

Kochman, Thomas. 1981. *Black and White Styles in Conflict.* Chicago: University of Chicago Press.

Kovel, Joel. 1970. *White Racism: A Psychohistory.* New York: Pantheon Books.

Kozol, Jonathan. 1991. *Savage Inequalities: Children in America's Schools.* New York: Crown Publishers.

Kristeva, Julia. 1982. *Powers of Horror: An Essay on Abjection.* Trans. Leon S. Roudiez. New York: Columbia University Press.

——. 1991. *Strangers to Ourselves.* New York: Columbia University Press.

BIBLIOGRAPHY

Kruks, Sonia. 2001. *Retrieving Experience: Subjectivity and Recognition in Feminist Politics*. Ithaca, N.Y.: Cornell University Press.

Lacan, Jacques. 1983. "Merleau-Ponty: In Memoriam." *Review of Existential Psychology and Psychiatry* 18(1–3): 73–81.

Lanouzière, Jacqueline. 2002–2003. "Breast-Feeding as Original Seduction and Primal Scene of Seduction." *New Formations* 48: 53–68.

Laplanche, Jean. 1989. *New Foundations for Psychoanalysis*. Trans. David Macey. Cambridge, Mass.: Basil Blackwell.

———. 1996. "Psychoanalysis as Anti-Hermeneutics." *Radical Philosophy* 79: 7–12.

———. 1999. *Essays on Otherness*. New York: Routledge.

———. 2002–2003. "Narrativity and Hermeneutics: Some Propositions." *New Formations* 28: 26–29.

Lauretis, Teresa de. 2000. "Gender, Body, and Habit Change." In *Peirce, Semiotics, and Psychoanalysis*. Ed. John Muller and Joseph Brent. Baltimore, Md.: John Hopkins University Press.

Lawson, Bill E., and Donald F. Koch, eds. 2004. *Pragmatism and the Problem of Race*. Bloomington: Indiana University Press.

Le Robert de Poche. 1995. Paris: Dictionnaires Le Robert.

Lee, Sandra Soo-Jin, Joanna Mountain, and Barbara A. Koenig. 2001. "The Meanings of 'Race' in the New Genomics: Implications for Health Disparities Research." *Yale Journal of Health Policy, Law, and Ethics* 1(1): 33–75.

Levitt, Morton. 1960. *Freud and Dewey on the Nature of Man*. Westport, Conn.: Greenwood Press.

Lewis, Amanda E. 2003. *Race in the Schoolyard: Negotiating the Color Line in Classrooms and Communities*. New Brunswick, N.J.: Rutgers University Press.

Liégeois, Jean-Pierre. 1994. *Roma, Gypsies, Travellers*. Strasbourg: Council of Europe Press.

Lifton, Robert Jay. 1986. *The Nazi Doctors: Medical Killing and the Psychology of Genocide*. New York: Basic Books.

Light, Andrew, and Jonathan M. Smith, eds. 1998. *Philosophies of Place*. Lanham, Md.: Rowman and Littlefield.

Lissak, Rivka Shpak. 1989. *Pluralism and Progressives: Hull-House and the New Immigrants, 1890–1919*. Chicago: University of Chicago Press.

Lugones, María C. 1987. "Playfulness, 'World'-Traveling, and Loving Perception." *Hypatia* 2(2): 3–19.

Lugones, María, and Elizabeth Spelman. 1983. "Have We Got a Theory for You! Feminist Theory, Cultural Imperialism and the Demand for 'The Woman's Voice.'" *Hypatia* (WSIF) 1: 573–81.

Lyons, Joseph. 1988. "The Lived Body in Phenomenology and Psychoanalysis." In *Phenomenology and Psychoanalysis: The Sixth Annual Symposium of the Simon Silverman Phenomenology Center*. Pittsburgh, Pa.: Simon Silverman Phenomenology Center.

Macey, David. 1999. "Fanon, Phenomenology, Race." *Radical Philosophy* 95: 8–14.

———. 1999. "The Recall of the Real." *Constellations* 6(1): 97–107.

Marks, Paula Mitchell. 1998. *In a Barren Land: American Indian Dispossession and Survival.* New York: William Morrow.

Martinez, Jacqueline M. 2000. *Phenomenology of Chicana Experience and Identity: Communication and Transformation in Praxis.* Lanham, Md.: Rowman and Littlefield.

Mendieta, Eduardo. 2004. "A Pyrrhic Victory: Racial Justice Not Aesthetic Diversity." Paper presented at Suffolk County Community College Spring Conference, April 24.

Merleau-Ponty, Maurice. 1962. *Phenomenology of Perception.* Trans. Colin Smith. New York: Routledge.

———. 1963. *The Structure of Behavior.* Trans. Alden L. Fisher. Boston: Beacon Press.

———. 1983. "Phenomenology and Psychoanalysis: Preface to Hesard's *L'Oeuvre de Freud.*" *Review of Existential Psychology and Psychiatry* 18(1–3): 67–72.

Mills, Charles. 1997. *The Racial Contract.* Ithaca, N.Y.: Cornell University Press.

———. 1998. *Blackness Visible.* Ithaca, N.Y.: Cornell University Press.

Mills, Jon, and Janusz A. Polanowski. 1997. *The Ontology of Prejudice.* Amsterdam: Rodopi Press.

Mitchell, Juliet. 1974. *Psychoanalysis and Feminism.* New York: Pantheon Books.

Morrison, Toni. 1972. *The Bluest Eye.* New York: Pocket Books.

———. 1987. *Beloved.* New York: Penguin Books.

———. 1990. *Playing in the Dark: Whiteness and the Literary Imagination.* Cambridge, Mass.: Harvard University Press.

Nash, Roderick. 1982. *Wilderness and the American Mind.* 3rd ed. New Haven, Conn.: Yale University Press.

O'Connor, Anahad. 2003. "Rise in Income Improves Children's Behavior." *New York Times on the Web,* October 21, www.nytimes.com.

Oliver, Kelly. 2001. *Witnessing: Beyond Recognition.* Minneapolis: University of Minnesota Press.

———. 2004. *The Colonization of Psychic Space: A Psychoanalytic Social Theory of Oppression.* Minneapolis: University of Minnesota Press.

Oliver, Kelly, and Steve Edwin, eds. 2002. *Between the Psyche and the Social: Psychoanalytic Social Theory.* Lanham, Md.: Rowman and Littlefield.

Olkowski, Dorothea. 1983. "Merleau-Ponty's Freudianism: From the Body of Consciousness to the Body of Flesh." *Review of Existential Psychology and Psychiatry* 18 (1–3): 97–115.

Olkowski, Dorothea, and James Morley, eds. 1999. *Merleau-Ponty, Interiority and Exteriority, Psychic Life and the World.* Albany: SUNY Press.

Osborne, Peter. 2000. *Philosophy in Cultural Theory.* New York: Routledge.

Outlaw, Lucius. 1996. *On Race and Philosophy.* New York: Routledge.

———. 2004. "Rehabilitate Racial *Whiteness*?" In *What White Looks Like: African-American Philosophers on the Whiteness Question.* Ed. George Yancy. New York: Routledge.

Pappas, Gregory. 1996. "Dewey's Philosophical Approach to Racial Prejudice." *Social Theory and Practice* 22(1): 47–65.

Perry, Twila L. 2003. "Transracial Adoption: Mothers, Hierarchy, Race, and Feminist Legal Theory." In *Critical Race Feminism: A Reader.* 2nd ed. Ed. Adrien Katherine Wing. New York: New York University Press.

Phillips, James. 1988. "Latency and the Unconscious in Merleau-Ponty." In *Phenomenology and Psychoanalysis: The Sixth Annual Symposium of the Simon Silverman Phenomenology Center.* Pittsburgh, Pa.: Simon Silverman Phenomenology Center.

——. 1996. "Lacan and Merleau-Ponty: The Confrontation of Psychoanalysis and Phenomenology." In *Disseminating Lacan.* Ed. David Pettigrew and François Raffoul. Albany: SUNY Press.

Pontalis, J. B. 1983. "The Problem of the Unconscious in Merleau-Ponty's Thought." *Review of Existential Psychology and Psychiatry* 18(1–3): 83–96.

Proctor, Robert. 1988. *Racial Hygiene: Medicine under the Nazis.* Cambridge, Mass.: Harvard University Press.

Rich, Adrienne. 1979. *On Lies, Secrets, and Silence: Selected Prose, 1966–1978.* New York: Norton.

Rieff, Philip. 1979. *Freud: The Mind of a Moralist.* Chicago: University of Chicago Press.

Risch, Neil, Esteban Burchard, Elad Ziv, and Hua Tang. 2002. "Categorization of Humans in Biomedical Research: Genes, Race, and Disease." *Genome Biology* 3(7): 1–12.

Robinson, Randall. 2000. *The Debt: What America Owes to Blacks.* New York: Plume.

Rorty, Richard. 1986. "Freud and Moral Reflection." In *Pragmatism's Freud: The Moral Disposition of Psychoanalysis.* Ed. Joseph H. Smith and William Kerrigan. Baltimore, Md.: Johns Hopkins University Press.

Roth, Michael S. 1987. *Psycho-Analysis as History: Negation and Freedom in Freud.* Ithaca, N.Y.: Cornell University Press.

Scott, Charles. 1997. *The Advantages and Disadvantages of Politics and Ethics.* Bloomington: Indiana University Press.

Seattle, Chief. 1984. *How Can One Sell the Air? The Manifesto of an Indian Chief.* Dorchester, England: Prism Press.

Seigfried, Charlene Haddock. 1999. "Socializing Democracy: Jane Addams and John Dewey." *Philosophy of the Social Sciences,* 29(2): 207–30.

——. 2001. "Introduction to the Illinois Edition." In *Democracy and Social Ethics.* By Jane Addams. Chicago: University of Illinois Press.

——. 2002. "John Dewey's Pragmatist Feminism." In *Feminist Interpretations of John Dewey.* Ed. Charlene Haddock Seigfried. University Park: Pennsylvania State University Press.

Shoemaker, Nancy. 1997. "How Indians Got to Be Red." *American Historical Review* 102: 625–44.

Shuford, John. 2001. "Four Du Boisian Contributions to Critical Race Theory." *Transactions of the Charles S. Peirce Society* 37(3): 301–37.

Smith, Maureen. 1998. "An Enduring American Indian Myth: The Exercise of Religious Freedom in America." *Maine Scholar: A Journal of Ideas and Public Affairs* 11: 191–208.

Southern Poverty Law Center. 2002. "The Year in Hate." In *Intelligence Report.* Issue 105. www.splcenter.org.

Staples, Brent. 1986. "Just Walk on By: A Black Man Ponders His Power to Alter Public Space." *Ms.,* September, 54, 88.

Sullivan, Shannon. 2001. *Living Across and Through Skins: Transactional Bodies, Pragmatism, and Feminism.* Bloomington: Indiana University Press.

———. 2001. "Pragmatism, Psychoanalysis, and Prejudice: Elisabeth Young-Bruehl's *The Anatomy of Prejudice.*" *Journal of Speculative Philosophy* 15(2): 162–69.

———. 2001. "The Racialization of Space: Toward a Phenomenological Account of Raced and Anti-Racist Spatiality." In *The Problems of Resistance: Studies in Alternate Political Cultures.* Ed. Steve Martinot. Atlantic Highlands, N.J.: Prometheus/Humanity Books.

———. 2003. "Reciprocal Relations between Races: Jane Addams's Ambiguous Legacy." *Transactions of the Charles S. Peirce Society,* 39(1): 43–60.

———. 2003. "(Re)construction Zone: Beware of Falling Statues." In *In Dewey's Wake: Unfinished Work of Pragmatic Reconstruction.* Ed. William Gavin. Albany: SUNY Press.

———. 2003. "Remembering the Gift: Du Bois on the Unconscious and Economic Operations of Racism." *Transactions of the Charles S. Peirce Society* 39(2): 205–25.

———. 2004. "Ethical Slippages, Shattered Horizons, and the Zebra Striping of the Unconscious: Fanon on Social, Bodily, and Psychical Space." *Philosophy and Geography* 7(1): 9–24.

———. 2004. "Racialized Habits: Dewey on Race and the Roma." In *Pragmatism and Values: The Central European Pragmatist Forum, Volume One.* Ed. John Ryder and Emil Višòovský. Amsterdam: Rodopi Press.

———. 2004. Review of Richard Kearney's *Strangers, Gods and Monsters. Teaching Philosophy* 27(1): 85–87.

———. 2004. "The Unconscious Life of Race: Freudian Resources for Critical Race Theory." In *Rereading Freud: Psychoanalysis Through Philosophy.* Ed. Jon Mills. Albany: SUNY Press.

Sullivan, Shannon, and Nancy Tuana, eds. Forthcoming. *Race and Epistemologies of Ignorance.* Albany: SUNY Press.

Tate, Claudia. 1998. *Psychoanalysis and Black Novels: Desire and the Protocols of Race.* New York: Oxford University Press.

Taylor-Guthrie, Danielle, ed. 1994. *Conversations with Toni Morrison.* Jackson: University Press of Mississippi.

Thompson, Warren S. 1919. "Discussion." *American Sociological Society Proceedings* 14: 214–15.

Tocqueville, Alexis de. 1990. *Democracy in America.* Vol. 1. New York: Vintage Books.

Turner, Frederick. 1962. *The Frontier in American History.* New York: Holt, Rinehart, and Winston.

Van de Port, Mattijs. 1998. *Gypsies, Wars, and Other Instances of the Wild: Civilisation and Its Discontents in a Serbian Town.* Amsterdam: Amsterdam University Press.

Van Haute, Philippe. 1995. "Fatal Attraction: Jean Laplanche on Sexuality, Subjectivity, and Singularity in the Work of Sigmund Freud." *Radical Philosophy* 73: 5–12.

Watson, Jamal E. 2001. "Lawyers Plan Suit for Slavery Reparations." *Boston Globe,* April 13, p. A1.

Weate, Jeremy. 2001. "Fanon, Merleau-Ponty, and the Difference of Phenomenology." In *Race.* Ed. Robert Bernasconi. Malden, Mass.: Blackwell Publishers.

Weber, David J., ed. 1973. *Foreigners in Their Native Land: Historical Roots of the Mexican Americans.* Albuquerque: University of New Mexico Press.

Webster's Encyclopedic Unabridged Dictionary of the English Language. 1989. New York: Portland House.

Weinburg, Meyer. 1977. *A Chance to Learn: The History of Race and Education in the United States.* New York: Cambridge University Press.

West, Cornel. 1993. *Keeping Faith: Philosophy and Race in America.* New York: Routledge.

White, Renée T. 1996. "Revolutionary Theory: Sociological Dimensions of Fanon's *Sociologie d'une revolution.*" In *Fanon: A Critical Reader.* Ed. Lewis R. Gordon, T. Denean Sharpley-Whiting, and Renée T. White. Maldon, Mass.: Blackwell Publishers.

Willett, Cynthia. 2001. *The Soul of Justice: Social Bonds and Racial Hubris.* Ithaca, N.Y.: Cornell University Press.

Williams, Patricia J. 1991. *The Alchemy of Race and Rights: Diary of a Law Professor.* Cambridge: Harvard University Press.

———. 1997. *Seeing a Color-Blind Future: The Paradox of Race.* New York: Farrar, Straus and Giroux.

Wilson, Bobby M. 2002. "Critically Understanding Race-Connected Practices: A Reading of W. E. B. Du Bois and Richard Wright." *Professional Geographer* 54(1): 31–41.

Wood, Manfri Frederick. 1973. *In the Life of a Romany Gypsy.* London: Routledge and Kegan Paul.

Yancy, George, ed. 2005. *White on White/Black on Black.* Ed. George Yancy. Lanham, Md.: Rowman and Littlefield.

Young, Iris Marion. 1997. "Asymmetrical Reciprocity: On Moral Respect, Wonder, and Enlarged Thought." In *Intersecting Voices: Dilemmas of Gender, Political Philosophy, and Policy.* Princeton, N.J.: Princeton University Press.

Young-Bruehl, Elisabeth. 1996. *The Anatomies of Prejudice*. Cambridge, Mass.: Harvard University Press.

Zack, Naomi. 1993. *Race and Mixed Race*. Philadelphia: Temple University Press.

———. 2002. *Philosophy of Science and Race*. New York: Routledge.

Zedler, Beatrice H. 1976. "Wonder in John Dewey." *Modern Schoolman* 54(1): 1–14.

INDEX

Abject, the, 73–74
Abraham, Nicholas, 96, 110, 113
Absolutely Fabulous, 182–83
Acredolo, Linda, 213n77
Addams, Jane, 167–74, 177
    and assimilation, 170–71, 225nn11,17
    and pluralism, 171, 225n17
    and reciprocity, 168–70, 171–74, 176,
        179–80, 184; asymmetrical, 173,
        226n23; hierarchical, 173, 226n26
    and separatism, 168, 169
    and transaction, 171, 176
Adoption, transracial, 181–83, 228n51
Affirmative action, 192–93, 195
African Americans
    commodified, 126
    and education, 27–30, 177–79
    gifts of, 122–24, 127, 129, 142
    and habits of communication, 28–30
    and reparations, 136–38, 141
    scientific investigation of, 19–20
    and separatism, 178–79
    treated as property, 125, 127
Alcoff, Linda Martín, 227n45
Alexander Technique, 8
American Indian Religious Freedom Act,
    135
Aristotle, 226n27
Aryan Nation, 55

Baldwin, James, 209n6
Beauvoir, Simone de, 216n39
Biologism, racial, 18, 32
Blackness, 123, 125–27, 140
    and the Roma, 156
Bodily schema, 102, 107, 117, 215n29
Body, 46
    and emotions, 53
    and epidermalization, 105

    and ethical slippage, 97, 101–10
    and the Roma, 155–56
    and seduction theory, 66–69
    as unconscious, 8
    and white privilege, 188–89
Bodying, 3
Bordo, Susan, 228n51
Boxill, Bernard, 201n10

Campbell, James, 201n17
Capitalism
    and the appropriation of the uncon-
        scious, 124–25
    and decolonization, 139–40
    and planned obsolescence, 126
    and racism, 127, 137
Césaire, Amié, 107
Cherokee, 139
Chief Seattle, 130, 219n29
Chief Toohoolhoolzote, 133
Chippewa, 169
Churchill, Ward, 91, 141, 224n60
Civilization
    versus savagery, 133
    versus wilderness, 150–51, 157–58,
        163, 172–73
Cleanliness, 72, 73–75
    and female genitalia, 74
    as obsessional, 74
Code, Lorraine, 214n84
Colapietro, Vincent, 205n92
Colonialism, 95, 101, 118
    and Africa, 139–40
    and colorblindness, 140
    Euro-American, 130
    French: in Algeria, 106–108; in Mar-
        tinique, 96–98, 99–104, 105, 107–
        108, 109–10
    and World War II, 121

Shannon Sullivan is Associate Professor of Philosophy and Women's Studies at Penn State University. She is author of *Living Across and Through Skins: Transactional Bodies, Pragmatism, and Feminism* (Indiana University Press, 2001) and co-editor (with Nancy Tuana) of *Race and the Epistemologies of Ignorance* (forthcoming) and a special issue of *Hypatia* on Feminist Epistemologies of Ignorance (Summer 2006).